IMAGES
of America

HESPERIA

On the Cover: The cover photograph was taken in 1888. The four men are presumably prospective land buyers of the new frontier named Hesperia. The image was taken by C. H. Shaffner, a highly sought-after photographer who helped record many communities' birth and development. (Courtesy Huntington Library.)

IMAGES
of America

HESPERIA

Gary "Old Town Griz" Drylie

ARCADIA
PUBLISHING

ISBN 978-0-7385-8107-1

Published by Arcadia Publishing
Charleston, South Carolina

Printed in the United States of America

Library of Congress Control Number: 2010921992

For all general information contact Arcadia Publishing at:
Telephone 843-853-2070
Fax 843-853-0044
E-mail sales@arcadiapublishing.com
For customer service and orders:
Toll-Free 1-888-313-2665

Visit us on the Internet at www.arcadiapublishing.com

This book is dedicated to people of all ages who believe in their community—those who give to their hometowns to maintain a good, family-oriented environment. Throughout Hesperia's history, many fine people have sustained these important values with faith and perseverance.

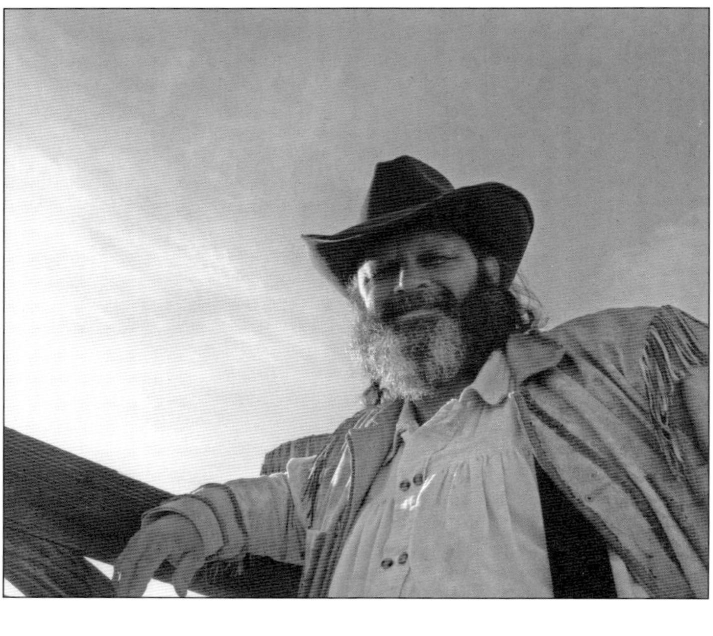

Gary "Old Town Griz" Drylie has been in the High Desert for 30 years. He is retired from the U.S. Air Force with a background and education in vocational education, safety, and teaching and with a love of history. The photograph was taken by Shelly Drylie while on location filming the second segment of *Hesperia: Past, Present, and Future.* (Courtesy Hesperia Old Town Museum.)

Contents

ACKNOWLEDGMENTS

In any project, there are people who have a very large impact on that project. This book is not any different. The writing of this book is just a portion of the overall project *Hesperia Past, Present and Future*. Hesperia has so many wonderful people who have made major contributions, and these come in many forms. Some contribute by making contacts, providing pictures or artifacts, researching, proofing, or bringing forth that life story that transforms a period of time from an obscure two-dimensional picture to a three-dimensional depiction filled with feeling. I wish to thank all those who helped in making this book something that will make a Hesperian say proudly, after reading it, "Hesperia is my hometown."

I would like to extend a special thanks to some people both past and present who have been an inspiration for many reasons. First are the historians of the area, who have all made major contributions to preserving Hesperia's history during their time, including Arleen Kallenburger, John Swisher, Leo Lyman, Myra McGinnis, and George Dewey Hedrick.

Thanks also go to a variety of very special people I have either collaborated in person or corresponded with whose families have resided in Hesperia as far back as 1900.

One very special person is my wife, Shelly, who has supported me in all the time spent putting this book together. She knows very well from personal experience that it takes a lot of time and effort to produce something of which one can be proud.

The photographs in the book come from many sources, and I wish to extend a heartfelt thank you to these people or groups. Credits for the source of the photographs are denoted as follows: California Railroad Museum (CRRM); Hesperia Recreation and Parks District (HRPD); Hesperia Old Town Museum (HOTM); Huntington Library (HL); Mary Ann Creason Rhodes (MACR); Mojave Historical Society (MHS); Route 66 Museum, Victorville (VVR66M); San Bernardino County Archives (SBCA); University of Southern California (USC); University of California at Los Angeles (UCLA); Tatum family (TF); Hedrick family (HF); Lillian Lee Stratton Platt (LSP); Jim Walker (JW); Lorraine Cottrell Moffat (LCM); Bascom family (BF); Hesperia Unified School District (HUSD); the Swanson family (SF); and F. X. McDonald (FXM).

INTRODUCTION

In this modern day, both time and technology seem to fly by at the speed of light. The old vanishes as the new springs into being. People find themselves asking, "What happened?" "How did we get here?" "Was there something here before?" The goal of this book is to look at the documented history and a variety of personal accounts to bring forth the magnificent history of Hesperia.

There are as many observations of an event as there are people witnessing it. Every event in history can be seen from many viewpoints. Each event affects individuals or groups differently. Some may prosper monetarily, while others may be tested by the event and grow from the adversity. Hesperia's history is filled with stories and achievements, from the extraordinary efforts of developing early water systems to the construction of a three-story hotel that towered over the Mojave Desert, as well as many other events that exemplify the pioneer spirit of the West.

Hesperia is known as the southern gateway to the High Desert and was known as such even along the trails of yesteryear. From time immemorial, living things have traveled beside, or in search of, water. Within the Mojave Desert region, the Mojave River has been the major source for water. Many a traveler or explorer has noted or written about the headwaters of the Mojave River. This great river, running along the eastern border of Hesperia, is one of the few in the world that runs from south to north. The new visitor might well ask, "What river?" due to the small amount of water that flows between the Mojave's banks most of the time, but a look at its expansive banks reveals that at peak flow, it is a great river. The river flows at bedrock level until it is time to handle that heavy flow, and then the sleeping giant awakens—hence many writings have referred to it as being "upside down."

When traveling the north or southeastern area and through the Cajon Pass, Hesperia is the first or last place one sees. In the past, Hesperia was the place to get supplies and water before continuing a treacherous trip down the Cajon or a place to rest before continuing the passage northward through the Mojave Desert. Hesperia throughout history has been a place in the middle of the journey, the shining star that one needed to reach before continuing with the second half of the trek. However, in 1885, the Santa Fe Railroad laid tracks through the Cajon Pass, then into this area, and Hesperia emerged by name. Thus Hesperia started a new chapter in its history, as a destination in itself rather than just a stopping point in the middle of one's travels.

The early 20th century for Hesperia was a time of growth and promise. In the 1920s, another great event occurred—the completion of Route 66—and this brought major changes and challenges for the young town. As Hesperia moved into the 1940s, agriculture was a major industry, with the Tatum/Walker potato fields on the mesa as well as a national-record onion crop that was fed to livestock. This was all irrigated with a water system that was constructed in the late 1880s and supplied Hesperia with water into the 1950s.

In the 1950s, two songs were written specifically about Hesperia; one by the father of F. X. McDonald and sung by F. X. and the other by Eddie Maxwell, performed by the West-O-Crates. These songs reached back into Hesperia's history and told of a place of rejuvenation, suggesting a time to "leave your hysteria and head for Hesperia." Most of modern-day Hesperia came from the mid- to late-1950s development of M. Penn Phillips in conjunction with the World Heavyweight Champion Jack Dempsey. Some of these developments were Hesperia Lakes (the only PGA golf course Victor Valley has had), the Leisure League, and the Hesperia Chamber of Commerce.

When it was time, in the 1980s, Hesperia made a move towards independence. Once cityhood was achieved in 1988, Hesperia dealt with a variety of situations, as does any new city. In its infancy, however, Hesperia maintained a positive outlook. As to the future, time will tell. History has proven that Hesperia will continue on in a constructive, upbeat manner. For that, we can thank the fine, caring people who have settled here and made Hesperia their home.

One

Early Days, Before 1885

References to the Hesperia area appear in recorded history as far back as the late 1770s, when pioneer Spanish priest Fr. Francisco Garces wrote of encountering the headwaters of the Great Mojave River as he explored the area in search of new mission sites. From the early to mid-1800s come stories of the great Piute chief Whakara and a mountain man named Peg-Leg Smith, who ran a horse-rustling ring. During this time, there was an estimated 5,000 head of horse run through the Summit Valley area. This series of events was of such a magnitude that what is known as Summit Valley was then called Horse Thief Canyon. Two of the frontier era's best-known explorers—Gen. John C. Frémont and Kit Carson—traveled in expeditions through the future site of Hesperia before traversing the Cajon Pass. In the late 1840s, Mormon immigrants passed through the area as they made their historic journey from Utah to the San Bernardino area.

On April 17, 1861, the state passed an act to build a toll road in the Cajon Pass; the road contract was awarded to John Brown, Henry M. Willis, and George L. Tucker. During the first year of construction, the road was devastated by the January 1862 flood. Over the next 20 years, the toll roads brought travelers into the area that would become Hesperia, "The Star of the West." The John Brown Toll Roads were a major improvement for travelers over the Cajon Pass and were the beginning of what became part of Route 66 and now Interstate 15.

By the 1860s, the railroads was laying track, and Southern California began to transform. Max Strubel bought the area to be known as Hesperia and worked to establish a German settlement there, but this endeavor never truly came to fruition. During these same years, the Widney brothers continued buying up land and water rights into the Inland Empire and on up through the Cajon Pass for the Santa Fe Railroad.

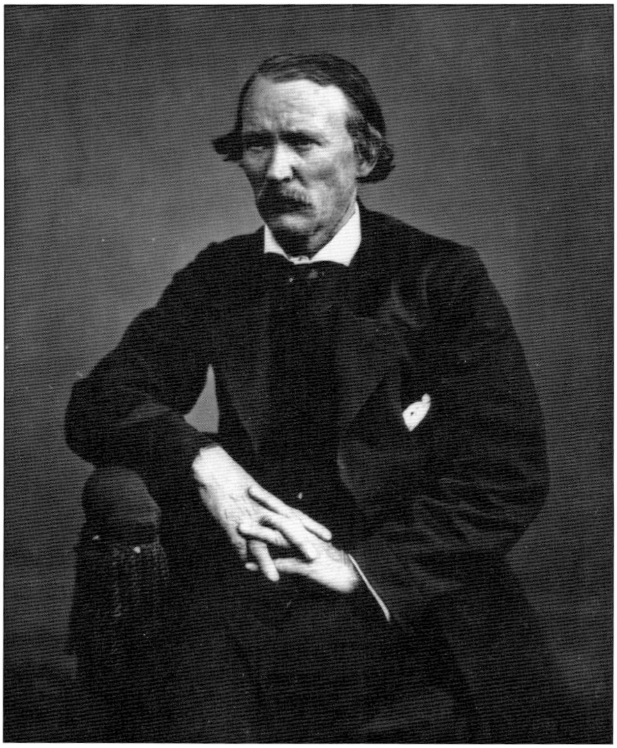

Christopher Houston "Kit" Carson was born in 1809 and died in 1868. He led many expeditions throughout the American West, including the southwestern area of the Mojave Desert. Contemporaries described him as a man whose "word is as sure as the sun coming up." Though he'd been trapping in the West since the 1820s, Carson came to national attention as John C. Frémont's guide into California and Oregon between 1842 and 1846. (Courtesy HOTM.)

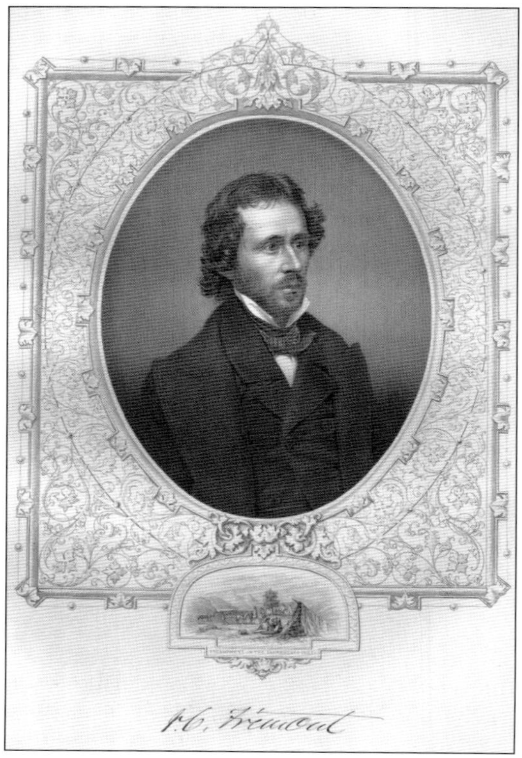

Former presidential candidate John C. Frémont was one of four major generals appointed by President Lincoln at the start of the Civil War. He had made a name for himself nearly 20 years earlier during his explorations into Southern California with Kit Carson. Frémont was instrumental during the campaign to acquire California from Mexico. He was also one of California's first senators and grew rich off the Gold Rush. (Courtesy HOTM.)

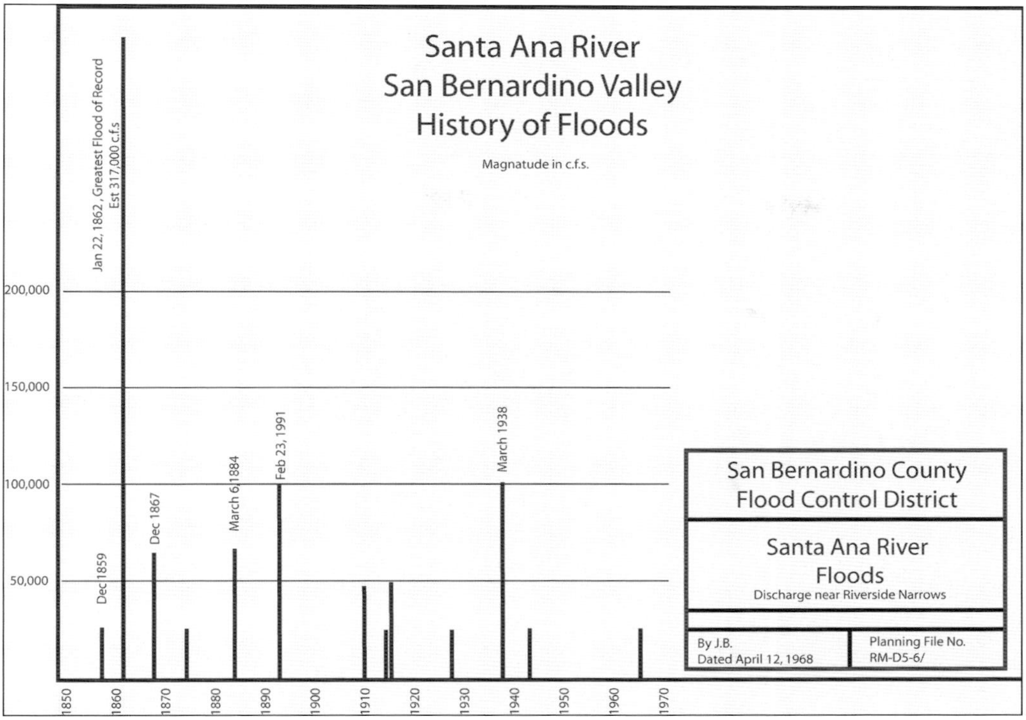

This graph highlights the magnitude of Southern California's great flood in the winter of 1861–1862. According to public flood control records, the storm dropped an estimated 50 inches of rain over just four days. Witnesses reported that the storm created four inland lakes that were each 4 feet deep. Many adobe homes succumbed to this event; contemporary illustrations show town residents boating through the streets. (Courtesy HOTM.)

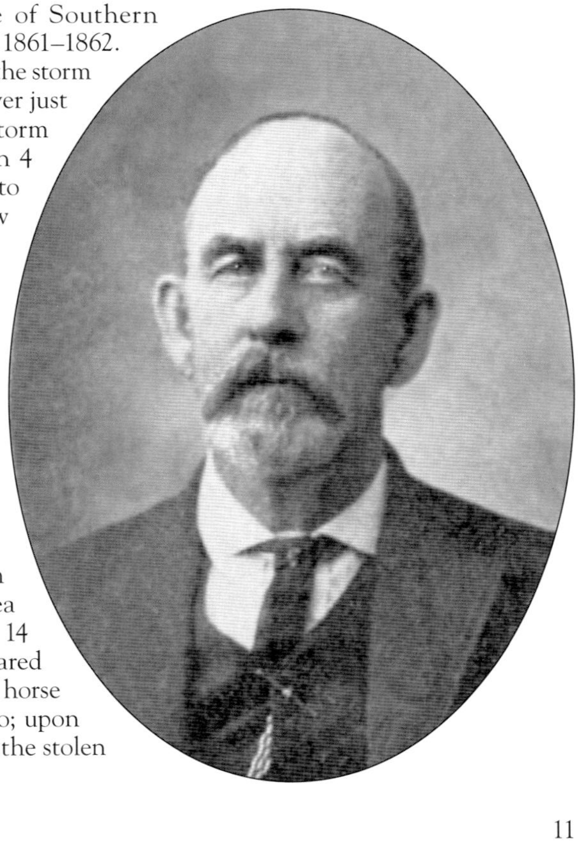

Silas Cox was born in 1843 and came to the High Desert and San Bernardino as a boy in 1851. Silas ran freight in and out of the area and was noted for killing his first bear at 14 years of age—which led to his being compared to Daniel Boone. Once, Silas chased some horse thieves who had stolen his horse Chappo; upon catching them, he freed many animals in the stolen herd. (Courtesy MHS.)

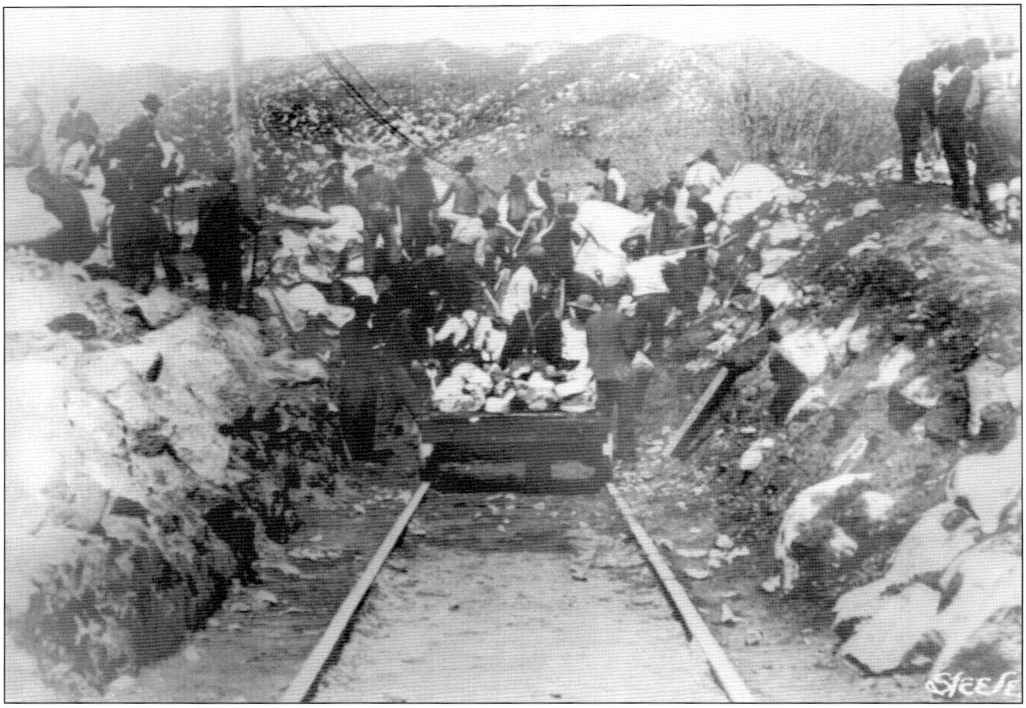

Construction of the railroad up Cajon Pass was a very tedious job. Much of the work was done with pick, shovel, horse, and wagon. The crews consisted of many Chinese workers to construct and lay the railroad tracks. The tracks followed the terrain of the Cajon and Summit Valley with twists and turns to accommodate the speed of the locomotives of the day. As the railroad passed through Summit Valley and finally crested on to the southeastern portion of the Mojave Desert, passengers saw what was soon to become known as Hesperia. As time went on, the tracks' tight turns would have to be straightened out to accommodate bigger and faster locomotives. (Both, courtesy VVR66M.)

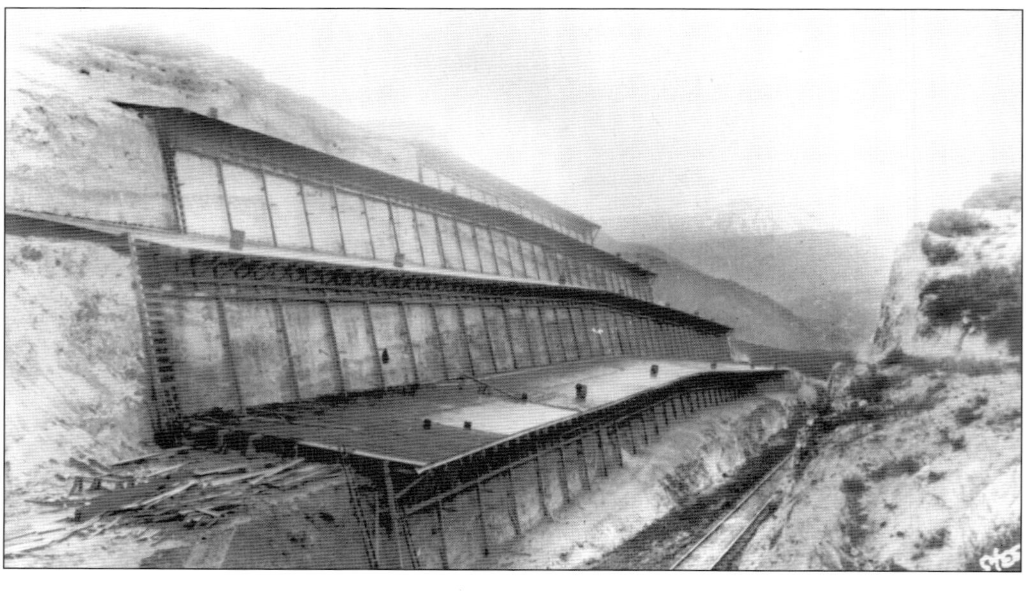

Two

Our Founders

In 1885, Hesperia was formally named and became a town. The primary person recorded in this event was Robert MaClay Widney. Robert and his brother, Joseph Palmaroy Widney, were instrumental in acquiring land and water rights as the railroad continued eastward from Los Angeles to the High Desert communities.

The Widney family came to California from Ohio. Robert MaClay Widney started out west around 1855 as a member of a trapping expedition through the Rockies and finally made it to Sacramento, where his first job was chopping wood. Although his education had started in Ohio, Widney continued his schooling at the College of the Pacific in Santa Clara. He graduated as class valedictorian with a bachelor's degree in 1863 and immediately earned a position as a professor. He taught at the College of the Pacific for several years.

Anybody researching the San Bernardino County Archive will find both of the Widney brothers' signatures recording transactions for land and water rights to lay way for the Santa Fe Railroad as it continued to move eastward and up the Cajon Pass. The Widneys were both Greek scholars, and this accounts for their choice of Hesperia as the name for their new development. The term means "star of the West," deriving from the Greek *Hesperus*, meaning "evening star." Presumably, the brothers were making reference to Hesperus from Greek mythology—the son of Cephalus (a mortal) and Eos, goddess of the dawn. The Widneys may also have been making reference to the mythical, idyllic Garden of Hesperides, site of the goddess Hera's orchard of golden apples.

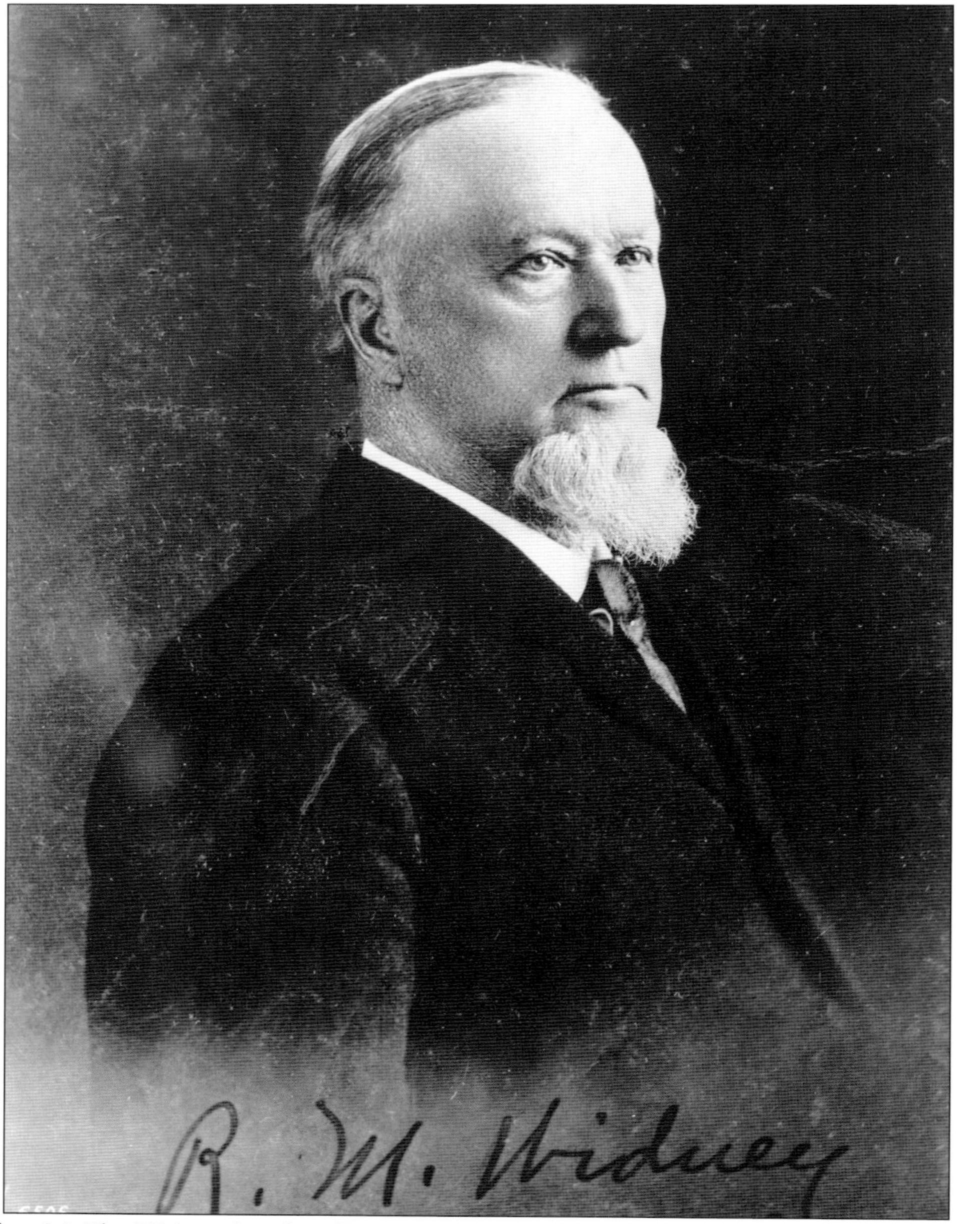

Robert MaClay Widney, founder of Hesperia, authored many books, helped found the University of Southern California, and helped negotiate many of the land deals and water rights as the Santa Fe Railroad progressed east and up the Cajon to the point where the western part of the railroad met the eastern portion in what would be named the town of Victor. R. M. Widney opened a law and real estate office and published real estate advertisements. That same year, he married his wife, the former Mary Barnes. During the 1871 Chinese riots, R. M. Widney was credited with helping pacify the rioters and saving many lives; subsequently, that December, he was appointed judge of the 17th Judicial District. Widney was instrumental in drawing up the articles of incorporation for the University of Southern California and was appointed to its first board of directors. Widney is also credited with starting the Los Angeles Chamber of Commerce. (Courtesy USC.)

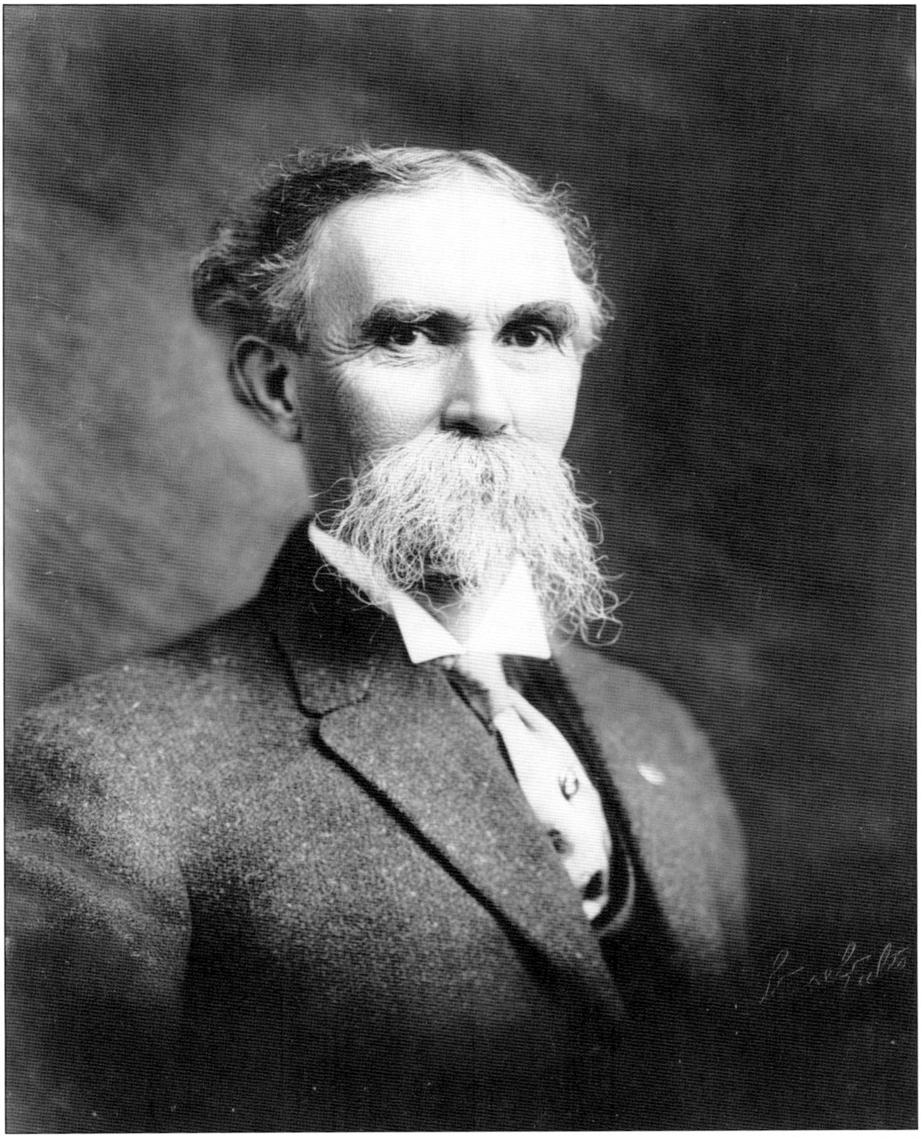

Joseph Palmaroy Widney, though not formally named as one of Hesperia's founders, worked side-by-side with his older brother, Robert MaClay, in acquiring land and water rights as the railroad was being built. Joseph was the founder of the USC Medical School and not only assisted in the founding of the Church of the Nazarene denomination but was the person who actually named it. After graduating from Tolland Medical College in San Francisco (California's only medical school at the time), Joseph Palmaroy Widney enlisted in the military and was detailed as the assistant surgeon for Arizona Territories during the Apache Wars. In 1868, he was discharged from the military and moved to Los Angeles, California. Both Widney brothers arrived in Los Angeles in 1868. Within the year of moving to Los Angeles, J. P. Widney opened a medical practice with Dr. John Strother Griffin at the corner of Temple and South Main Streets in Los Angeles. Two of his more noted patients were Gen. William Tecumseh Sherman and California bandit Tiburcio Vasquez. Dr. Widney was also a strong proponent of medical licensing and treatment for the indigent. (Courtesy USC.)

R. M. WIDNEY, President.
S. H. MOTT, Secretary.
E. F. SPENCE, Treasurer.

G. H. BONEBRAKE.
DR. W. L. WILLS.
C. GANAHL.
J. M. DAVIES.
H. L. MACNEIL.

HESPERIA

Land and Water Company.

OFFICE, UNIVERSITY BANK.

HESPERIA is situated on the northern slope of the Sierra Madre Mountains about 35 miles from San Bernardino on the A. T. and S. F. Railroad.

The elevation is about 3,000 feet above the sea, the soil, a rich, sandy loam of a reddish color and the very best adapted for the cultivation of deciduous fruit.

The colony of 23,040 acres of ground is supplied with an abundance of pure, mountain water, conducted by steel and iron pipes, and the Hesperia Ditch from Lake Adelene and Hesperia Cañon.

The Hesperia Ditch is one of Southern California's Wonders; at first, it seemed like a Col. Sellers scheme, but now a reality. Standing on the banks of Hesperia Creek, hundreds of feet above, you can see the faint outline of this great piece of engineering, with its numerous sand-gates overflowing with the abundance of cool, mountain water. The greater part of the Ditch was tunneled and cut through the solid granite wall of the mountain side, the precipitous character of which was so great that the surveyor was compelled to do the work from the opposite side of the cañon.

VICTOR is beautifully located on the banks of a large stream always full of cool, mountain water, and surrounded by groves of cotton wood trees.

Near Victor is the finest Granite Quarry anywhere near Los Angeles.

Photo by

C. H. SHAFFNER,

26 South Spring Street. P. O. Address: 509 Sixth Street.

LOS ANGELES, CAL.

This document was affixed to the back of all the photographs of Hesperia taken by C. H. Shaffner in 1888. Shaffner photographically recorded the birth and growth of many of Southern California's emerging townships in the late 1800s and early 1900s. The top of the document notes the Hesperia Land and Water Company's officers and board of directors, with town founder Robert MaClay Widney as president. It gives a description of the new settlement and its location relative to surrounding areas. Many of the areas described in this document have different names today: Hesperia Creek, for instance, is now known as Deep Creek; the town of Victor became Victorville in 1903. (Courtesy HL.)

Three

Little-Known Wonders of the High Desert

In this new railroad town, there were many things required for Hesperia's continued growth, but first the community needed a water source. Thus began the monumental endeavor that would supply Hesperia with water for 65 years. The ditch was constructed in two basic phases. The first was carried out in the late 1880s, when workers dug a 5-mile-long ditch along the southern exposure of a hillside some 500 feet above the Hesperia Creek. The ditch connected to a reservoir 7 miles away through a 14-inch pipe. The second phase began in 1911 under foreman Columbus Frank Hedrick, when workers installed a second pipe alongside the original 14-inch pipe. This 30-inch pipe covered the same 7 miles, doubling the amount of water delivered to the reservoir.

With the water came new residents and new building. Foremost among the latter was the Hesperia Hotel. It took two and a half years to build; at just three stories, it stood as a skyscraper overlooking the surrounding area. In the 1930s, residents invested in drilling wells on their properties. Today water is delivered by the City of Hesperia. Some properties still retain water rights and have their own wells.

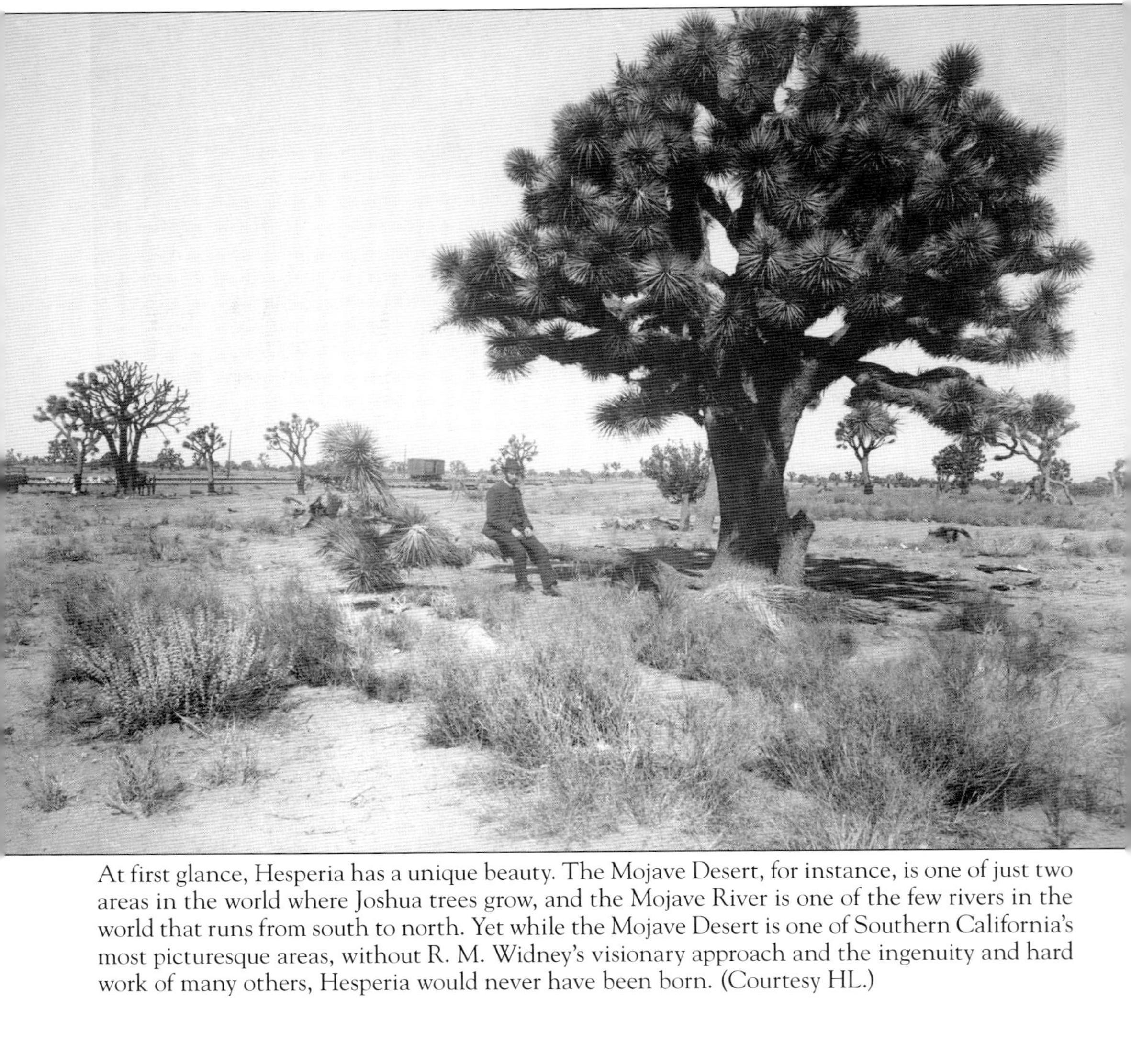

At first glance, Hesperia has a unique beauty. The Mojave Desert, for instance, is one of just two areas in the world where Joshua trees grow, and the Mojave River is one of the few rivers in the world that runs from south to north. Yet while the Mojave Desert is one of Southern California's most picturesque areas, without R. M. Widney's visionary approach and the ingenuity and hard work of many others, Hesperia would never have been born. (Courtesy HL.)

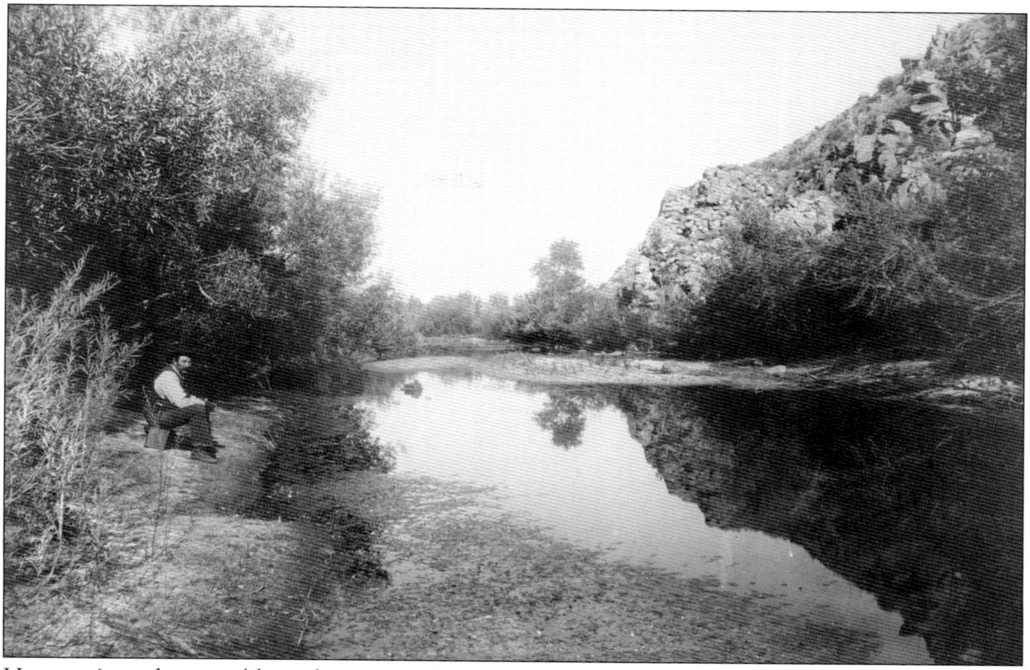

Hesperia's settlers would need water, and so would the railroad's steam engines. Surveyors found a source of cool and fresh water at the southeast corner of the Hesperia area but pondered how to get this water to the heart of the new township itself. (Both, courtesy HL.)

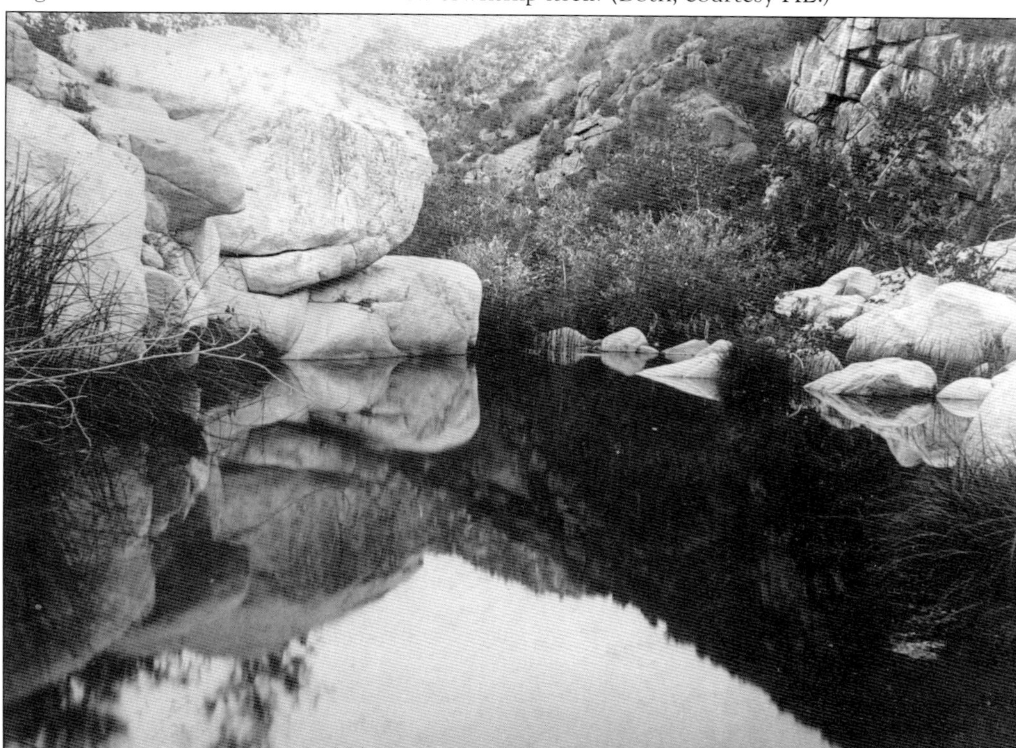

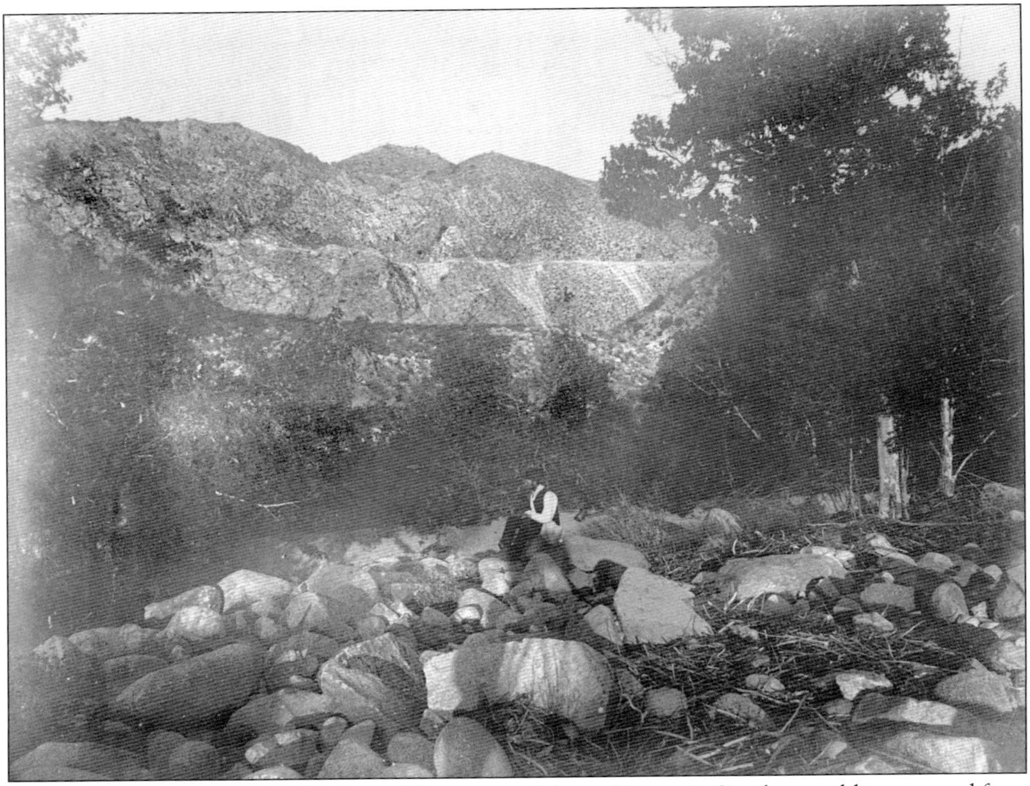

Engineers likely spent many hours trekking up and down Hesperia Creek, stumbling around for a way to get the water to the town site. As this man sits alongside the creek, he seems to be racking his brain for an answer. (Courtesy HL.)

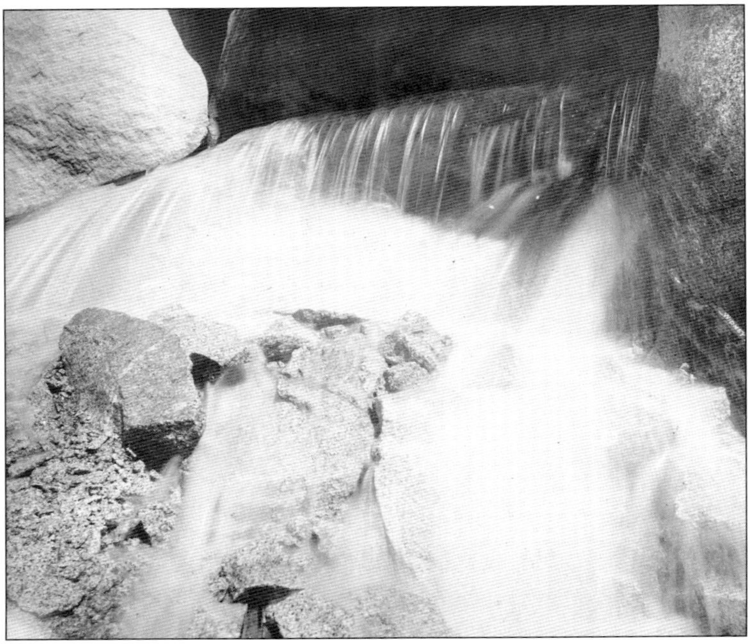

Traveling to the headwaters of Hesperia Creek, engineers struck upon an idea: if they created a ditch at the same elevation as the headwaters and sloped it along the southern exposure of the hillside, they could reroute the water from Hesperia Creek towards the middle of Hesperia. It would take a lot of work, but it could be done. The engineers had found Hesperia's water source. (Courtesy HL.)

During the first year after Hesperia's founding, notices of appropriations of water were filed by the Hesperia Land and Water Company. The one shown here is dated August 20, 1885; it is signed by company president R. M. Widney and H. L. Macneil. (Courtesy SBCA.)

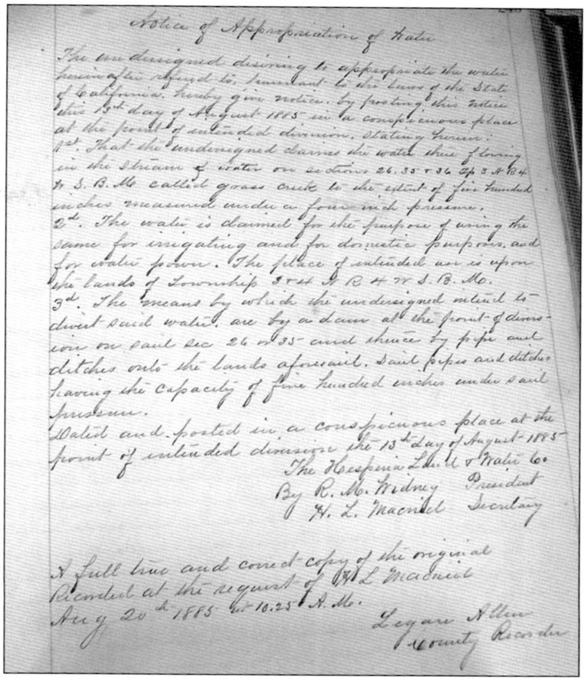

Notice of Appropriation of Water

The undersigned desiring to appropriate the water hereinafter referred to, pursuant to the laws of the State of California, hereby give notice, by posting this notice this 13th day of August 1885 in a conspicuous place at the point of intended diversion, stating herein:
1st. That the undersigned claims the water there flowing in the stream of water on sections 26. 35 & 36 Tp 3 N R 4 W S. B. M. called grass creek to the extent of five hundred inches measured under a four inch pressure.
2d. The water is claimed for the purpose of using the same for irrigating and for domestic purposes, and for water power. The place of intended use is upon the lands of Township 3 & 4 N R 4 W S. B. M.
3d. The means by which the undersigned intend to divert said water, are by a dam at the point of diversion on said sec 26 or 35 and thence by pipe and ditches onto the lands aforesaid. Said pipes and ditches having the capacity of five hundred inches under said pressure.
Dated and posted in a conspicuous place at the point of intended diversion the 13th day of August 1885

The Hesperia Land & Water Co.
By R. M. Widney President
H. L. Macneil Secretary

A full true and correct copy of the original
Recorded at the request of H L Macneil
Aug 20th 1885 at 10.25 A. M.

Legare Allen
County Recorder

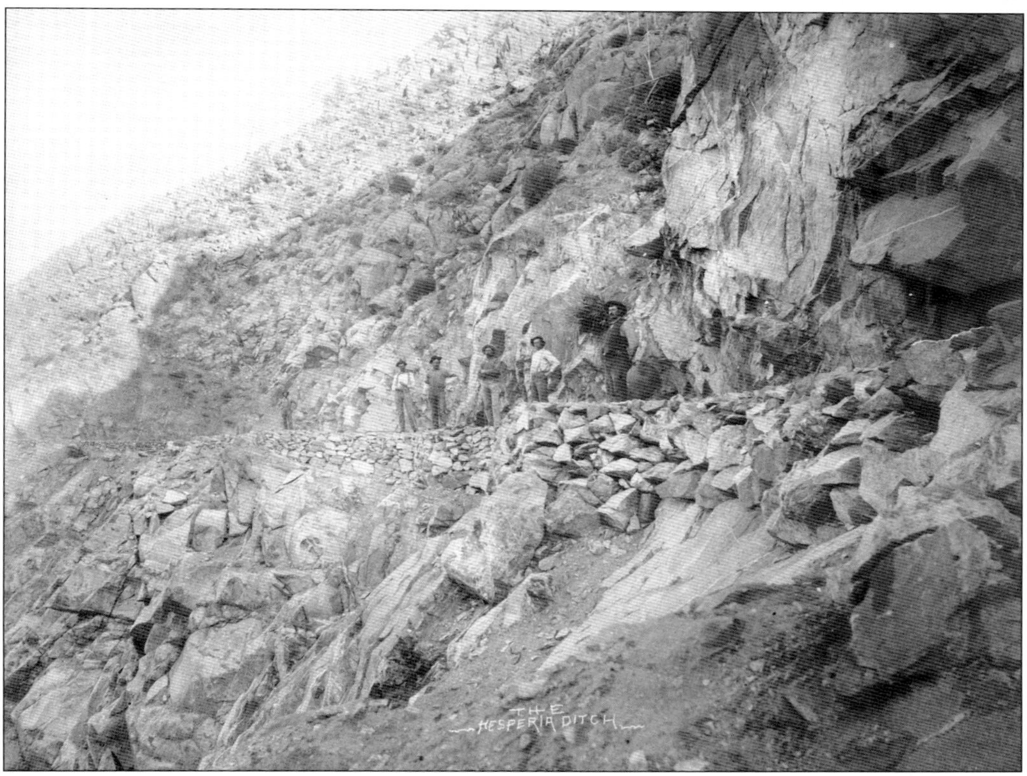

With the idea formulated, work began on the ditch. The men would end up trenching along the hillside approximately 2.5 feet deep and 3 feet wide for nearly 5 miles. (Courtesy HL.)

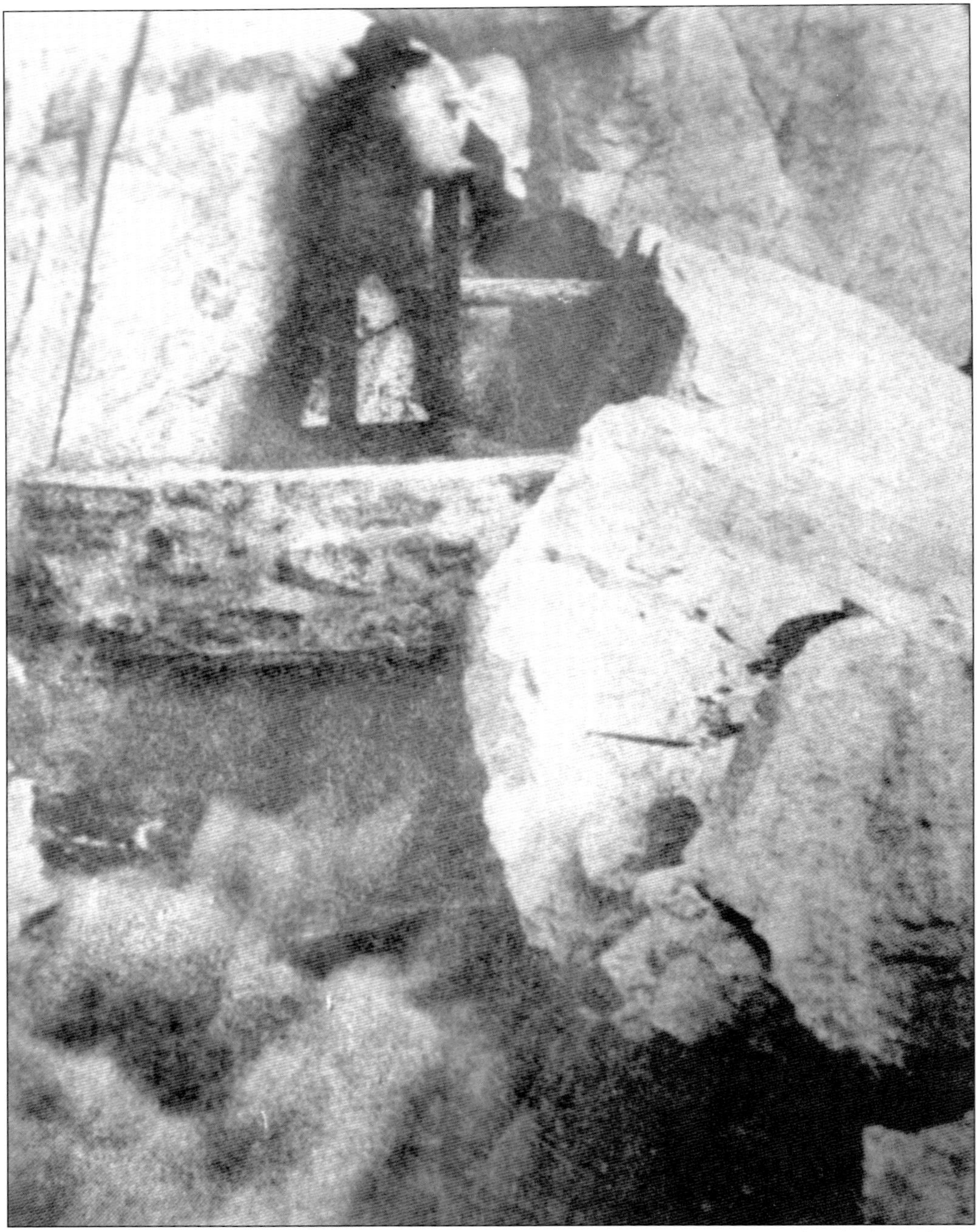

As part of this project, a valve was installed to direct the water either down the ditch or down Hesperia Creek. The water appropriations document dated August 20, 1885, allowed the Hesperia Land and Water Company to transport water from an agreed-upon location via ditch and pipe to an area described as Hesperia Township. The Arrowhead-area water table supplies Hesperia Creek and then flows into the Mojave River. The water appropriation documents dictated how much water could be drawn and the frequency of the draws. Hesperia was allowed to draw 500 inches of water at 4 inches of pressure for domestic purposes and irrigation. (Courtesy MHS.)

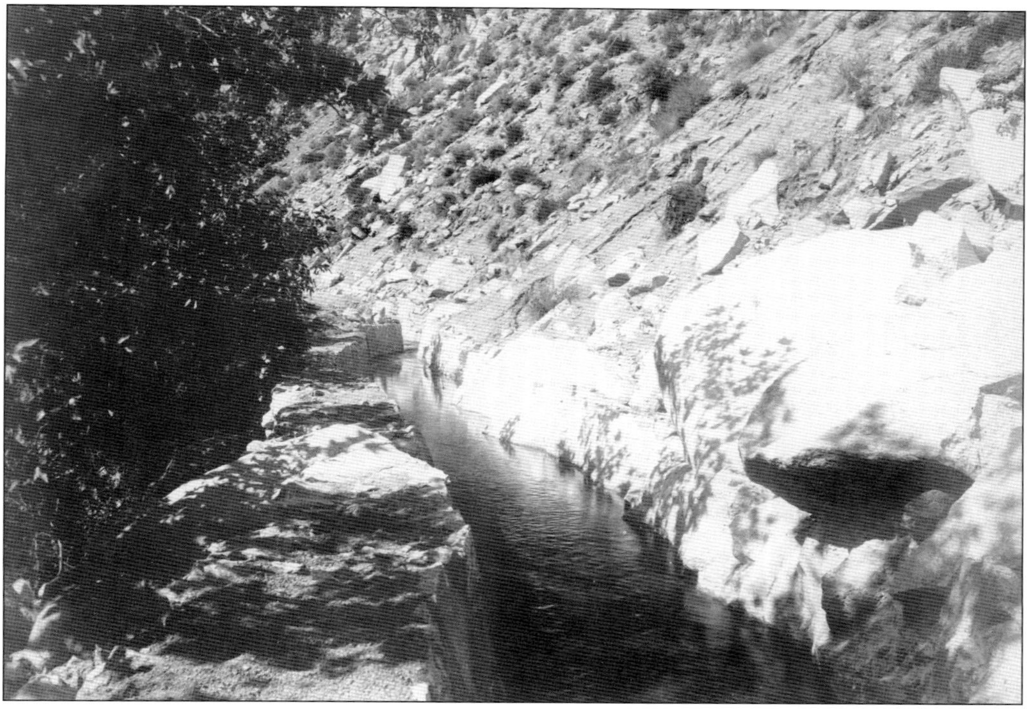

When the ditch was finished, the valve was opened and the water flowed down the newly sculpted delivery system and gradually traversed the side of the hill, making sweeps in and out of the crevices and contours of the slope. After a nearly 5-mile journey, the water funneled into a 14-inch pipe and dropped at a 50-to-60-degree angle for about 150 feet, creating a good amount of head pressure to push the water on its path through the pipeline and northward under the Mojave River to Hesperia Lake. It would then continue on up today's Honda Valley over the mesa and down into the wash area (along modern-day Jenkins Avenue) and to the awaiting reservoir at Lime Street Park. The entire journey was a system of pressure and suction to get the water to its destination. (Both, courtesy HL.)

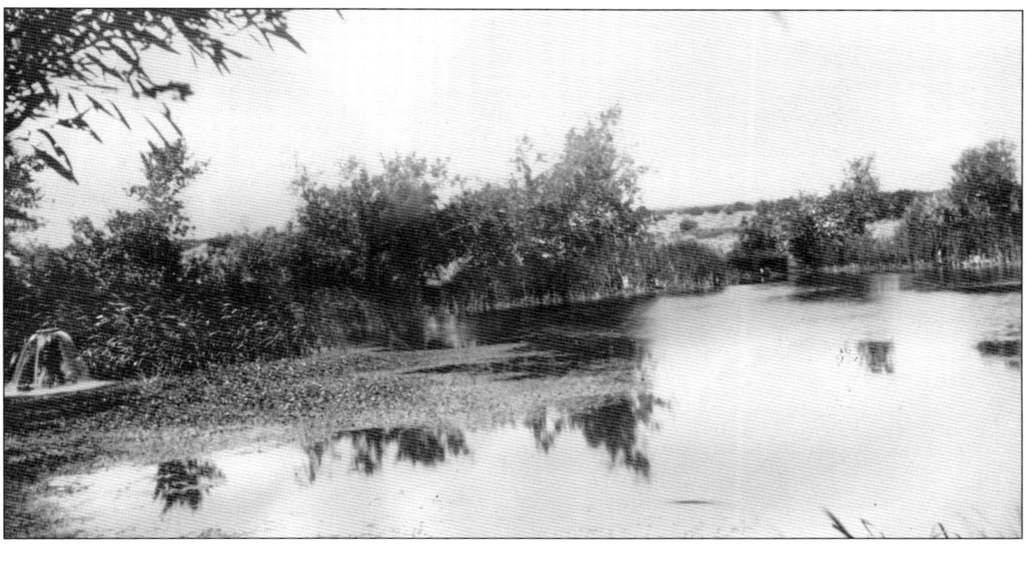

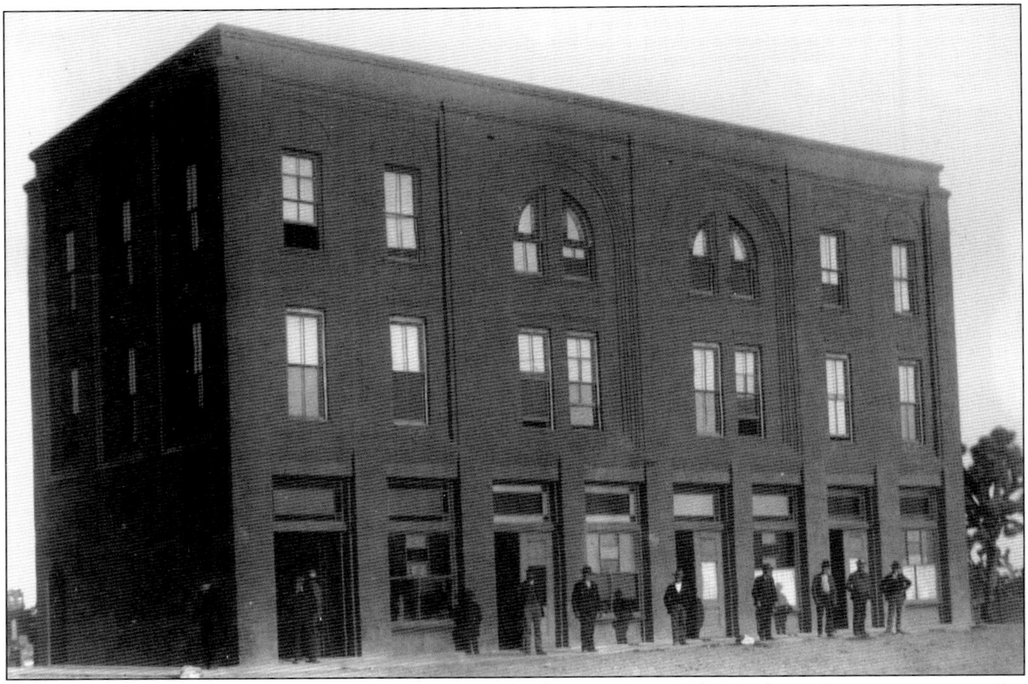

The Hesperia Hotel stood as a magnificent sight for weary travelers riding the train across the desert or up the Cajon Pass. It stood roughly 65 feet long, 45 feet deep, and 45 feet tall, and its wonders included hot and cold running water and a communication system that connected all three floors. A center stairway reached from the basement to the third floor. The second and third levels offered guests shared restrooms (with indoor plumbing), and the ground floor featured a dining room and lobby. The basement housed the kitchen and storage. (Both, courtesy HOTM.)

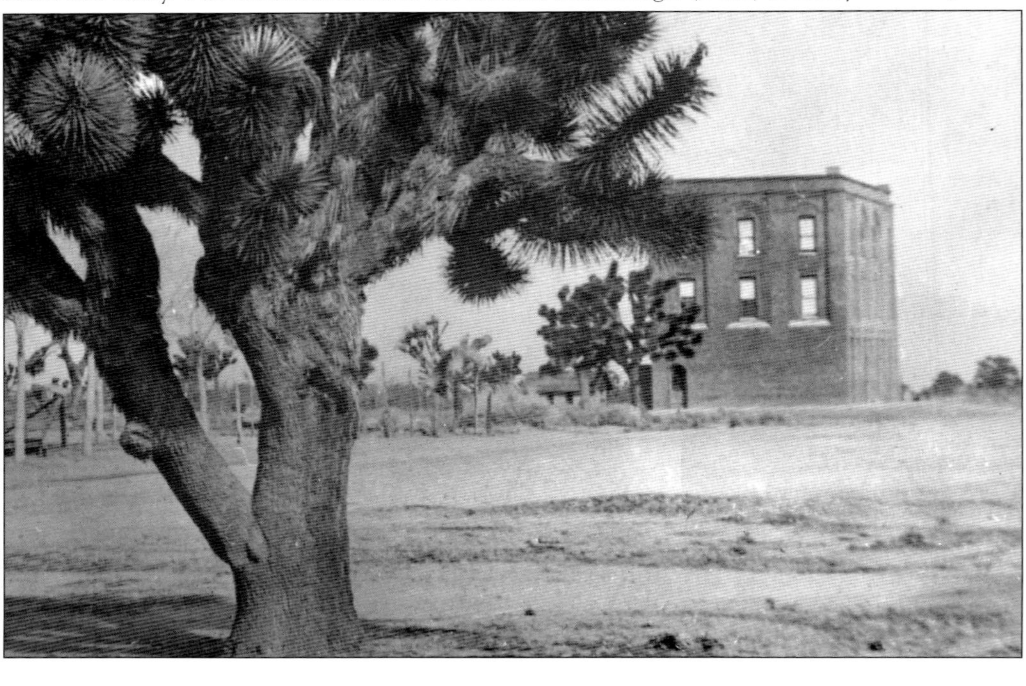

Four

Turning the Century

As the hotel and the ditch were being built, many other things were underway as well. New maps revealed plans for the town's water system, parks, hotel, and many other proposed civic improvements. Farmers grew grapes for wine. The first town business directories were produced, and the first censuses were taken.

As Hesperia—and its need for water—continued to grow, the ditch was expanded to include a 30-inch pipe in its delivery system. The Walters family started the town's first general store, which doubled as Hesperia's post office for nearly 50 years. Due to the area's clean, dry air, the new White Hotel housed many tuberculosis patients. Meanwhile, the Hesperia Hotel was thriving as a quality hotel for travelers on their way into the High Desert. AAA guides of the day recommended the Hesperia Hotel to motorists as well as Hesperia Garage for those in need of repairs. In the early 1920s, the Hesperia Hotel was the place of an impromptu recital by the world famous pianist Ignacy Paderewski.

This would not be the last noteworthy event in Hesperia during the 1920s. All through the decade, events and projects took place that would affect Hesperia's future. Miller's Corner became a favorite stop for aviators flying into and out of the Mojave Desert. Oil speculators drilled wells. The trip up the Cajon Pass—designed for horse-drawn wagons and riders on horseback—was now proving popular with motorists. Travelers of the day wrote about the importance of carrying a water bag on the radiator for additional cooling and how navigating the roads was made tricky by the width of ruts left by wagon wheels, which was different from the axle width of the new automobiles.

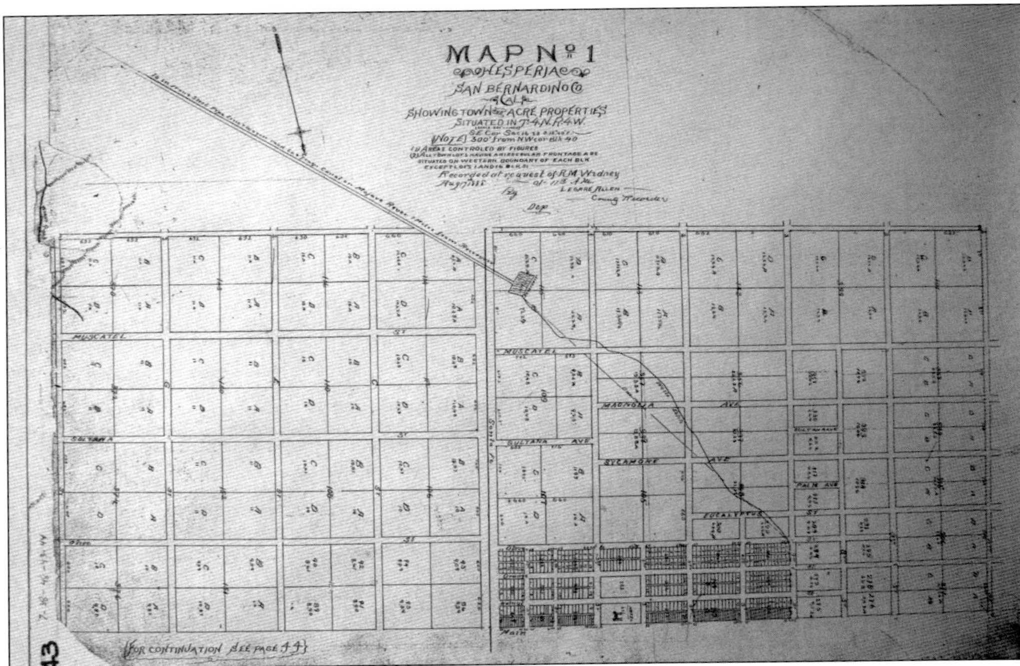

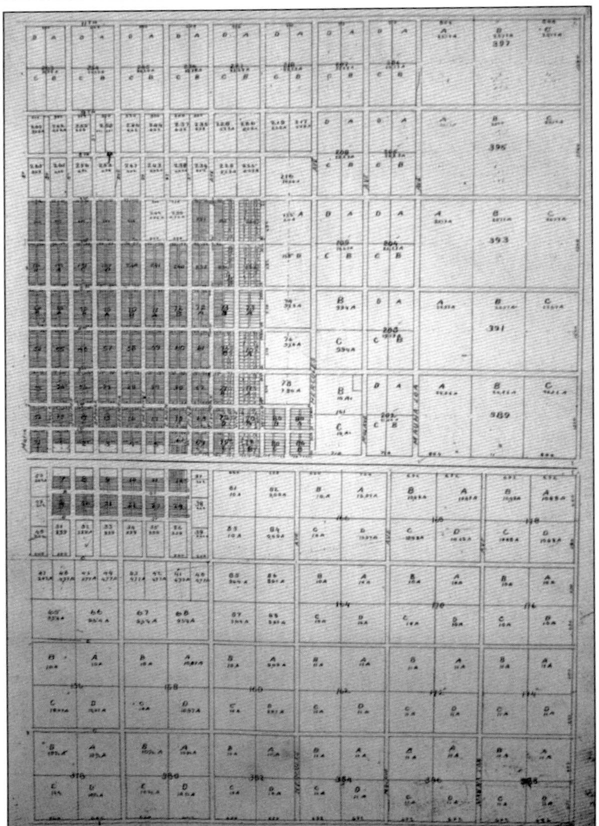

The original township subdivisions stretched from Eleventh Avenue to I Avenue and from Mojave Street to Lime Street. Drawn up at the request of R. M. Widney and recorded with San Bernardino County recorder Legare Allen on August 17, 1888, these maps show the 14-inch water pipe coming from the ditch to the reservoir at what is now Lime Street Park. They also show the original planned location of the Hesperia Hotel, which ended up instead at the corner of Hesperia Road and Spruce Street. Note that at the time of this map, the location of the original schoolhouse has not yet been determined. (Both, courtesy SBCA.)

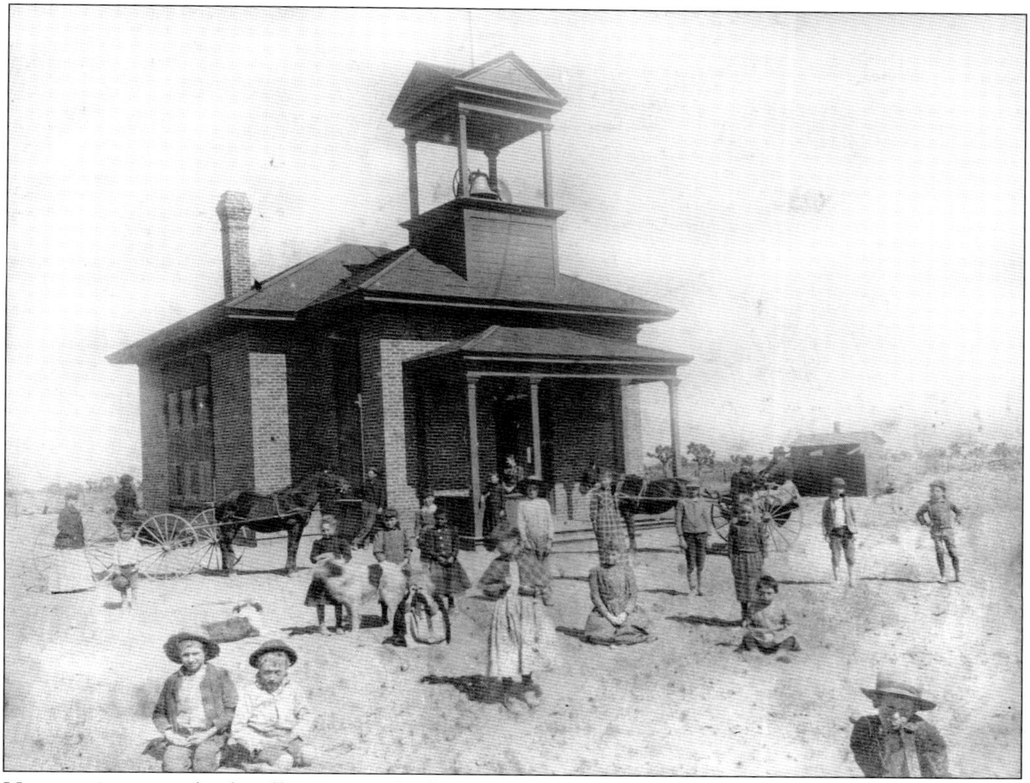

Hesperia's original schoolhouse was built in the mid- to late 1880s and is located at C Avenue and Main Street. From the town's first days until 1926, the schoolhouse served all the children in the area, no matter what grade they attended. This photograph is one of very few from the era. Unlike the adobe-brick Hesperia Hotel, the schoolhouse was made of fired bricks brought up from Colton by wagon. (Courtesy HOTM.)

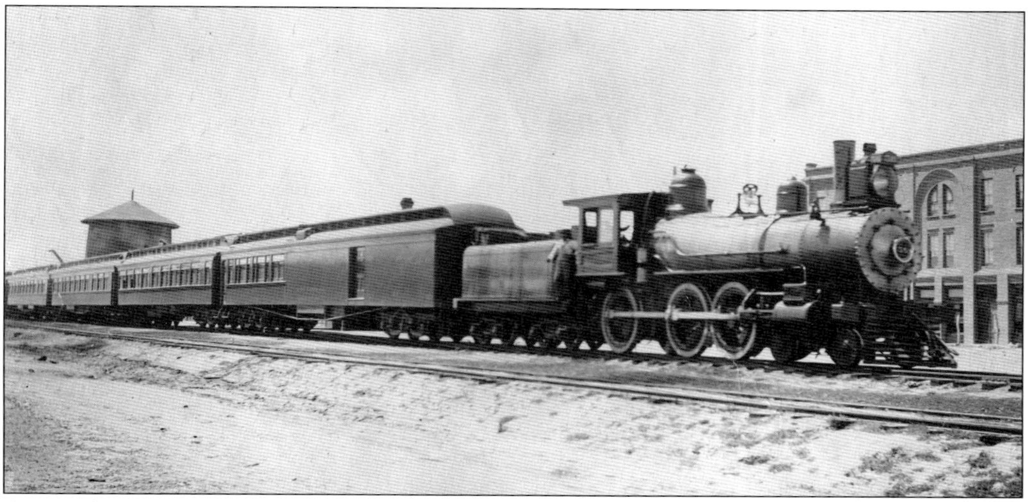

On an afternoon in the early 1900s, engine No. 56 pulls a string of railcars past the Hesperia Hotel. Two operators are visible in the cab of the locomotive. In the background, on the left, stands the water tower used to service the engines after they pulled into Hesperia. (Courtesy HRPD.)

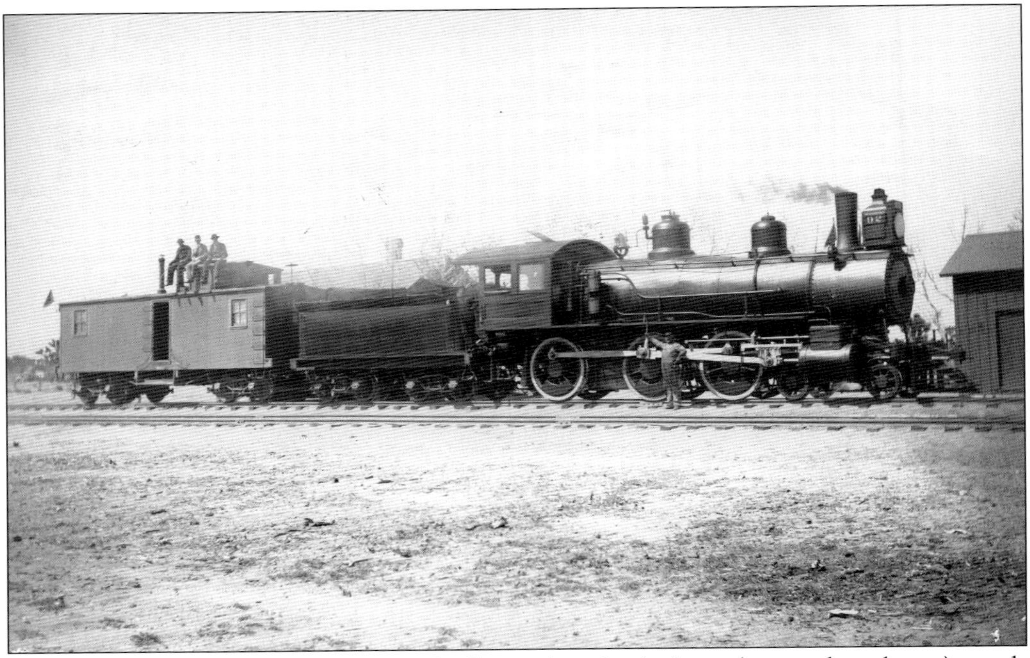

The crew of locomotive engine No. 92 (pulling a short load of a coal car and a caboose) stands and sits for a portrait at the Hesperia rail depot. The depot stood on skids, so it appears in different configurations in various pictures. In the background is the Hesperia Hotel. (Courtesy HRPD.)

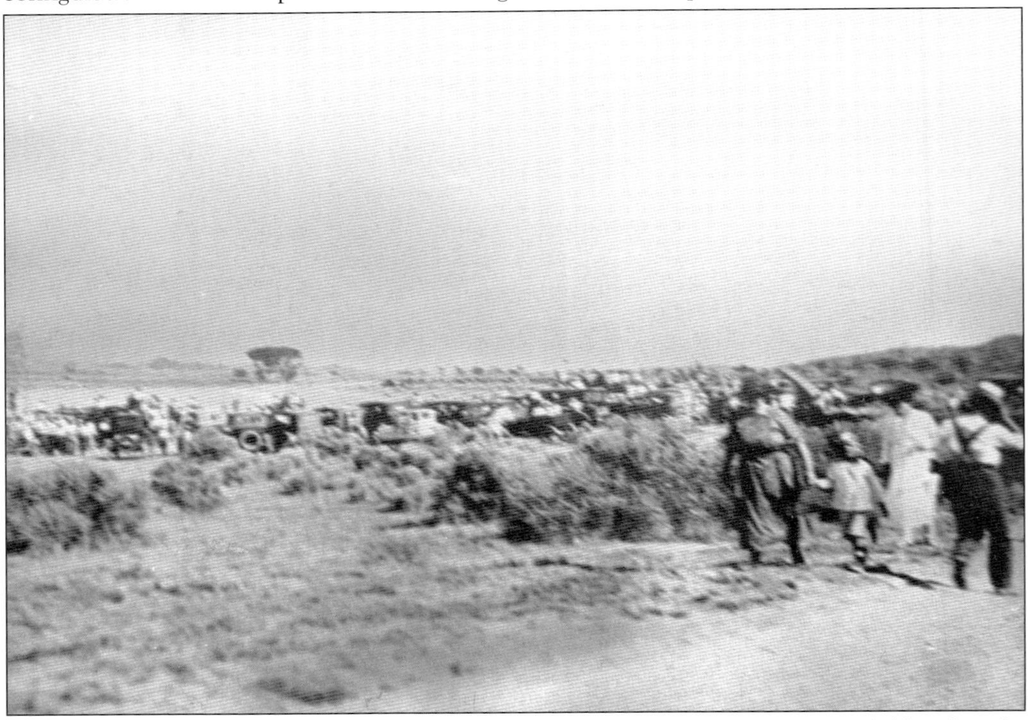

On this Fourth of July around 1900, the people of Hesperia have gathered beneath blue skies for an Independence Day celebration. (Courtesy HRPD.)

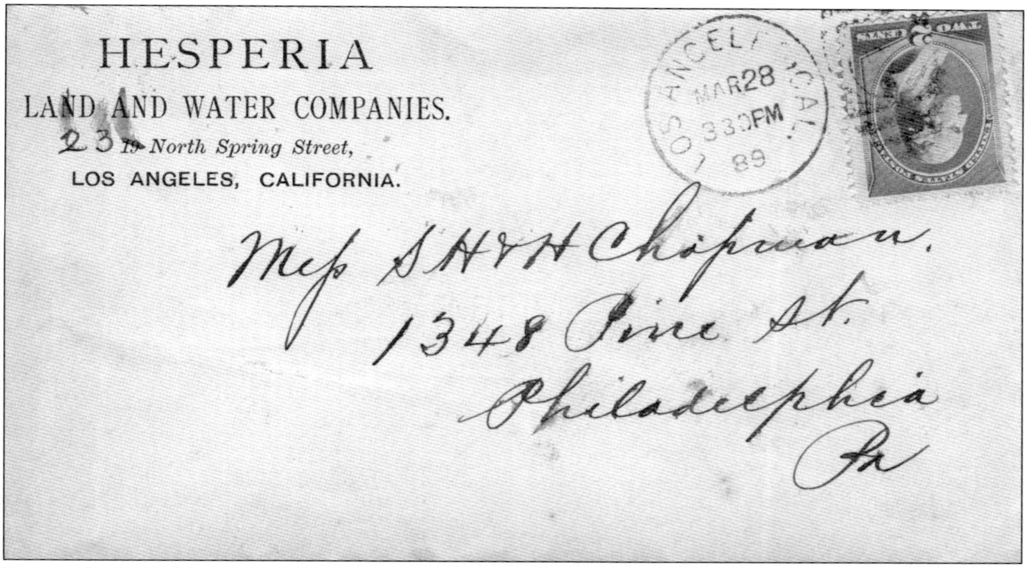

Postmarked at 3:30 p.m. on March 28, 1889, this envelope was mailed from the offices of the Hesperia Land and Water Company, which were at that time still in Los Angeles. The intended recipient appears to have resided in Philadelphia, Pennsylvania. Take note of the return address—the Hesperia Land and Water Company must have had a recent address change. (Courtesy HOTM.)

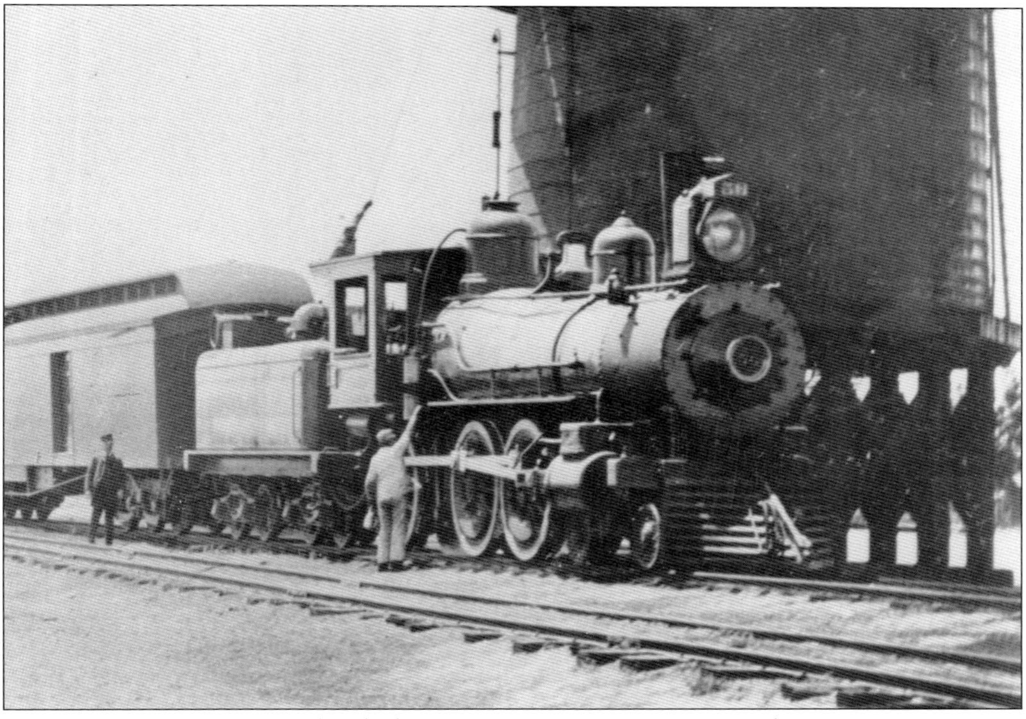

Locomotive engine No. 56 sits beside the Hesperia water tower as its crew takes on water to continue the trip across the Mojave Desert. One man is inspecting the engine just forward of the cab, and the conductor appears to be coming forward to check with the crew. (Courtesy HOTM.)

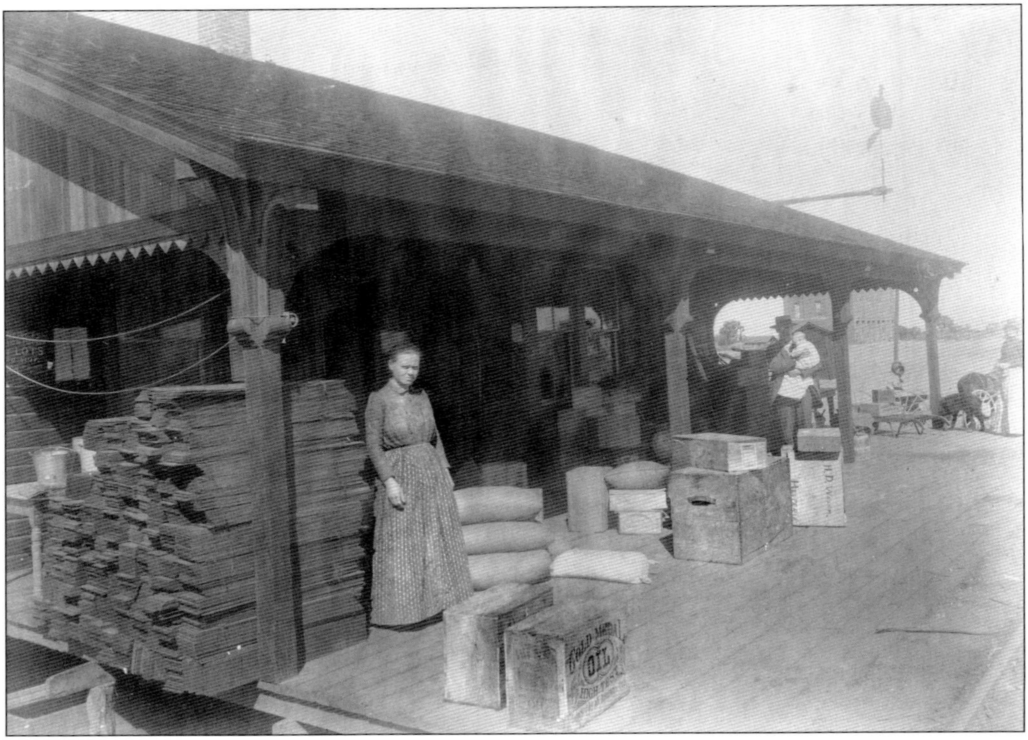

This *c.* 1890 photograph shows the Hesperia depot with several deliveries on the decking. In the background on the right stands the Hesperia Hotel. The sign on the left side of the station advertises "Low-Priced Lots for Sale" and "Will Build to Suit." (Courtesy HRPD.)

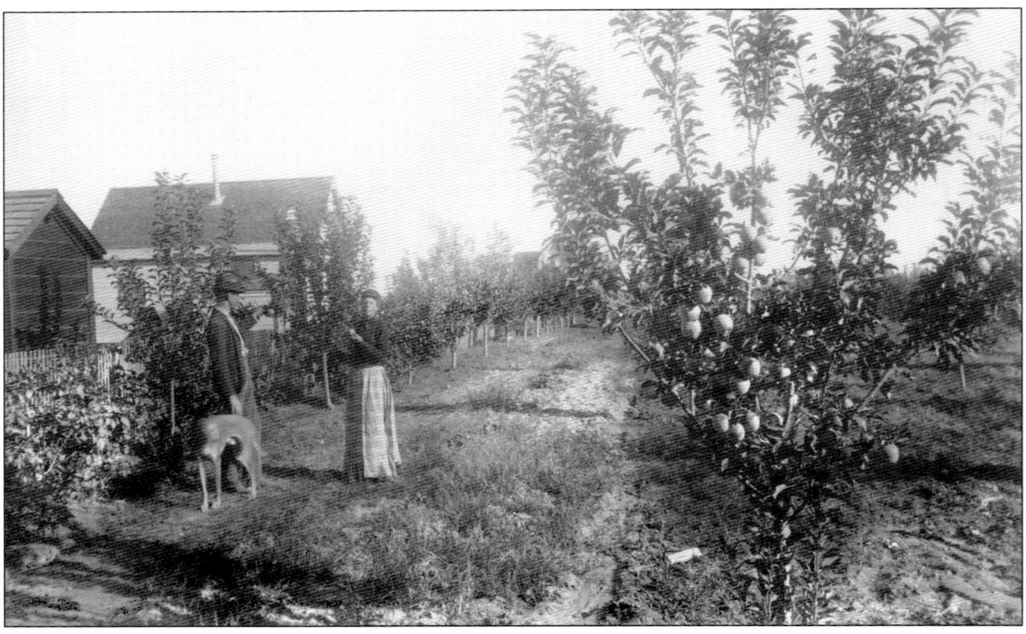

Hesperia farmers have grown a variety of crops throughout history. Here is a Hesperia apple orchard, seen around 1890. (Courtesy HRPD.)

As the railroad stations were built, the Santa Fe Railroad used topography peg books to document how its depots were built and where they were located. The peg books also showed tool inventories. The cover and inside pages here—preserved at the California Railroad Museum in Sacramento–date to about 1900 and show not only the original drawings but subsequent changes, which were marked in red pencil. (Courtesy CRRM.)

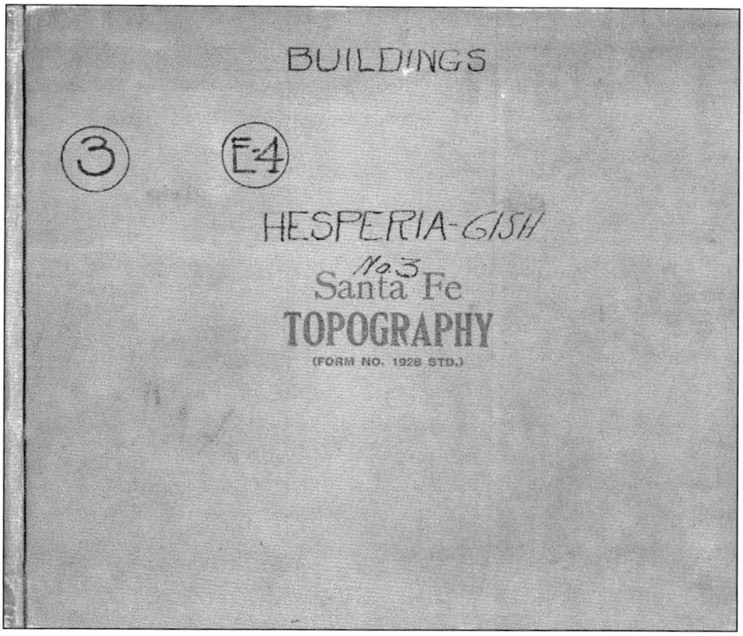

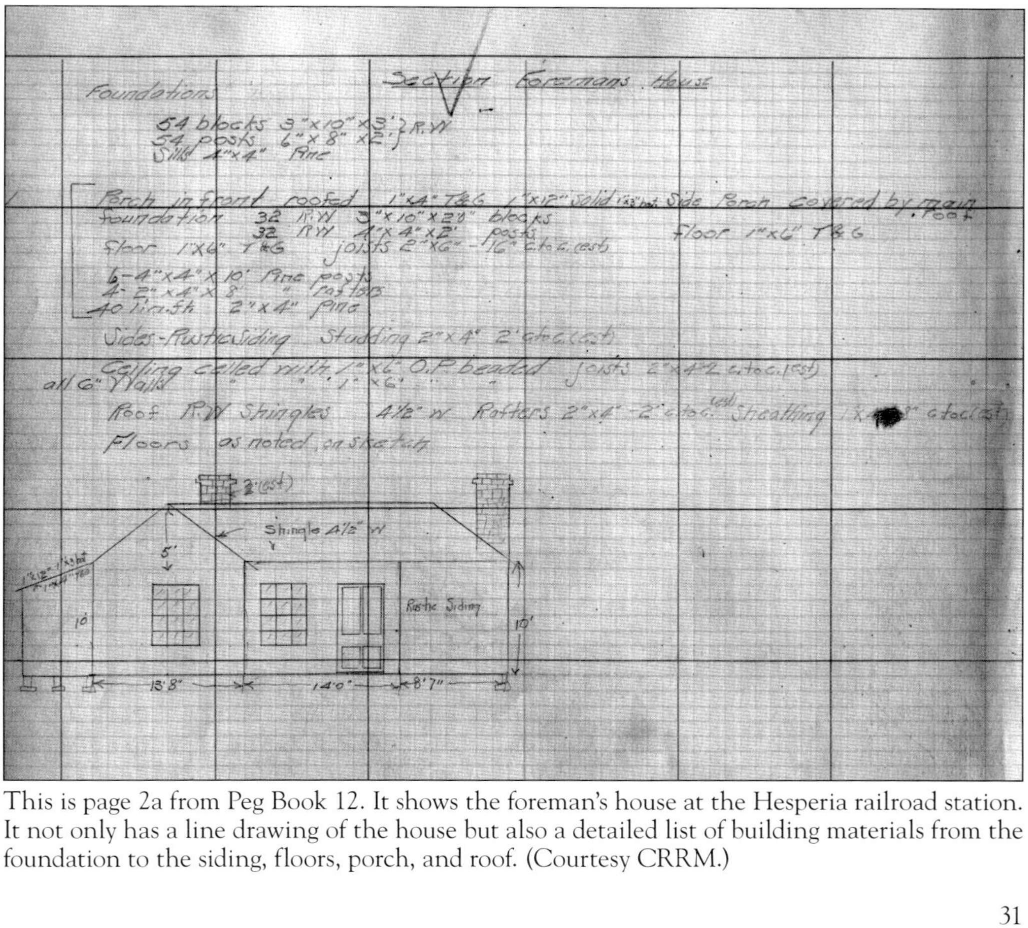

This is page 2a from Peg Book 12. It shows the foreman's house at the Hesperia railroad station. It not only has a line drawing of the house but also a detailed list of building materials from the foundation to the siding, floors, porch, and roof. (Courtesy CRRM.)

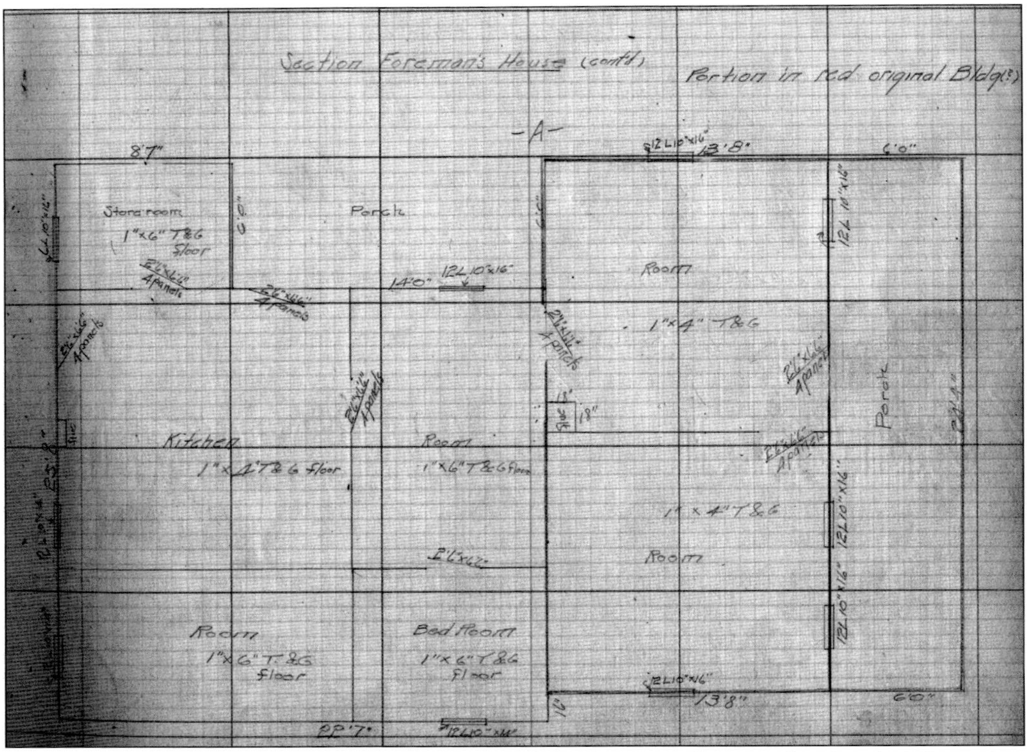

This is Peg Book 12, page 2b—a continuation of the foreman's house. The detailed floor plan shows seven rooms and two porches. The rooms include a kitchen, bedroom, general-use rooms, and a storeroom. (Courtesy CRRM.)

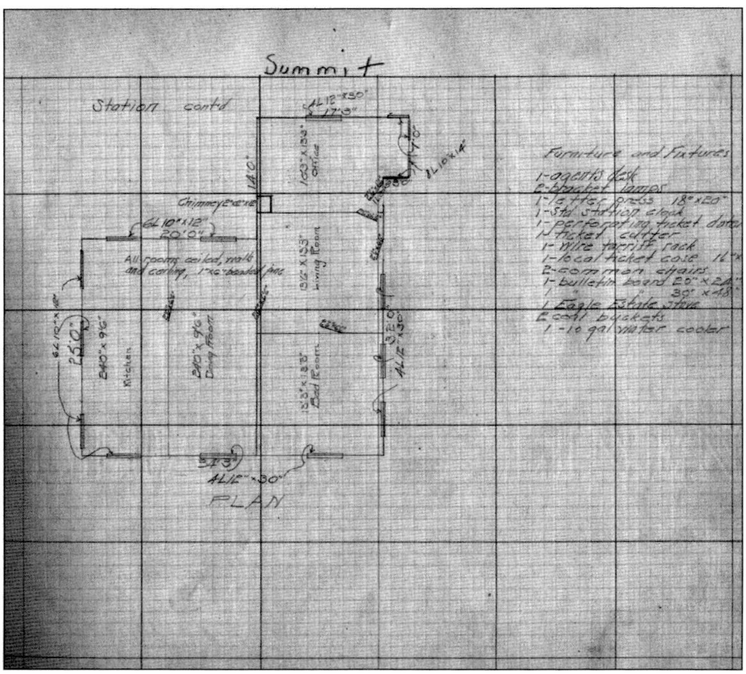

In Peg Book 12, page 8b, Summit Valley railroad station appears to differ from Hesperia station in that it is a combination living quarters and rail station. Summit Valley station sat approximately 4 miles east of Interstate 15 and 6 miles southwest of Main Street and Hesperia Road. (Courtesy CRRM.)

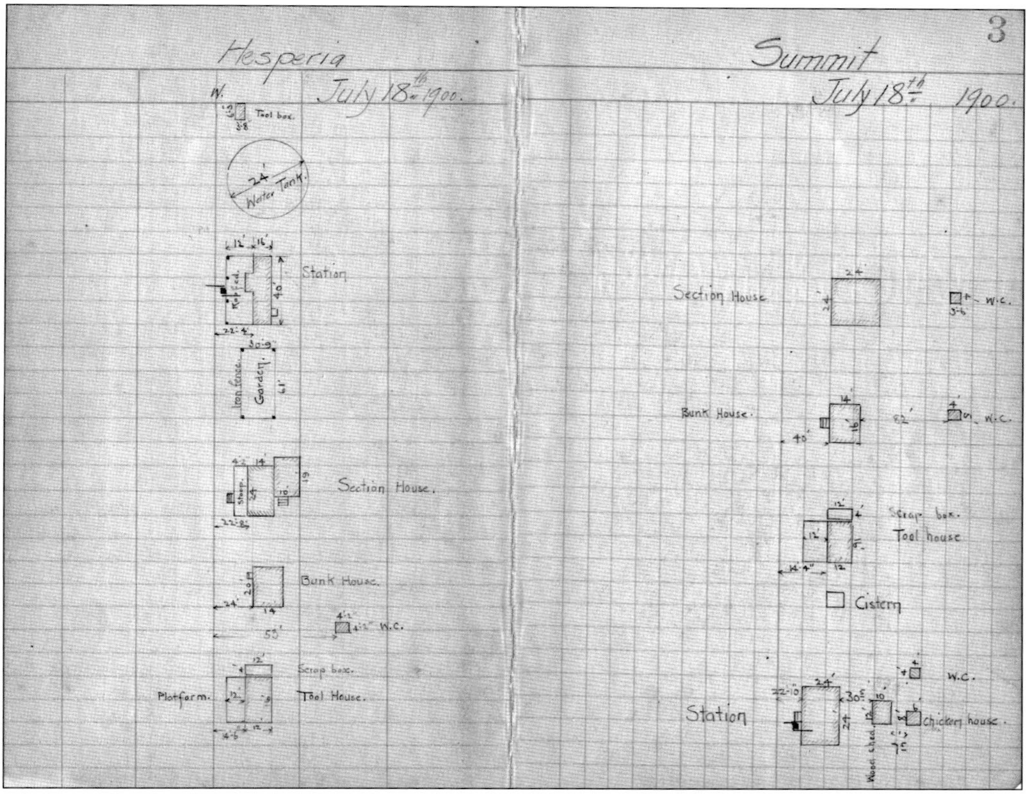

Here, on the third page of Peg Book 43, it is possible to compare the Hesperia and Summit Valley stations. Hesperia shows a water tower and bigger buildings to accommodate its larger crew. According to its description here, the Summit Valley station was not set up for transferring cargo, nor did it offer any lodging for passengers. (Courtesy CRRM.)

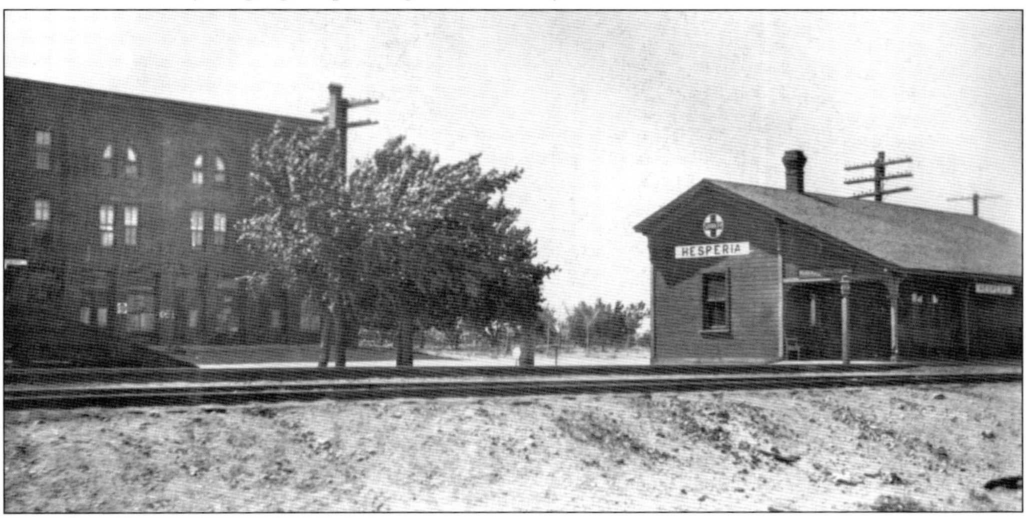

The Hesperia railroad station is shown here with the Hesperia Hotel in the background. This photograph was taken about 12 years after the hotel was finished; power poles have been installed, and the trees that were planted are starting to mature. (Courtesy HOTM.)

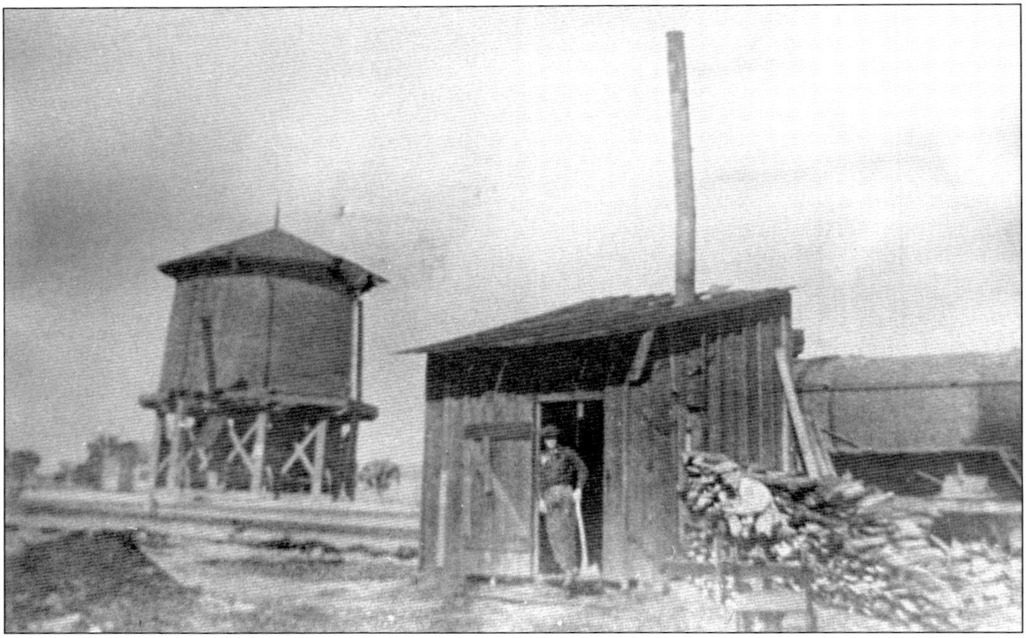

Seen around 1900 are two of a steam railroad's most vital structures: a woodshed and a water tower. In the shed lay the split timber needed to fuel the locomotives (and for cooking and heating in the station). The tower held the water needed to propel the steam engines. (Courtesy MHS.)

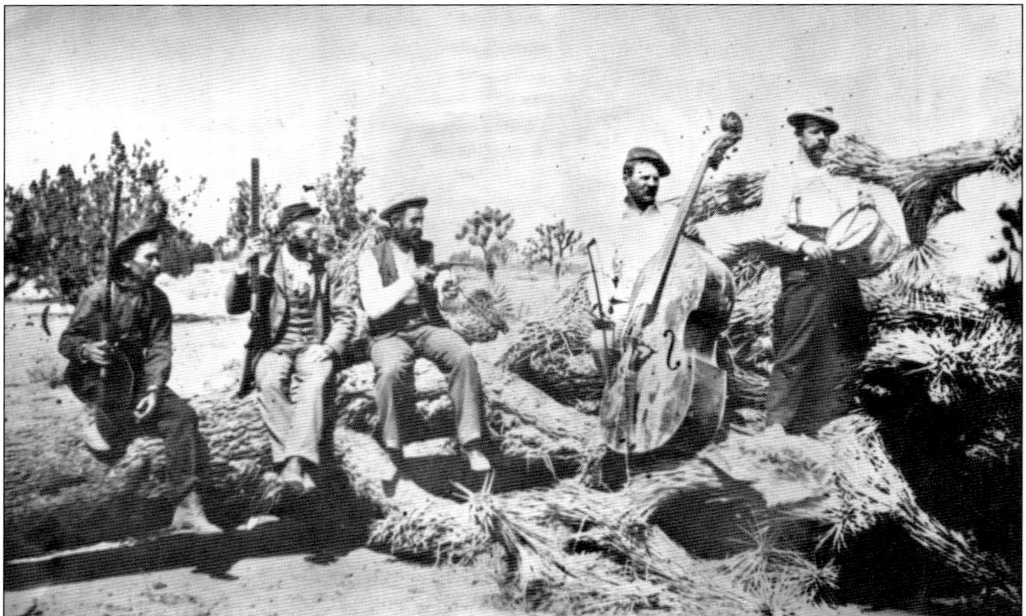

After a good grape harvest at the Sefton Ranch, it was customary to have a festive time, always accompanied by music. Pictured here is one of those times, but things look a little less than festive: while two men hold instruments, two others hold rifles, and a fifth is pointing a pistol at the musicians. (Courtesy HRPD.)

Chas. E. Walker. John Flagg. W. R. McIntosh.

McIntosh, Flagg & Walker's

SAN BERNARDINO CITY AND COUNTY

DIRECTORY

AND ALSO A

CLASSIFIED BUSINESS DIRECTORY

— OF —

SAN BERNARDINO, RIVERSIDE AND COLTON.

PART I.

A GENERAL RESIDENCE AND OCCUPATION DIRECTORY OF THE CITY OF SAN BERNARDINO; A STREET DIRECTORY OF SAN BERNARDINO; NATIONAL, STATE, COUNTY AND MUNICIPAL OFFICIAL DIRECTORY; PUBLIC AND PRIVATE SCHOOLS; STREET RAILWAYS; FRATERNAL SOCIETIES; CHURCHES; RAILROADS, ETC., ETC.

PART II.

NAME, OCCUPATION AND POSTOFFICE ADDRESS OF THE COUNTRY PEOPLE, AND RESIDENTS OF THE TOWNS AND CITIES OF THE COUNTY, AND ALSO A SKETCH OF EVERY POSTOFFICE SITE IN THE COUNTY.

SAN BERNARDINO, CAL.:
Flagg & Walker, Printers and Binders.
1889.

In 1889, this classified business directory was published for San Bernardino, Riverside, and Colton, but it also covered Hesperia due to its close proximity via the Santa Fe Railroad. In its description of Hesperia, the directory mentions both the "Hesperia Mountains" and the "Hesperia Valley." It proclaims that the town's climate makes it a wonderful health resort for "consumptives"—people suffering from tuberculosis—and notes that Hesperia features the modern conveniences of telegraph service and daily mail delivery. The directory only lists about 32 laborers and businessmen, but there may be a few more that are not listed. J. F. Edwards is named as the manager of the new water system, known simply as "the ditch" or "the flume." The wood business must have been very good in Hesperia, as there are two wood dealers listed. (Both, courtesy HRPD.)

HESPERIA.

This place has an elevation of 2,500 feet above sea level, and is on the main line of the California Southern (Santa Fe) railroad, about twenty-five miles north of San Bernardino in the beautiful Hesperia valley, surrounded by the San Bernardino and Hesperia mountains. The climate is delightful all the year round, and is a health resort for consumptives. The place has a telegraph, express, and postoffice with a daily mail.

Caleff H, wood dealer
Cook R L, carpt
Dutton Jas, farm
Edwards J F, mgr water syst
Elliott Walter, teamster
Gaskell Edwin A, labr
Harris J A, teamster
Howard A L, operator
Hunt Frank, teamster
Lemon Chas S, wood dealer
Lytle Chas, farm
Martin J B, poultryman
McDonald J B, woodchopper
McFeely Jas, farm
McInnis —, labr
Michalson O, labr
Moore J T, hort
O'Malley Chas, miner
Pier Thos, farm
Porter Jos G, labr
Pringle Geo, sec foreman
Reed C A Miss
Reynolds Wm, farm
Richards —, labr
Rockwell Chas, mercht
Rockwell Priscilla W Mrs
Schmees Wm, farm
Seaton Wm
Sifton A L Mrs
Sifton Hon J W, M P P
Sifton J W Mrs
Whitthorn W R, farm

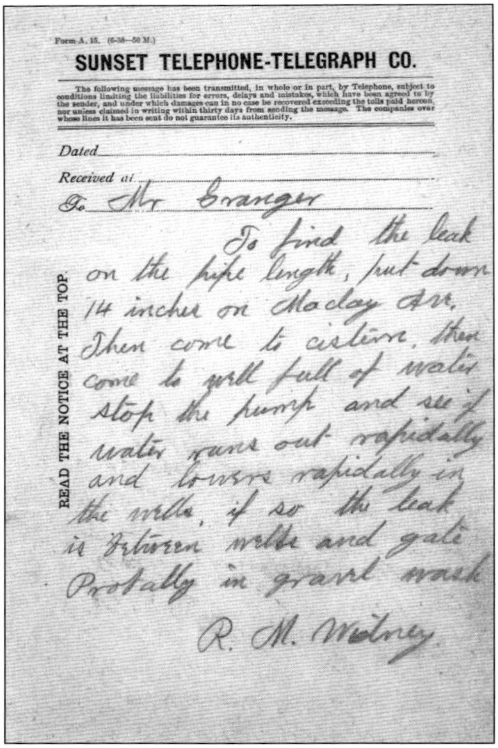

Form A. 15. (6-38—50 M.)

SUNSET TELEPHONE-TELEGRAPH CO.

The following message has been transmitted, in whole or in part, by Telephone, subject to conditions limiting the liabilities for errors, delays and mistakes, which have been agreed to by the sender, and under which damages can in no case be recovered exceeding the tolls paid hereon, nor unless claimed in writing within thirty days from sending the message. The companies over whose lines it has been sent do not guarantee its authenticity.

Dated

Received at

To Mr Granger

To find the leak on the pipe length, put down 14 inches on Maclay Av. Then come to cistern, then come to well full of water stop the pump and see if water runs out rapidally and lowers rapidally in the wells, if so the leak is between wells and gate Probably in gravel wash

R. M. Widney

READ THE NOTICE AT THE TOP.

Though based in Los Angeles, R. M. Widney stayed apace with the managers he had put in charge at Hesperia through regular use of the telegraph. He also used the railroad to meet with his on-site managers on a routine basis. Shown here are a few 1890s telegraph messages sent by Widney. The main subject of these, predictably, was the water system. (Both, courtesy UCLA.)

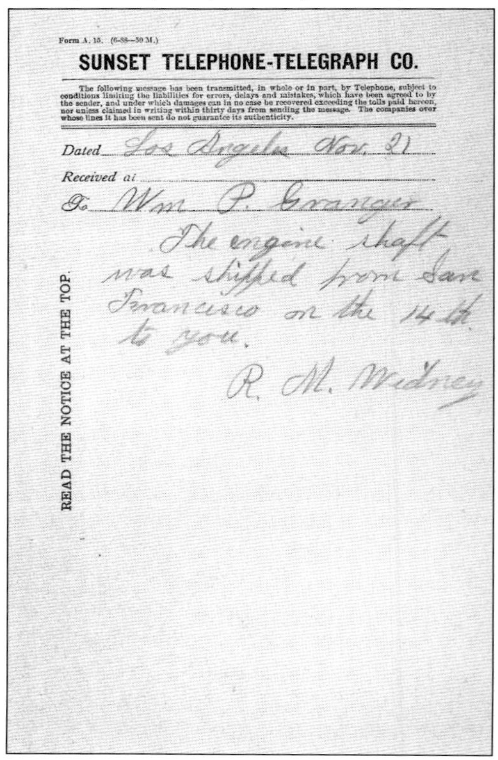

Form A. 15. (6-38—50 M.)

SUNSET TELEPHONE-TELEGRAPH CO.

The following message has been transmitted, in whole or in part, by Telephone, subject to conditions limiting the liabilities for errors, delays and mistakes, which have been agreed to by the sender, and under which damages can in no case be recovered exceeding the tolls paid hereon, nor unless claimed in writing within thirty days from sending the message. The companies over whose lines it has been sent do not guarantee its authenticity.

Dated Los Angeles Nov. 21

Received at

To Wm P. Granger

The engine shaft was shipped from San Francisco on the 14th to you.

R. M. Widney

READ THE NOTICE AT THE TOP.

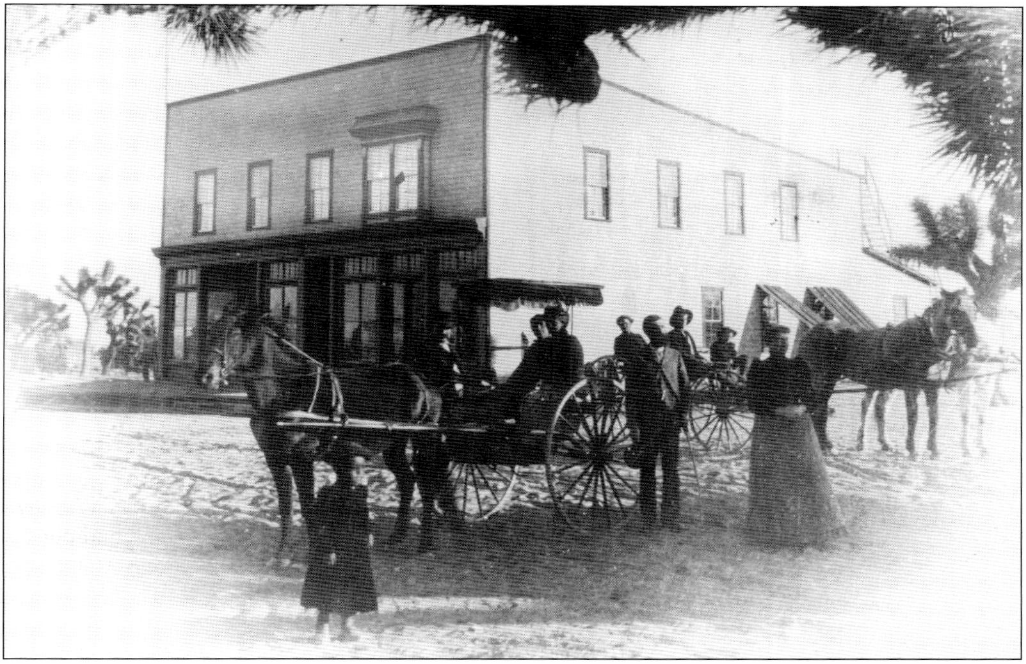

The White Hotel, shown here around 1900, was located near the intersection of Second Avenue and Juniper Streets, only a few blocks southwest of the Hesperia Hotel. The White Hotel was touted as Hesperia's health resort for tuberculosis patients, but it is unclear whether the hotel's name derived from one of the nicknames for the dread disease—"the White Plague," a reference to the pallor common among the afflicted. (Both, courtesy MHS.)

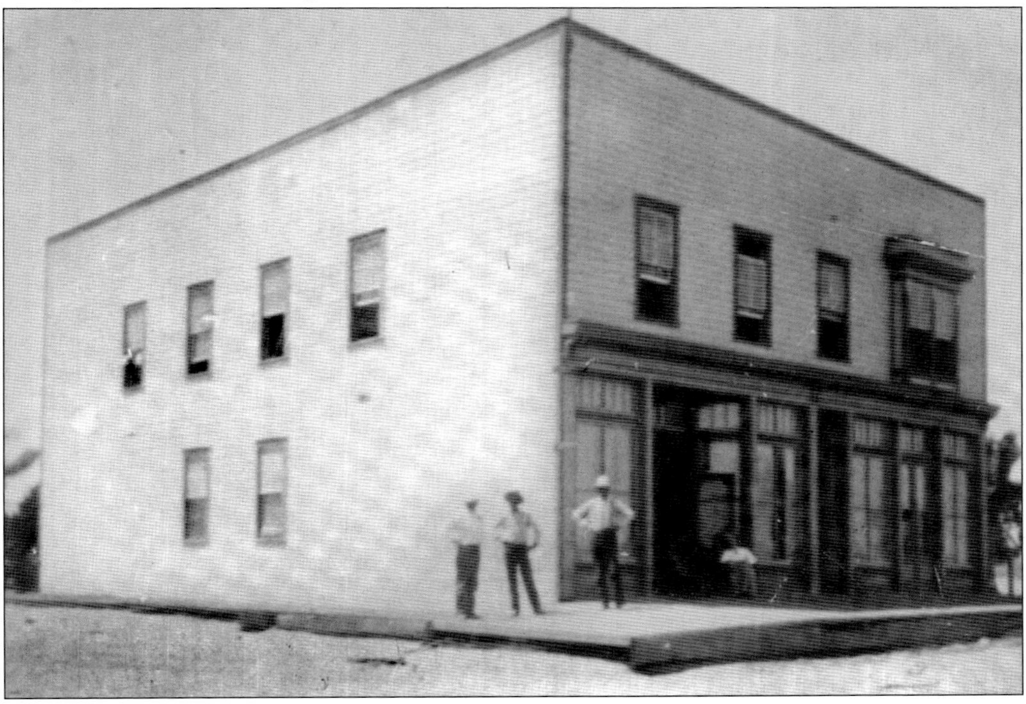

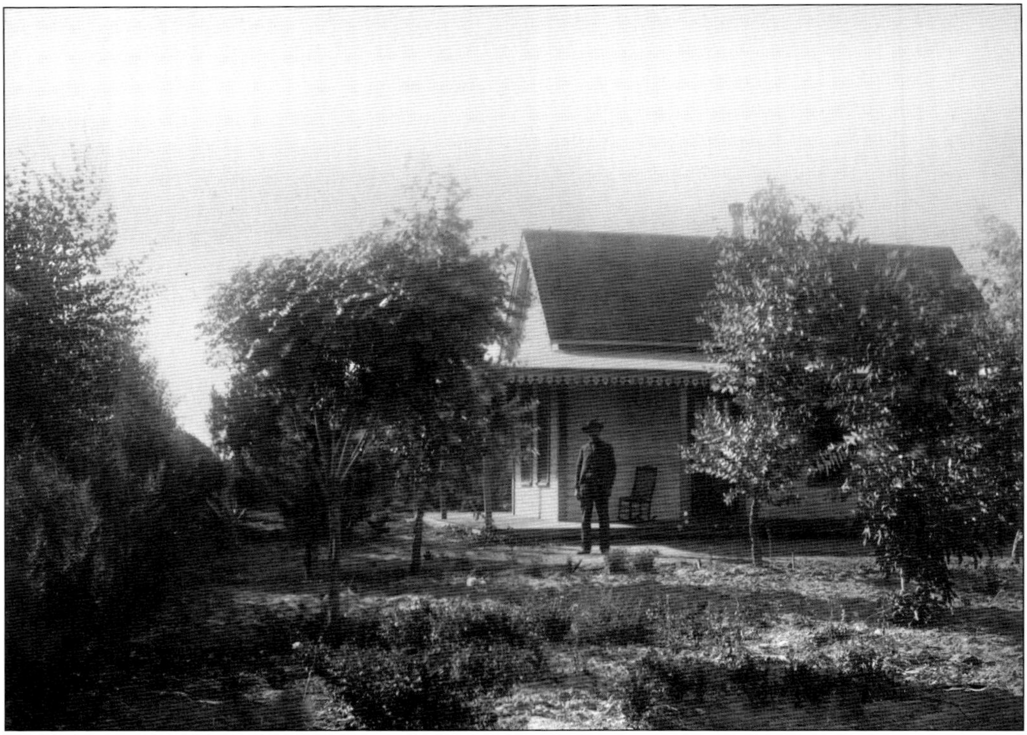

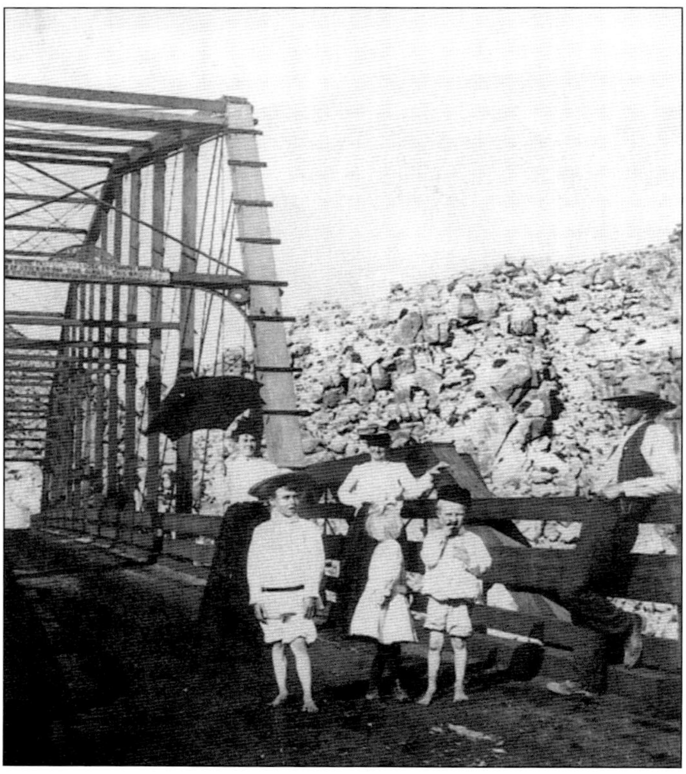

The local resident seen here is Sylvester McInnis, who built his home between 1888 and 1890. At least six generations of McInnises have lived in Hesperia. (Courtesy HRPD.)

This photograph was taken at the Narrows Bridge about 1906. The man on the far right is Columbus Frank Hedrick. His wife Charlotte stands against the bridge railing, and their son George Dewey Hedrick is the child in the front left. Frank would play an important part in the 1911 upgrade of Hesperia's water system. (Courtesy HF.)

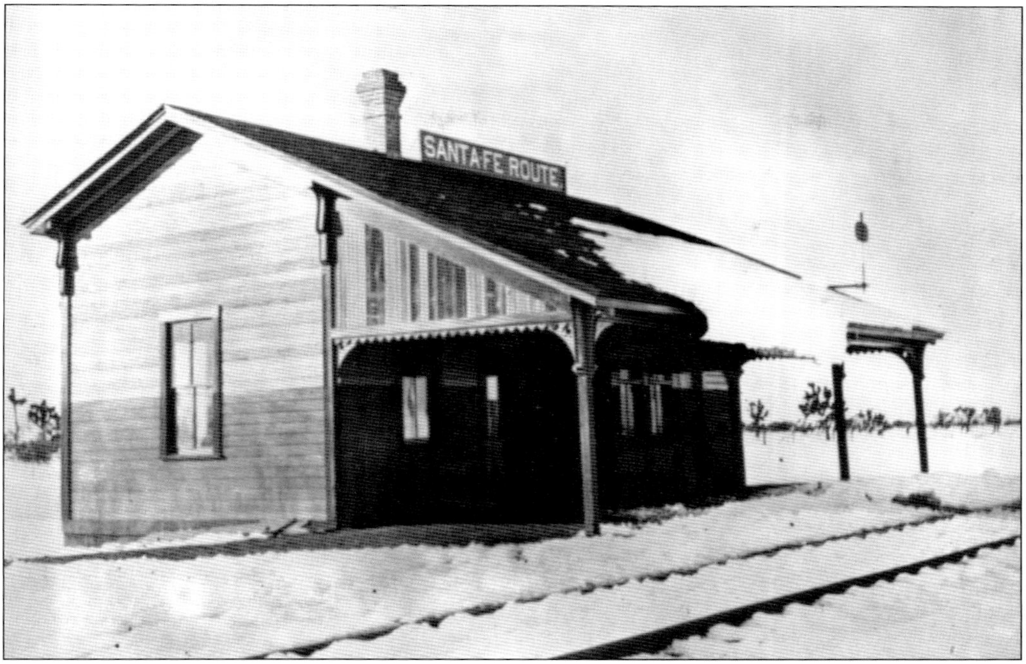

Most people think of the desert as hot, sandy, and desolate. The High Desert, however, has a beauty all its own. While it is true that summers can be very hot and dry, winters can bring snowfalls, which place a beautiful white blanket across the land. Seen here is the Hesperia Santa Fe rail station one winter day in the early 1900s. (Courtesy HRPD.)

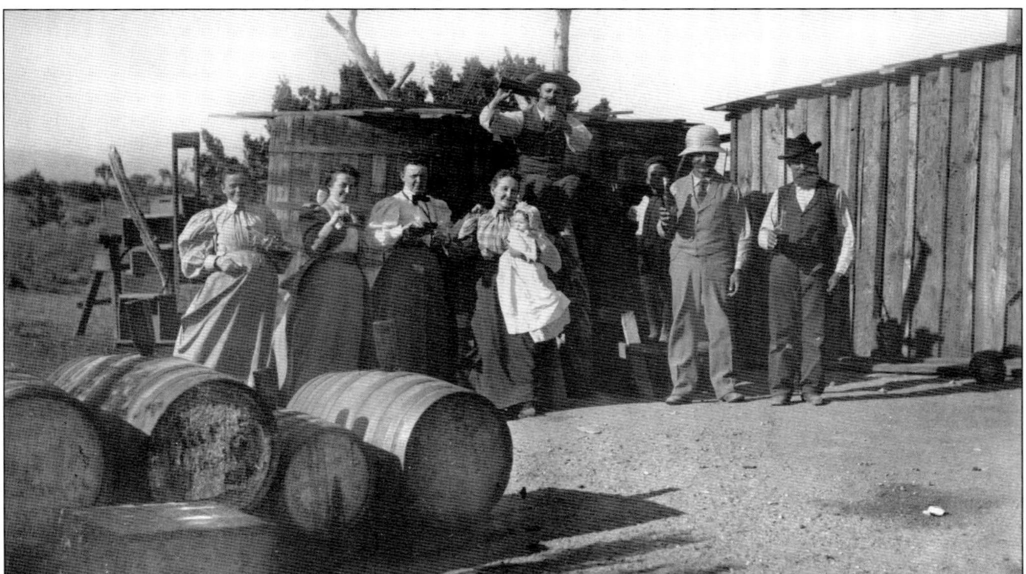

In the 1890s, one of the area's crops was grapes. Given the expressions on their faces here, one wonders whether the Seftons and their friends have been enjoying the fruits of their own labor. In the 1940s, remnants of wine presses and grapevines were found near Sultana Street between E Avenue and east of Santa Fe Avenue. (Courtesy HOTM.)

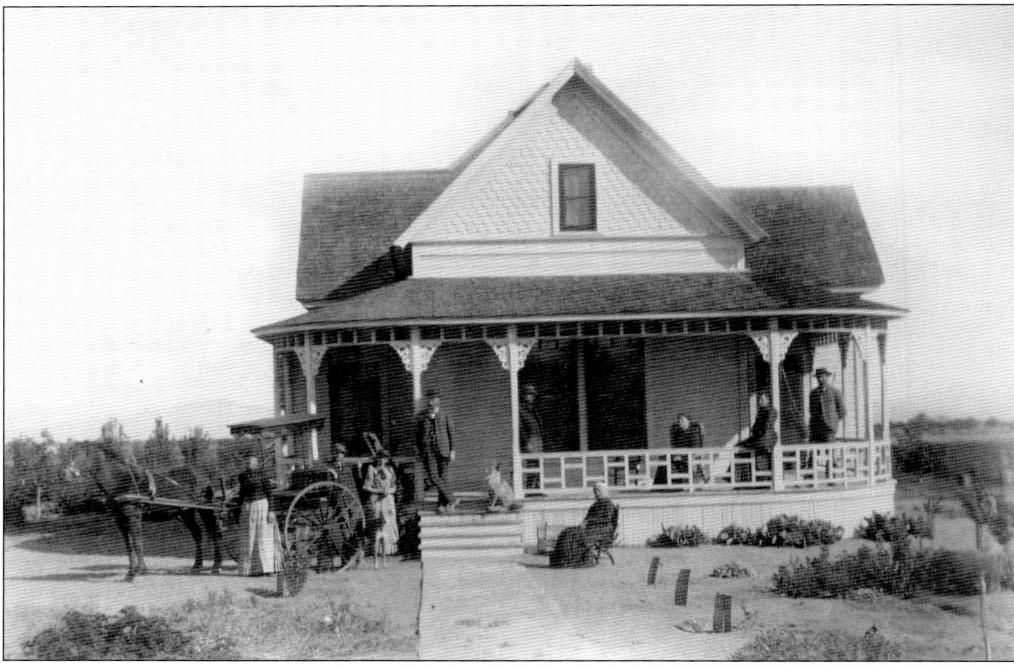

This *c.* 1895 photograph of Mrs. Shaw's cottage was taken by C. H. Shaffner with a backdrop of clear High Desert skies and the San Bernardino Mountains. About 180 acres of the Shaws' property was planted in grapes. (Courtesy HRPD.)

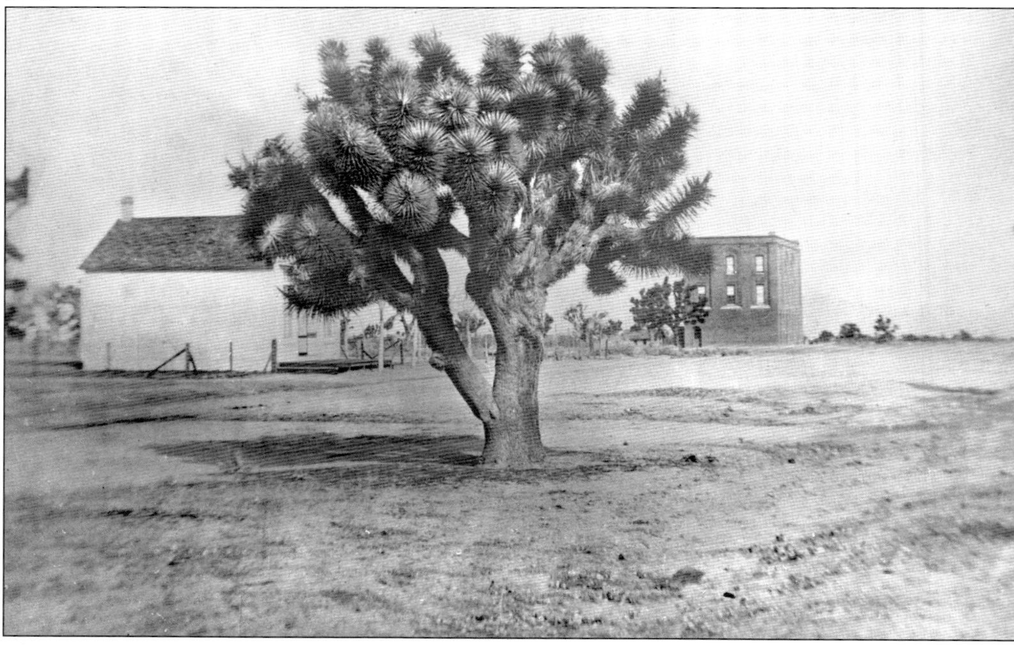

This may be one of the earliest photographs of the Hesperia Hotel, shown here sitting beside the National Old Trails Highway. The road has also gone by such names as Old Government Road, Old Indian Road, and Old Spanish Trail. This photograph shows the hotel around 1887, just after it was completed. (Courtesy HRPD.)

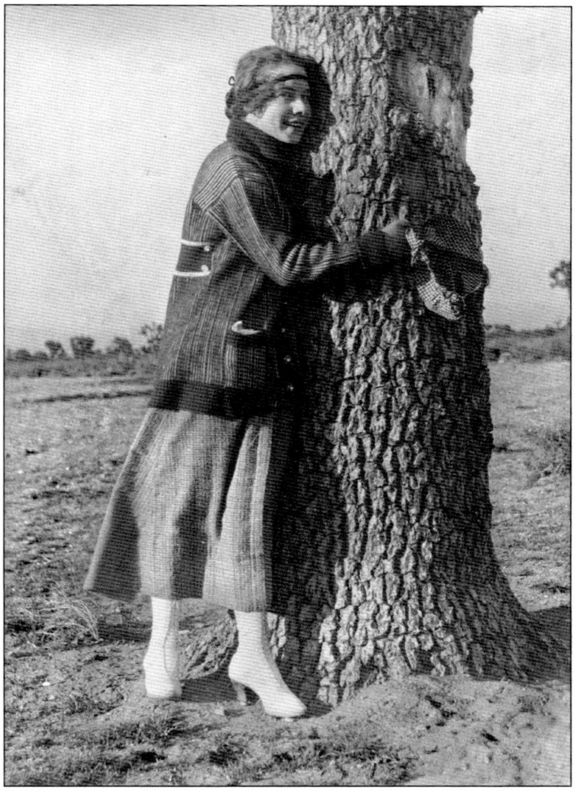

Hesperia's first "tree-hugger" is seen here around 1913. This photograph has appeared in several articles and books, but it took some investigation to identify the woman seen hugging that Joshua tree. A 1981 article in The *Hesperia Resorter* identified her as Verial Walters Ormand, sister of Roy Walters. In 1917, Verial Walters Ormand was the postmistress at the Walters Store. (Courtesy HRPD.)

When the Walters family first moved to Hesperia, they lived and worked at the Hesperia Hotel. Later they built their home just down the street. They started their store around 1916. This c. 1917 photograph shows the hotel, Hesperia Garage, the Walters home, and Walters Store. (Courtesy HRPD.)

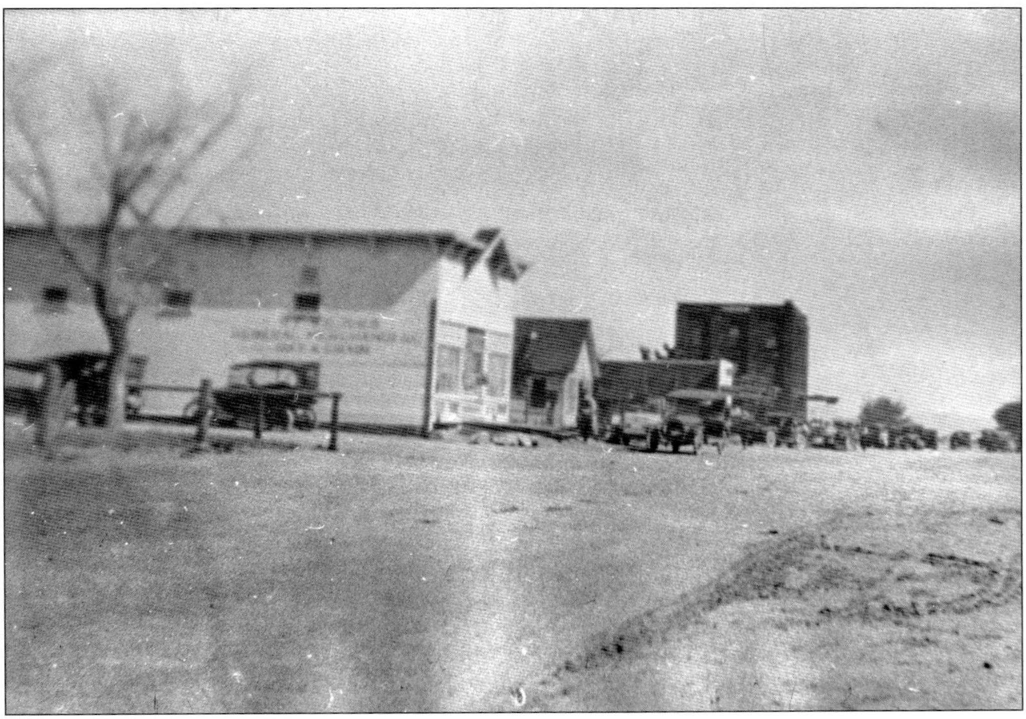

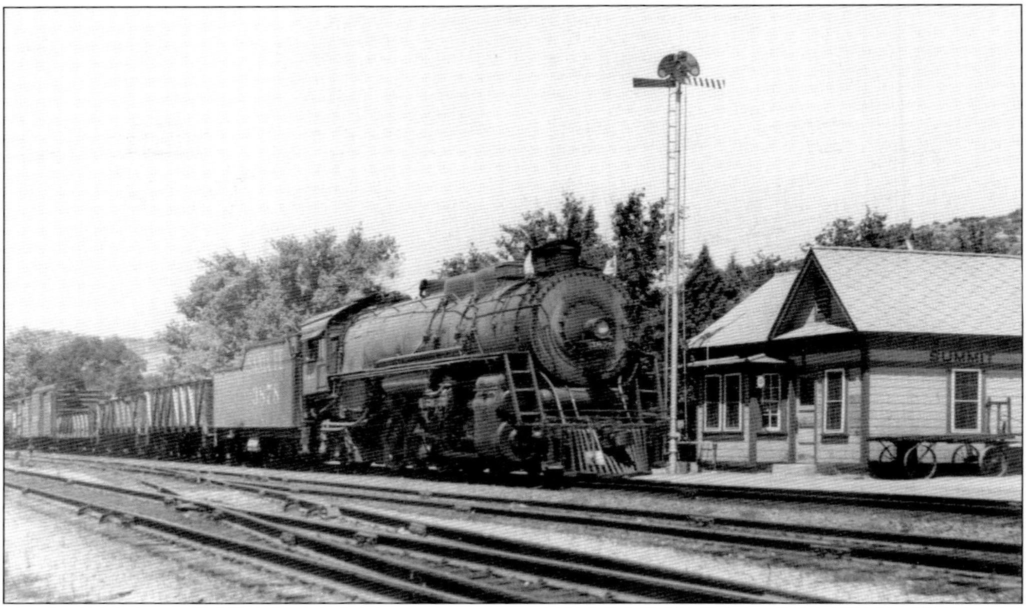

The photograph was taken in the 1920s. There were a few stops that the trains would make as they progressed up the Cajon to Hesperia. Locomotive No. 3878 is seen here stopped at the Summit Valley station before it continues on to Hesperia. When the trains stopped at Summit Valley, they would pick up and deliver mail and receive and send telegraph messages. (Courtesy HOTM.)

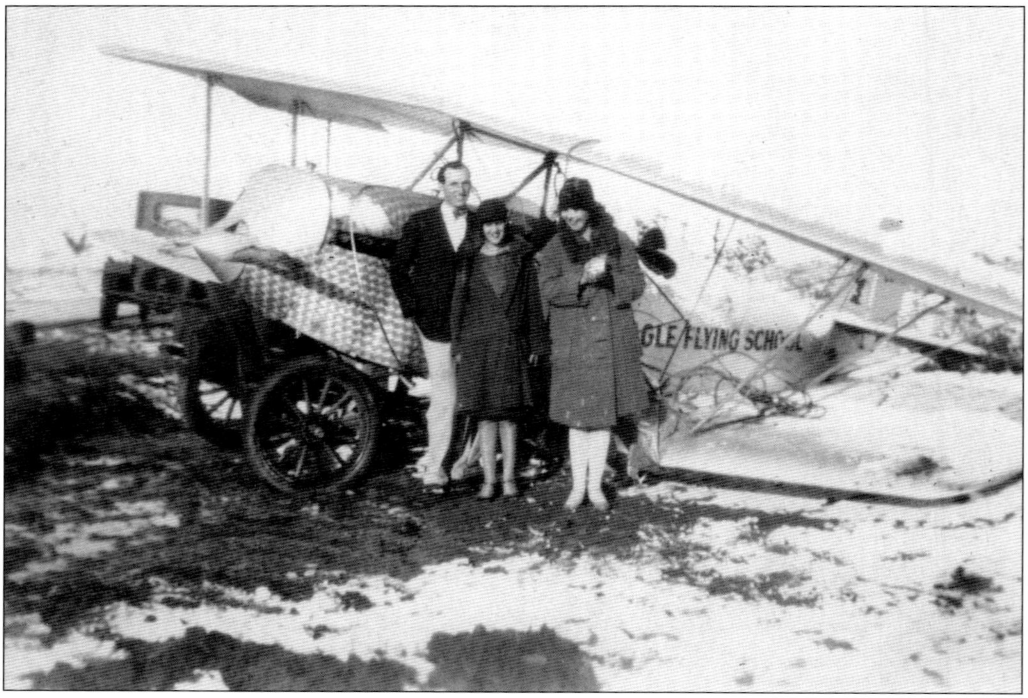

In 1928, the Nay family made an emergency landing just north of Miller's Corner and just south of Victorville. According to the signage on the small biplane, this was an aircraft used by a flight school in the area. (Courtesy HRPD.)

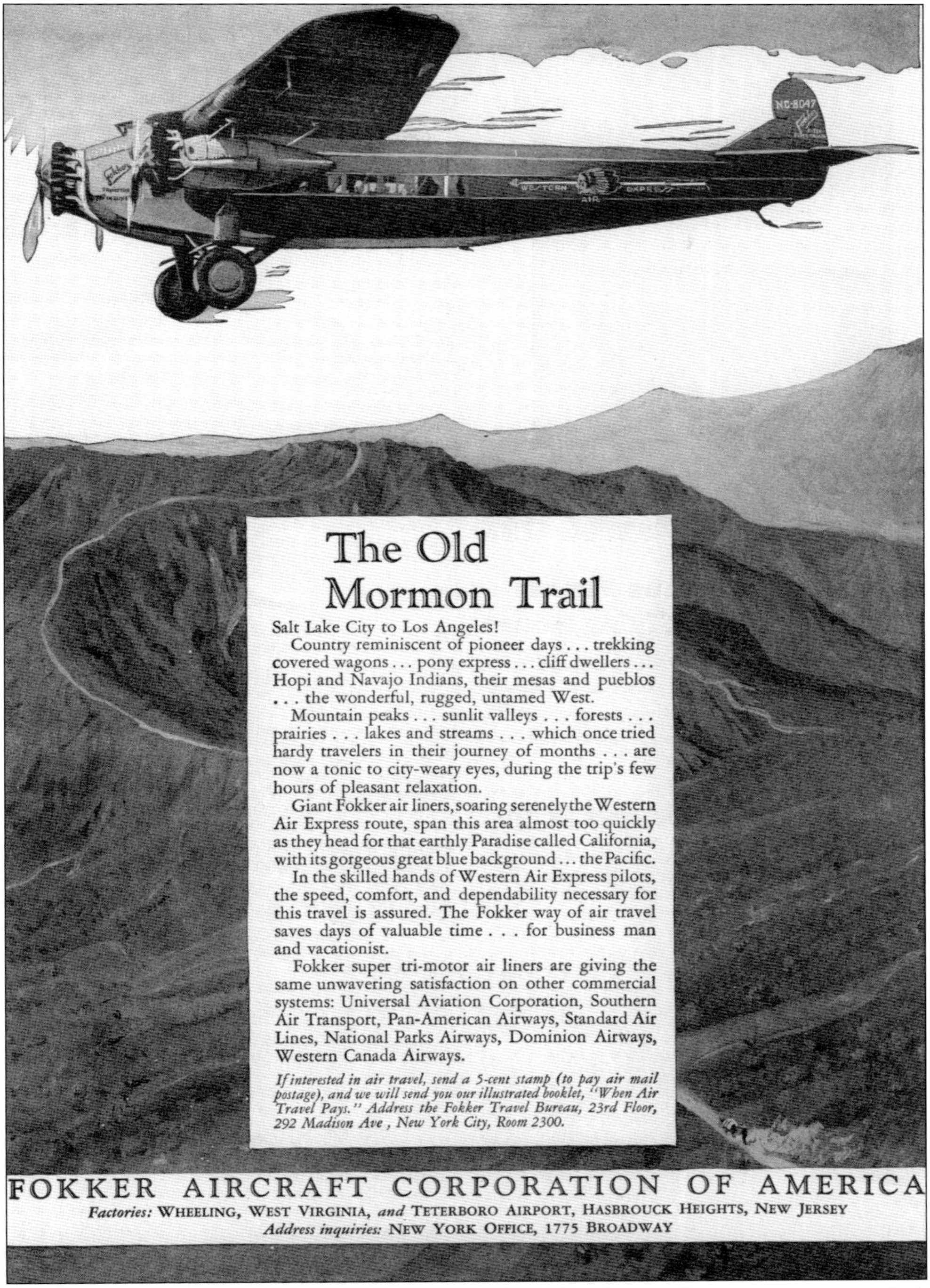

Miller's Corner was a very important landing strip in the 1920s. Air travel was growing in popularity, but the range of the aircraft was limited. Miller's Corner lay in the strategic place right before a pilot flew over the Cajon Pass from either the north or south. The Fokker Tri-Motor made flights over the Old Mormon Trail in the 1920s, as verified by this recently discovered advertisement in a 1929 edition of *Western Flyer* magazine. (Courtesy HOTM.)

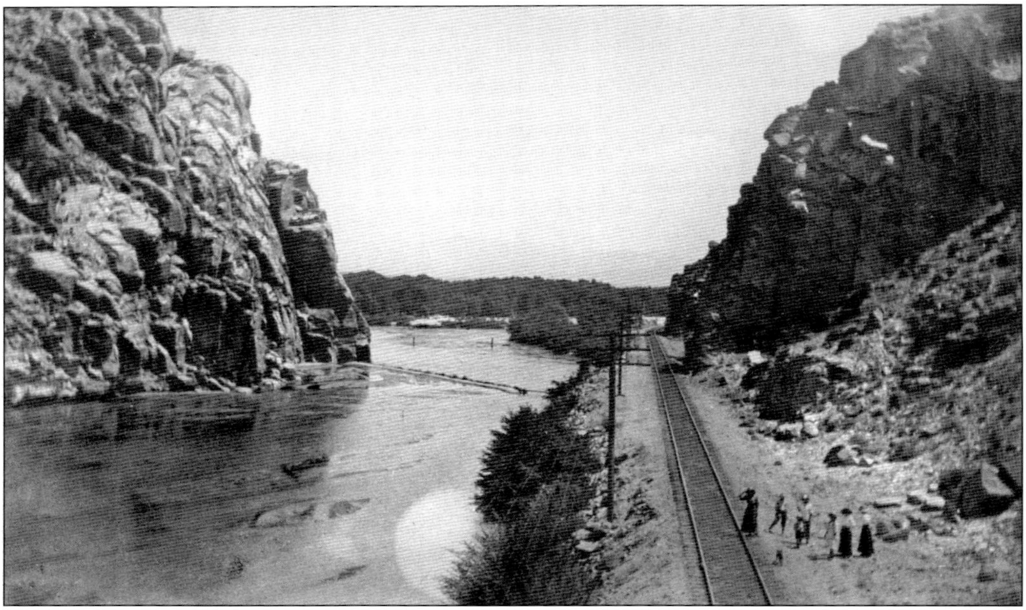

The Mojave River Narrows are shown here around 1914. Though people today often wonder why the Mojave River is even called a river, numerous historic photographs verify that it deserves the title. (Courtesy HRPD.)

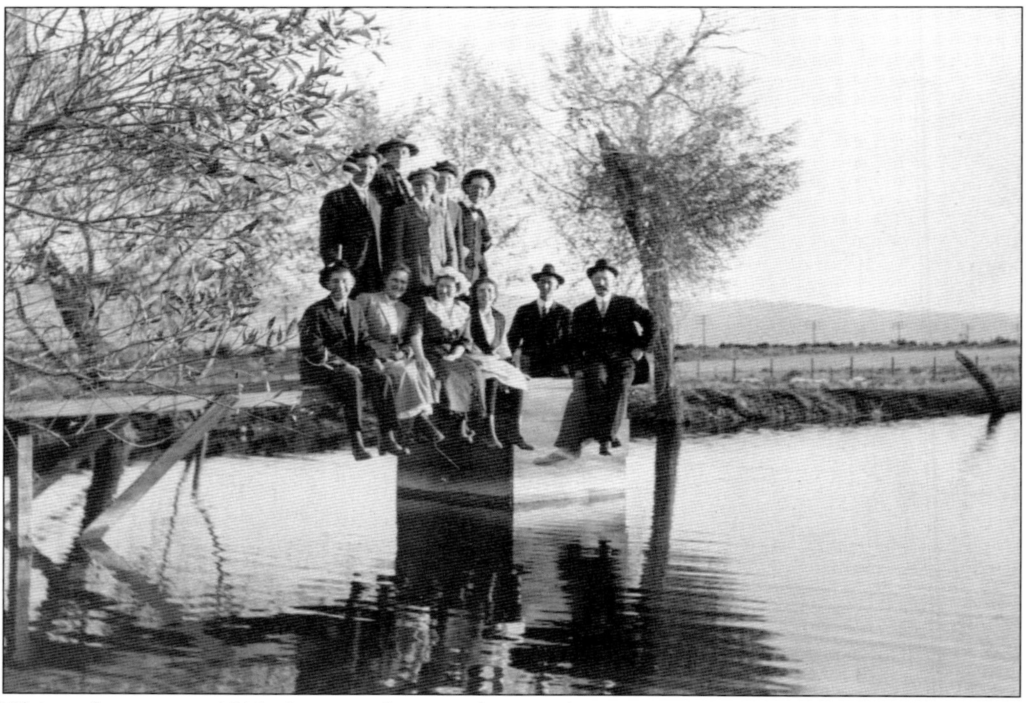

This rather rare *c.* 1914 photograph was taken at the reservoir at Lime Street and Hesperia Road—the site of today's Lime Street Park. Pictured here are service station owner-operators Leroy and Della Rolars (first row at left) with their family and some friends at Christmastime. (Courtesy HRPD.)

Leroy Rolars stands by the old Joshua tree near his property around 1925, which would be just before Route 66 was officially opened. In the 1940s, this would become the site of Rolars Gas Station. (Courtesy HRPD.)

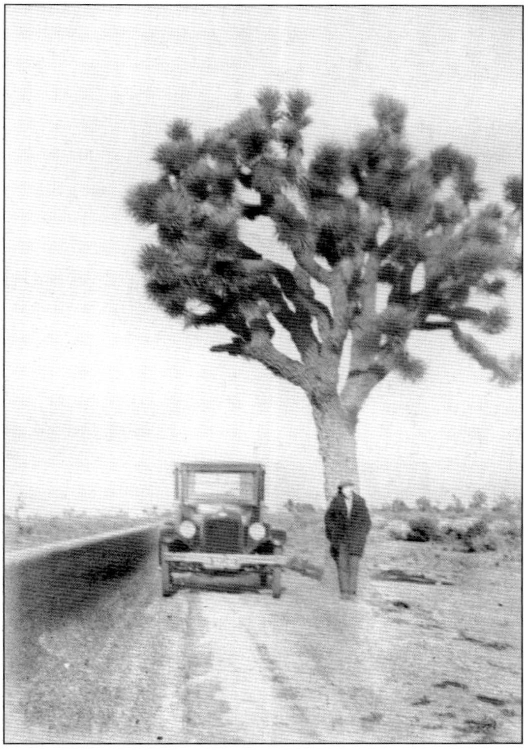

Hesperia Garage, shown here in the early 1920s, stood on Hesperia Road just down from the Hesperia Hotel. During this period, Leroy Rolars worked as a mechanic for the Walters family, who owned the Hesperia Garage. (Courtesy HRPD.)

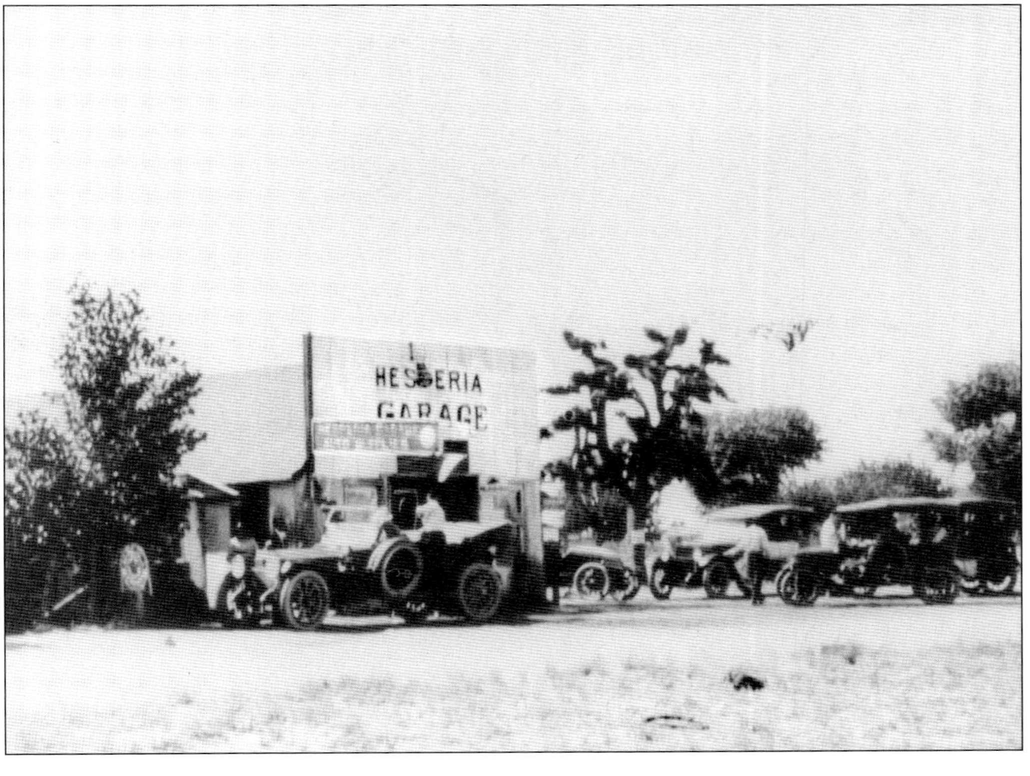

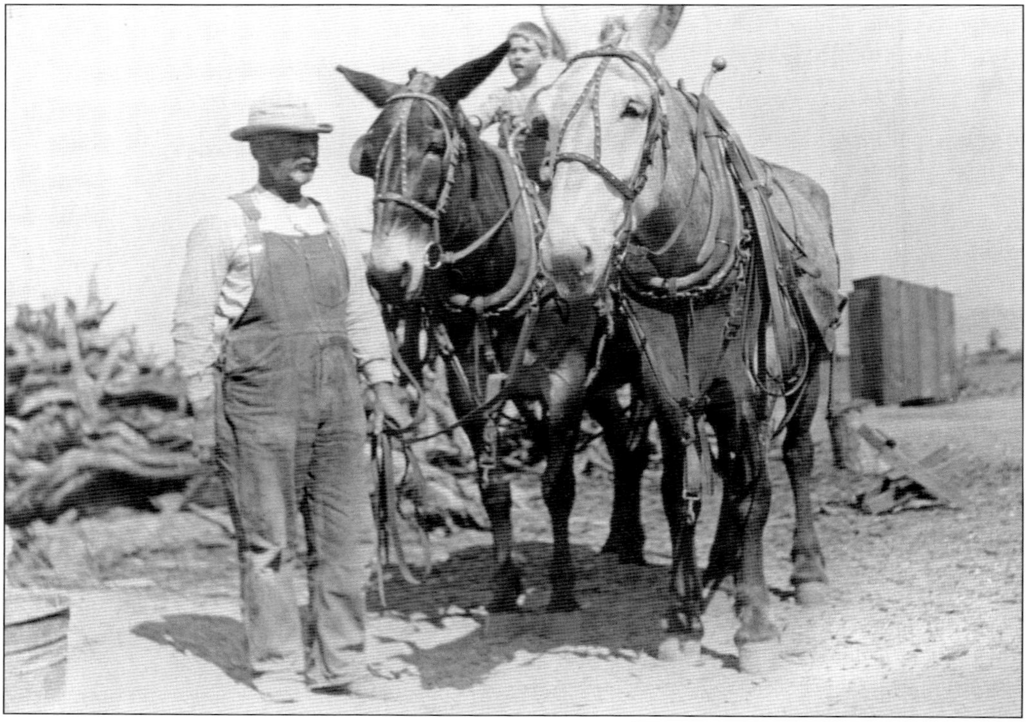

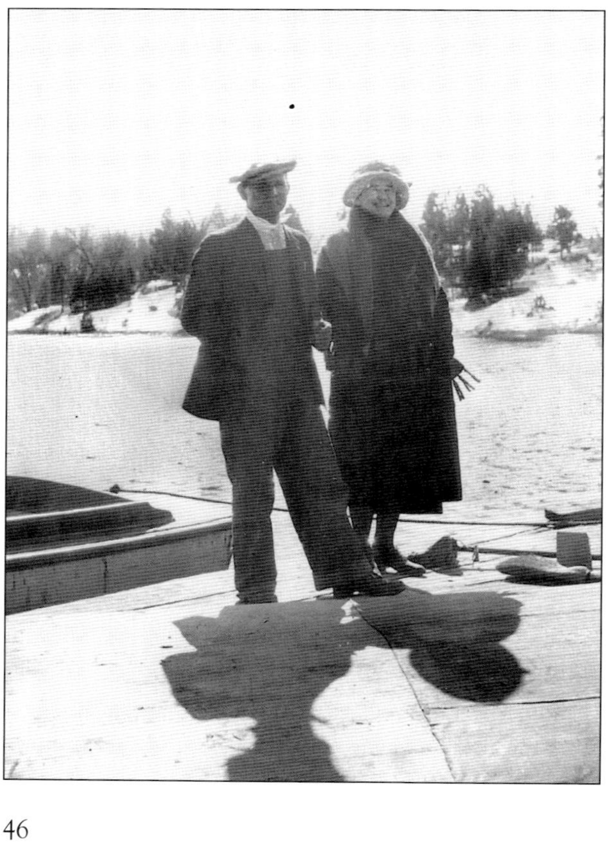

"Grandpa" Waggener is seen here leading his pair of mules in draft harnesses with a young boy riding atop one of them. Waggener homesteaded in Hesperia about 1913. The Waggener farm was in the area of Ranchero Road and Kourie Way. (Courtesy HRPD.)

This 1925 photograph of Columbus Frank Hedrick and Charlotte Hedrick shows the two hardworking Hesperians taking some time to relax at Lake Arrowhead—mother source of the Arrowhead water table, which fed the 30-inch pipeline that Columbus Frank Hedrick had installed from 1911 to 1913. (Courtesy HF.)

In the 1920s and into the 1930s, oil fever swept across the High Desert, and several exploratory wells were drilled. About 1931, the Rolars family erected its own oil rig. Their venture was unsuccessful—as were those of everyone else. In addition to the general lack of oil beneath the ground, vandals obstructed the shafts of some rigs, rendering them useless. (Courtesy HRPD.)

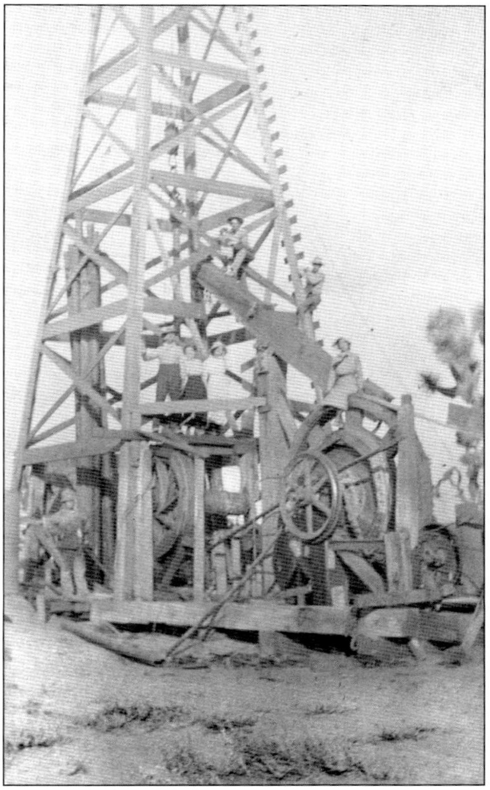

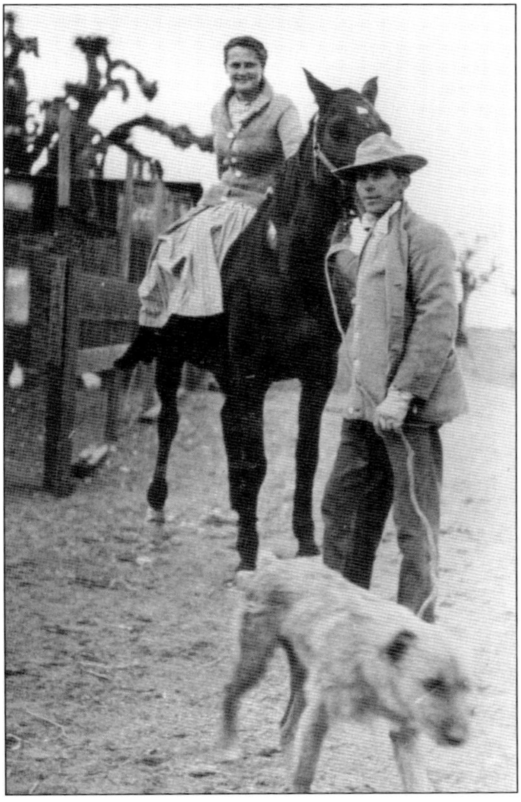

This 1914 photograph shows Leroy and Della Rolars and their dog out on their property. (Courtesy HRPD.)

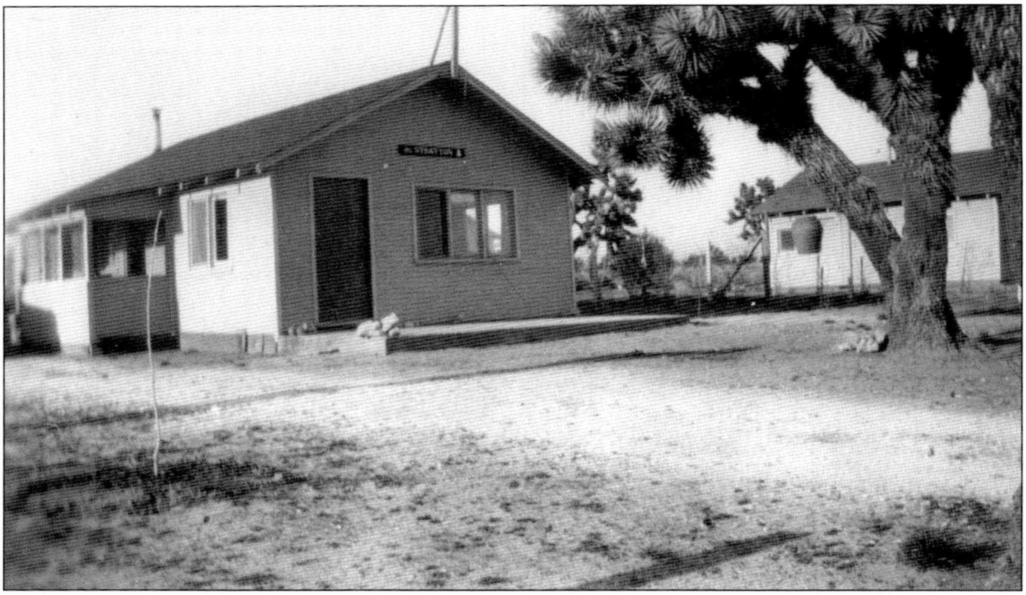

This home was built in the early 1920s by the Stratton family. The photographs were taken in 1926 and 1936. From 1925 to 1935, the Strattons rented the home to friends who wanted to get away from the Los Angeles area. After this, the Strattons used it as their own permanent residence, except for a couple of years during World War II. June Stratton Deutschman was an artist and head of the art department for the Terri Lee Dolls company from 1953 to 1958. She used the home as a studio until her death in 1971. Her daughter, Lillian Lee Stratton Platt, carried on the tradition of hand-painting the Terri Lee Dolls and was featured in a 2002 edition of *Doll* magazine. The Strattons also owned Knights Landing and Stratton's Camp in Big Bear. Their house is now the home of the Hesperia Old Town Museum. (Both, courtesy LSP.)

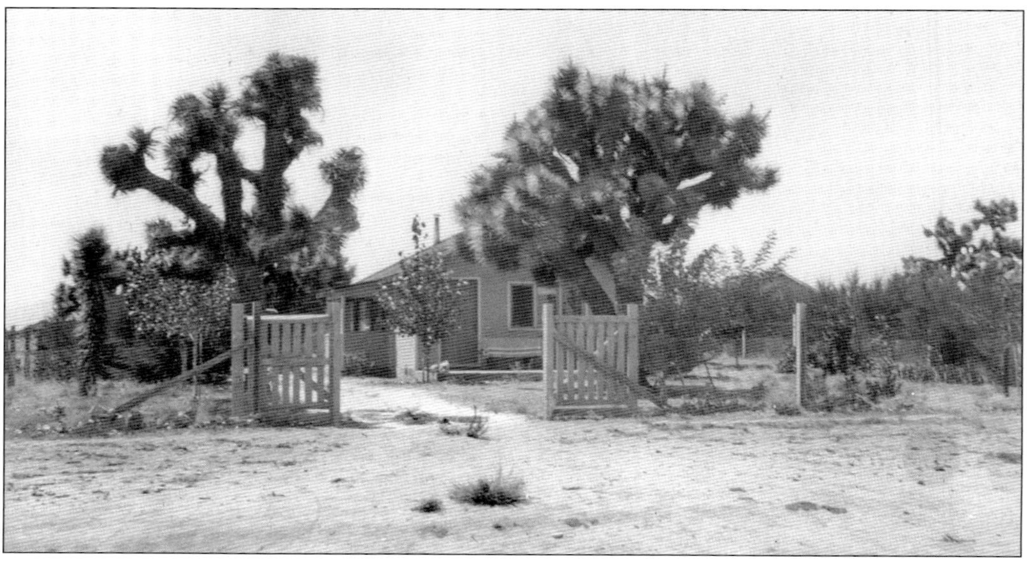

Seen in this 1936 Stratton family photograph from left to right are June, Lillian Lee, and Leroy Stratton. Leroy Stratton was born in Thomasville, New York. After moving to California he started several businesses, included an auto livery in Pasadena. He offered trips all over Southern California in five-to-seven-passenger vehicles. He especially advertised trips into the Inland Empire and San Bernardino Mountains. (Courtesy LSP.)

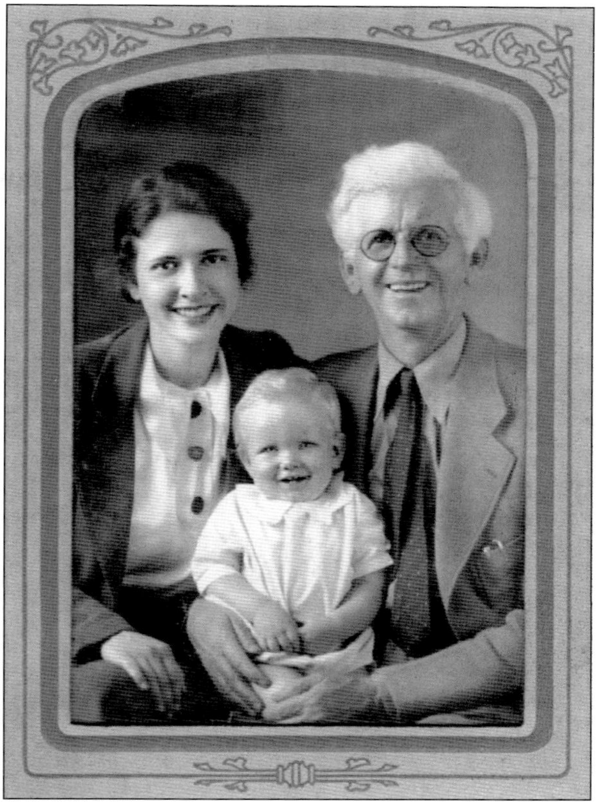

The March 1938 flood devastated much of the High Desert. Several inches of rain fell in just three days. The Bear Valley Bridge succumbed to this downpour, and the owners of this vehicle got a car wash that they didn't really expect. (Courtesy HF.)

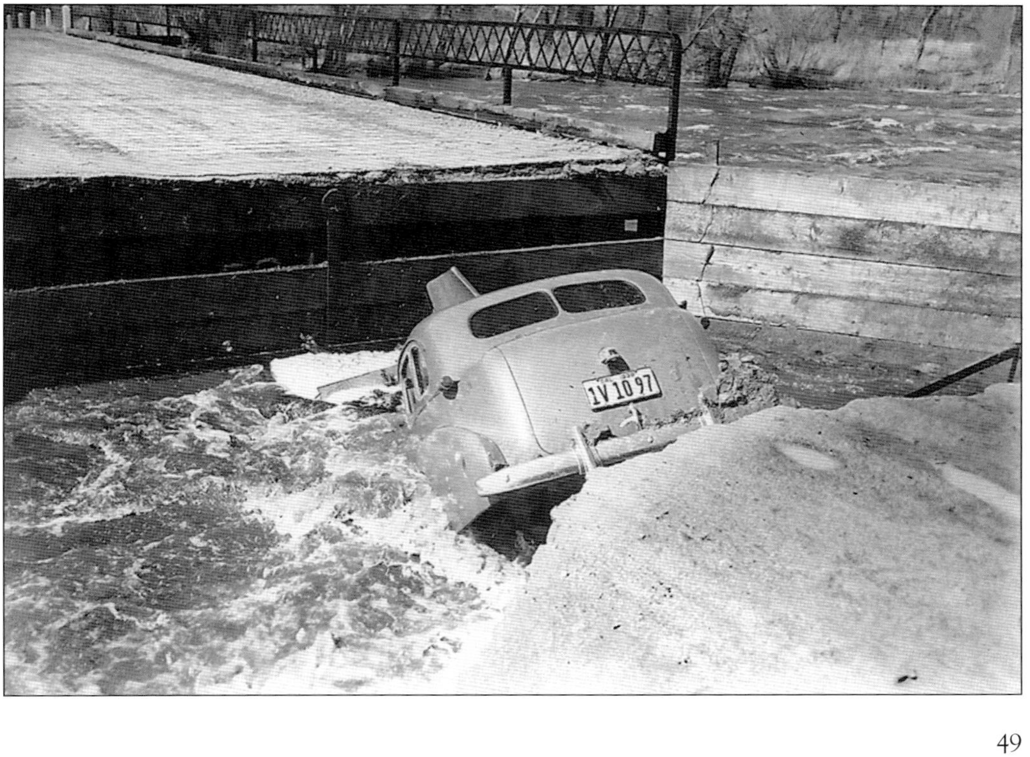

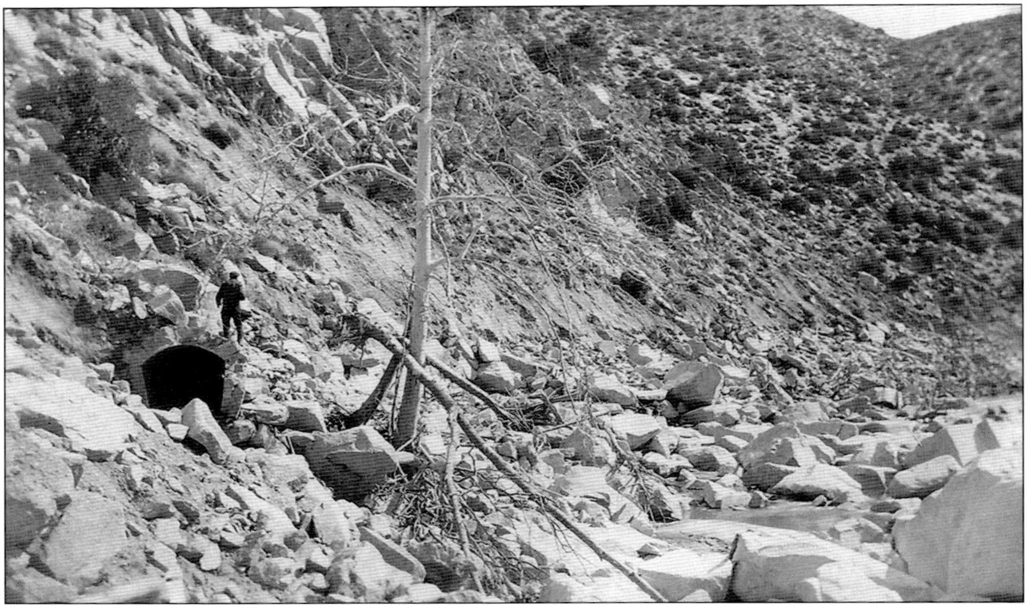

During the 1938 flood, the ditch suffered tremendous damage. In this picture taken soon afterward, a worker begins to assess the repairs that will be needed. (Courtesy HF.)

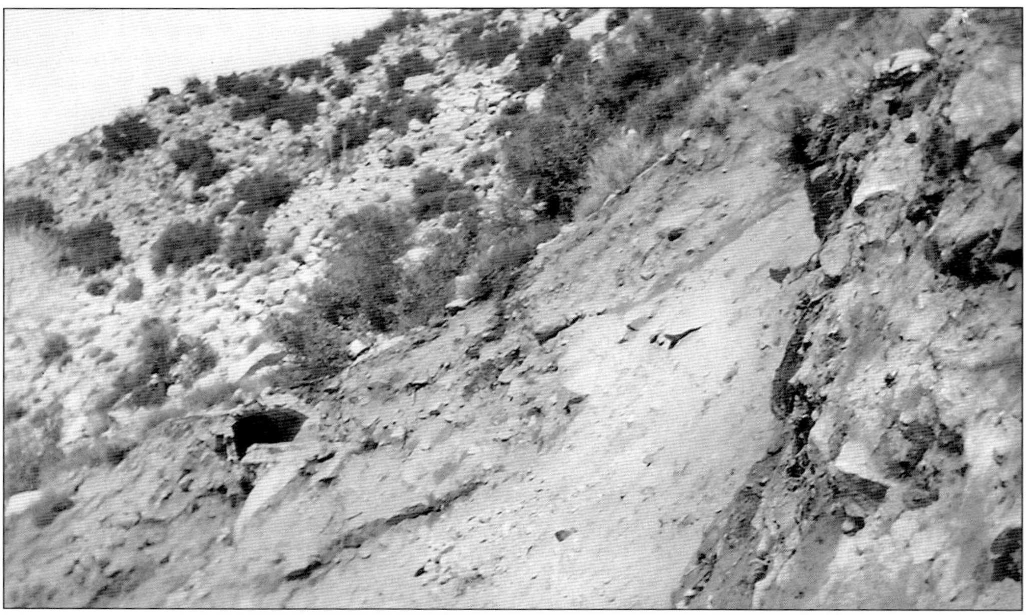

The damage to the ditch pipe continued along the Mojave River to today's Hesperia Lake, up through what is now known as part of Honda Valley, and across the mesa towards the reservoir, which was located about where Lime Street Park is today. (Courtesy HF.)

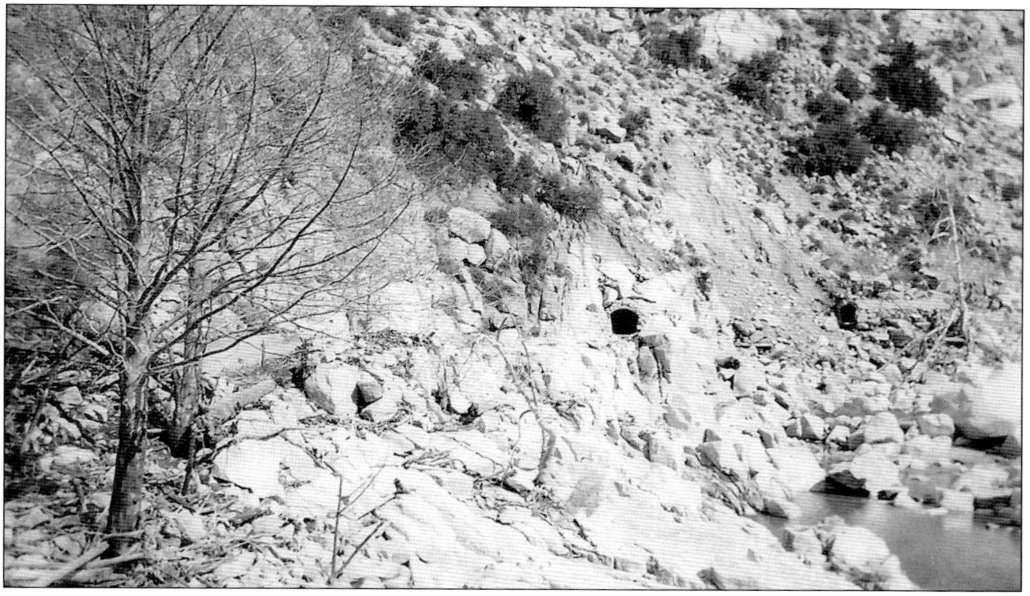

In 1938, the open ditch ran for about 5 miles (with some tunneling) before it reached the 30-inch pipe that ran to the reservoir. As the past few photographs attest, the March 1938 flood caused catastrophic damage to Hesperia's water system. (Courtesy HF.)

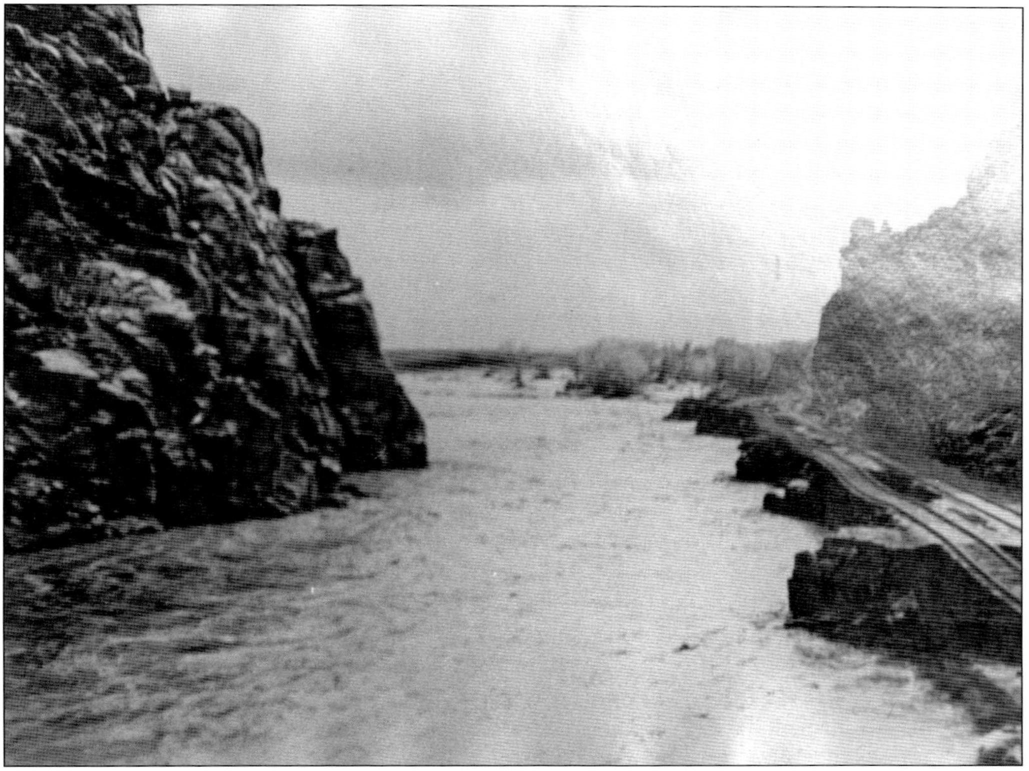

This photograph shows the Mojave River at the narrows just north of Hesperia during the March 1938 flood. Note the severe damage to the railroad tracks on the right side. (Courtesy VVR66M.)

Table 32.- Damage in southern California caused by storm of February 27 to March 4, 1938

Drainage basin	Drainage area (sq.mi.)	Damaged area (acres)	Direct damage: Residential	Business	Industrial	Agriculture	Roads, bridges	Railroads	Utilities	Other	Total
ia Juana River	461	1,920	None	None	None	$ 1,000	60,000	None	None	$ 3,000	$ 64,000
an Diego River	518	6,520	None	None	None	6,000	45,000	None	$ 10,000	5,000	66,000
an Luis Rey River	565	19,200	None	None	None	87,000	74,000	None	9,000	3,000	173,000
tay, Sweetwater, San Dieguito, and Santa Margarita Rivers and San Clemente and Escondido Creeks	1,736	5,390	None	$ 5,000	None	92,000	191,000	$ 3,000	8,000	5,000	304,000
an Juan and Aliso Creeks and miscellaneous Orange County streams	284	660	$ 2,000	None	$ 44,000	64,000	165,000	13,000	26,000	29,000	343,000
anta Ana River	2,476	182,303	1,159,000	564,000	806,000	2,670,000	3,227,000	1,175,000	1,856,000	2,501,000	13,958,000
oyote Creek (San Gabriel Basin)	181	61,056	899,000	518,000	30,000	1,446,000	172,000	106,000	125,000	65,000	3,361,000
an Gabriel River, except Coyote Creek	515	6,249	183,000	137,000	39,000	243,000	367,000	116,000	245,000	975,000	2,305,000
os Angeles River, except Rio Hondo	783	25,231	2,166,000	1,020,000	70,000	447,000	6,135,000	511,000	1,952,000	4,675,000	16,976,000
io Hondo	141	6,280	380,000	137,000	61,000	176,000	240,000	72,000	180,000	483,000	1,729,000
allona and Topanga Creeks and miscellaneous coastal streams in Los Angeles County	491	9,379	369,000	249,000	15,000	63,000	850,000	None	1,593,000	31,000	3,170,000
alleguas Creek	228	-	1,000	3,000	None	141,000	116,000	3,000	None	None	264,000
anta Clara River	1,598	5,000	46,000	40,000	188,000	1,264,000	1,254,000	605,000	90,000	71,000	3,558,000
entura River	227	1,200	54,000	72,000	163,000	170,000	272,000	3,000	31,000	12,000	777,000
oastal streams in Ventura County	76	-	4,000	None	35,000	45,000	54,000	None	6,000	10,000	154,000
ojave River	545	60,392	131,000	15,000	62,000	471,000	None	1,678,000	65,000	59,000	2,481,000
hitewater River	516	36,520	587,000	50,000	None	44,000	238,000	52,000	163,000	12,000	1,146,000
iscellaneous areas	-	-	30,000	None	1,000	None	314,000	10,000	3,000	2,000	360,000
otal direct damage	11,341	427,300	6,011,000	2,810,000	1,514,000	7,430,000	13,774,000	4,347,000	6,362,000	8,941,000	51,189,000
stimated indirect damage	-	-	13,223,000	7,313,000	1,968,000	1,485,000	None	1,592,000	1,631,000	201,000	27,413,000
Total direct and indirect damage	-	-	-	-	-	-	-	-	-	-	78,602,000

This table from flood control records shows the 1938 flood's devastation, which spread across some 60,000 acres. The residential damage came to about $131,000, and railroad damage came to about $1.6 million. Total damage was estimated at $2.4 million. Adjusted for inflation, $131,000 in 1938 would be $2,025,064 in 2010. (Courtesy HOTM.)

Five

Pathways, Waterways, Railways, Roadways, and Highways

People have always made and followed paths. At first, humans and their paths stayed close to water. People followed paths beside the water or used the waterways as paths themselves. As new means of travel were found, such as wagons (which could carry a small water supply), travelers were able to venture farther from their water sources. The steam engine allowed people to range even farther from water sources—making it possible to cross in hours deserts that would have once taken days. Ironically, however, the railroad itself required water to operate—in large quantities. Since trains sometimes required water far from any natural water source, engineers would have to create a "source" beside the railroad. And even though it had arrived there by unnatural means, water still brought life with it, turning these railroad stops into oases, which in turn became towns surrounded by formerly arid lands that water had turned into farms, orchards, and vineyards.

As the automobile came onto the scene, things really changed. Where the new automobile roads veered away from the railroads, once-bustling railroad towns saw fewer and fewer travelers coming through. As time continued to progress, the first scenic automobile roads were abandoned for new, better, faster, and more direct roads.

How many towns and business have been left in the dust of the old trails? As time goes on, one wonders how soon the airways will leave today's superhighways in that same dust of obscurity and desolation. As each path has given way to the next, some communities have blossomed, and others have stagnated, becoming frozen in a time that has passed and finally fading into history.

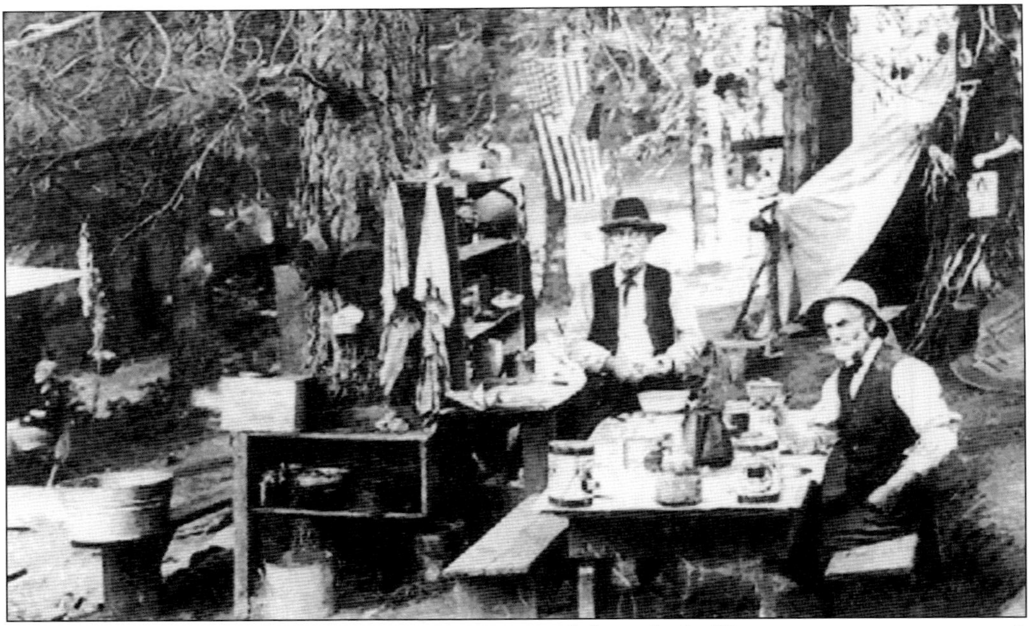

After statehood, the trails up the Cajon Pass, into and through the Hesperia area were improved. Pictured here are John Brown Sr. (right) and Silas Cox, two mid-1800s pioneers. Brown was responsible for improving the trail up the Cajon, despite encountering some setbacks caused by the devastating flood of 1861–1862. (MHS.)

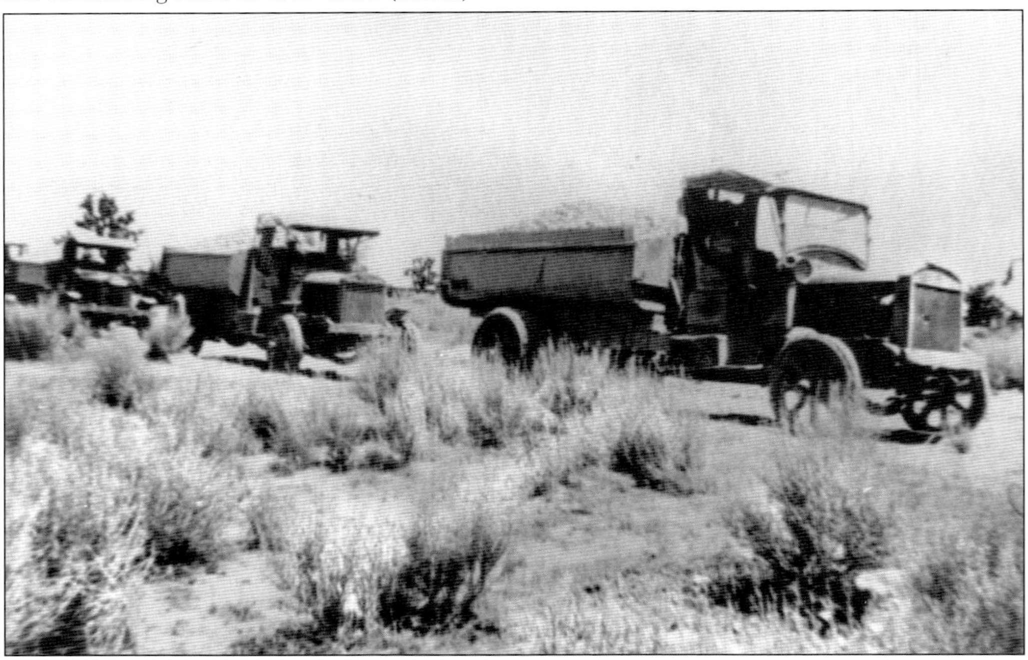

These trucks are shown working on the new Route 66 in 1923. The area under construction stretches from Cajon's summit to Victorville. As seen in the following maps, the new route would detour from part of the Old John Brown/Old National Trails Road, bypassing the township of Hesperia and the grand Hesperia Hotel. (Courtesy HRPD.)

Locals are seen spending a pleasant day fishing from the Deep Creek Bridge. This bridge was demolished and replaced in 1968. The Deep Creek area is now considered part of the Pacific Crest Trail and Nature Area, and its wildlife and vegetation are protected—though fishing is still allowed. (Courtesy HRPD.)

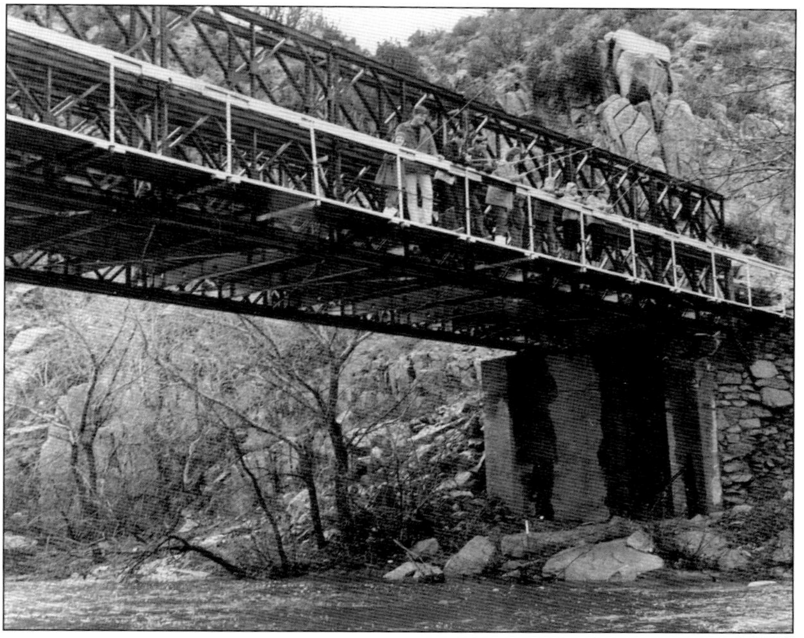

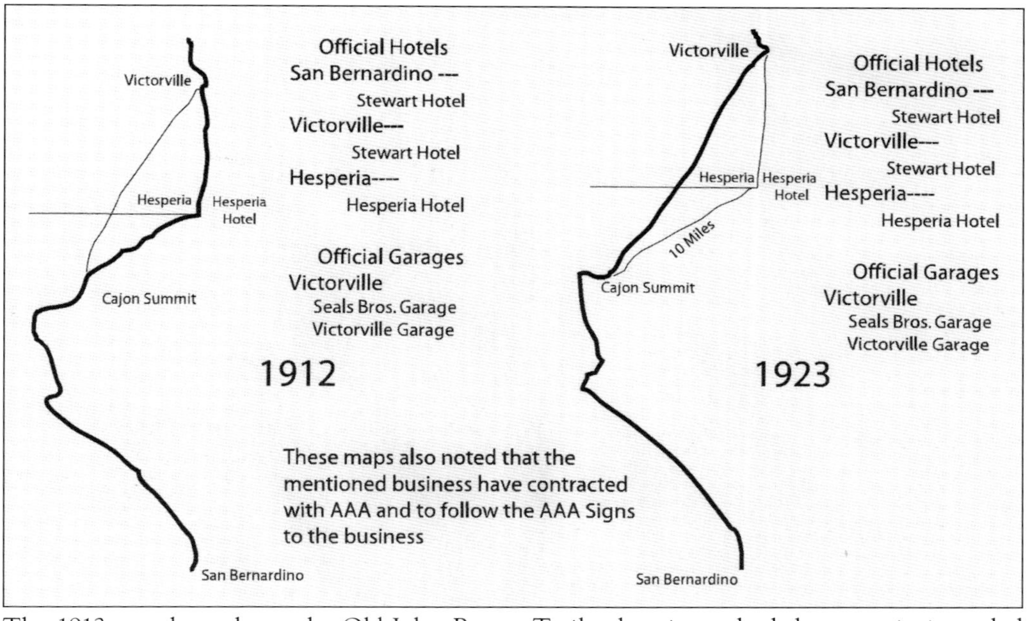

The 1912 map here shows the Old John Brown Trail; when it reached the summit, it angled 45 degrees to join Hesperia Road, following the National Old Trails Highway. The back of the map shows the Hesperia Hotel, which was located on Hesperia Road and popular with traveling motorists. The 1923 AAA map features an important change—it shows Route 66 (still under construction) as the primary road through the area. Hesperia Road had then become a secondary route, and this fact alone greatly reduced the amount of traffic down Hesperia Road, which in turn affected its businesses—including the hotel. Three years later, when Route 66 was officially commissioned, the Hesperia Hotel officially closed its doors. (Maps redrawn by HOTM, for illustrative purposes only.)

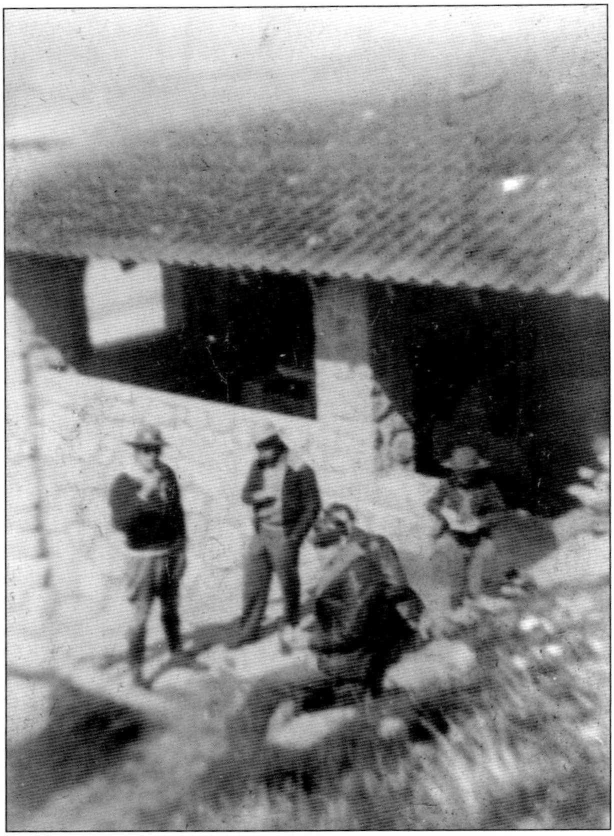

Fort Cajon stood down in the lower part of the Cajon Pass, known today as Blue Cut—shown here in 1937. This was also the approximate location of the lower tollhouse on the John Brown Trail. Some of the old Fort Cajon remnants remain standing and can be seen by travelers following Old Route 66 between Cleghorn and Kenwood. (Both, courtesy HRPD.)

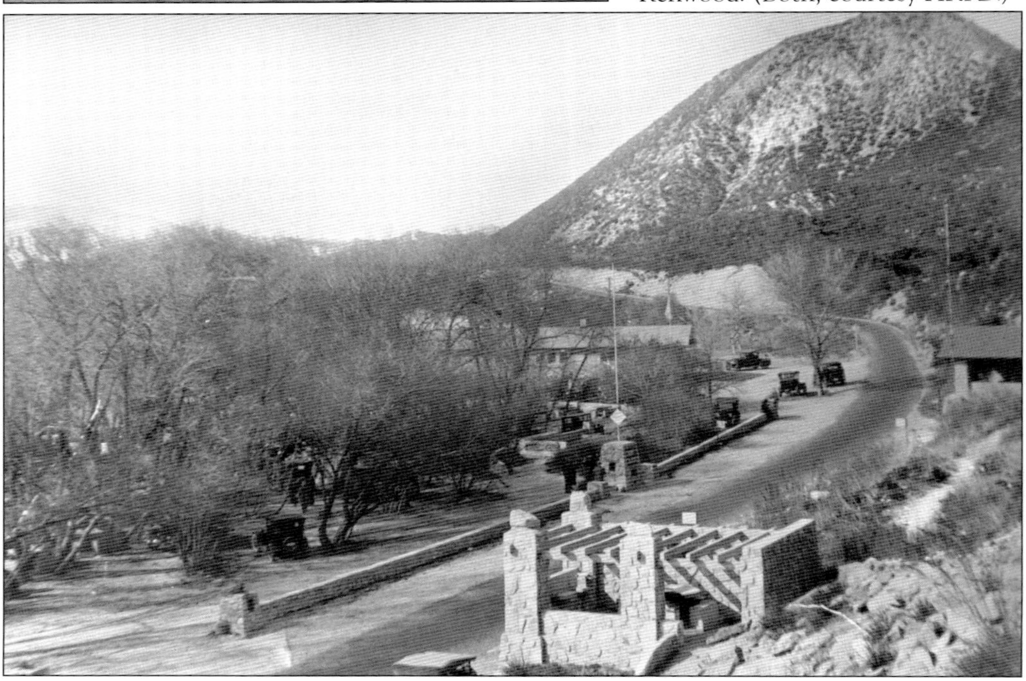

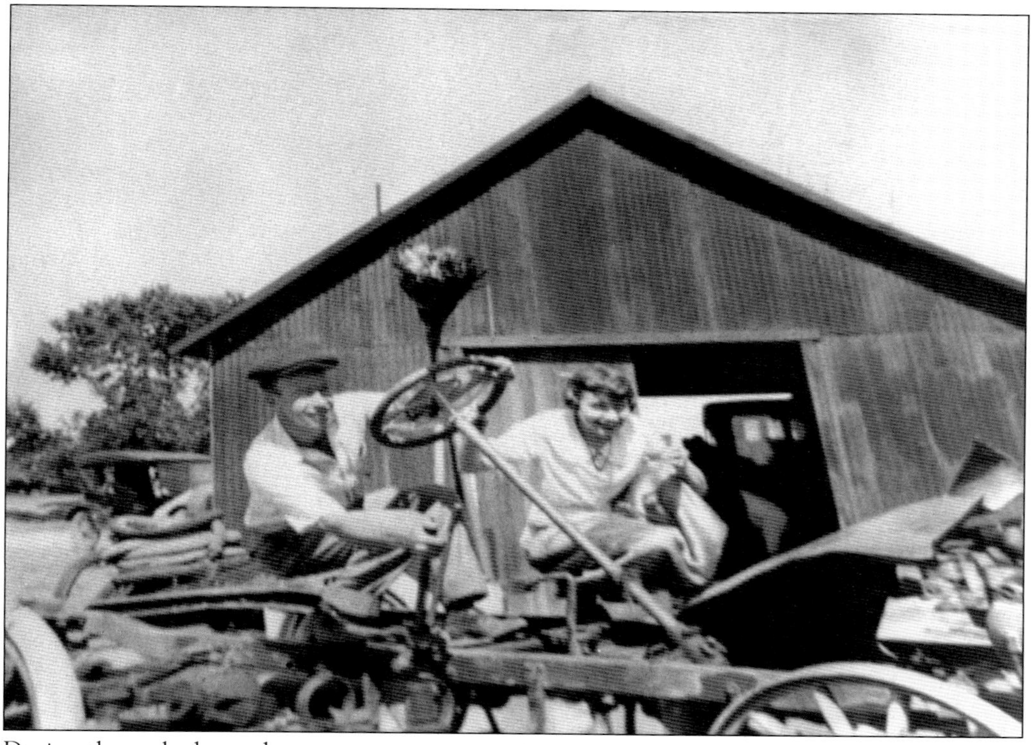

During the early days, when someone was looking for automobile parts or a mechanic, they could generally be found at Hesperia Garage on Hesperia Road between Walters Store and the Hesperia Hotel. Seen in this photograph atop the tractor are garage owners Roy and Verial Walters. (Courtesy HRPD.)

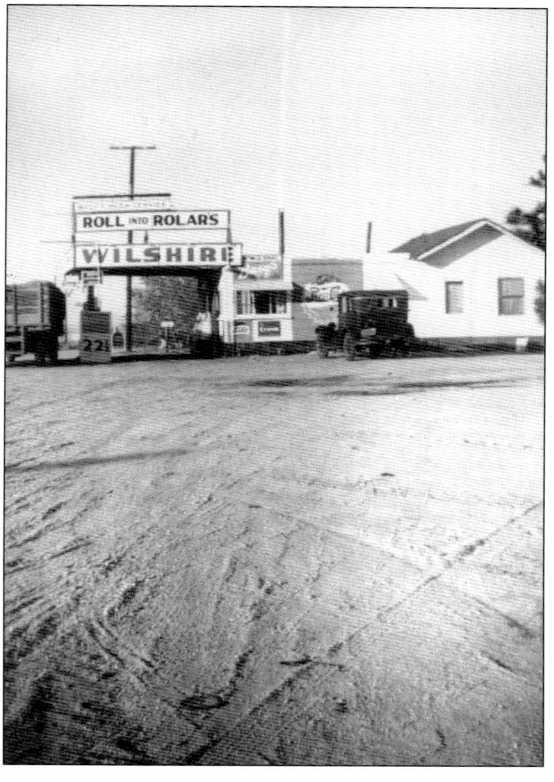

Leroy and Della Rolars opened up their service station along Route 66 around 1941. Its signage included the catchy slogan, "Roll into Rolars." The station stood just between Mariposa Road and today's Interstate 15 on Joshua Street. Leroy Rolars was a mechanic at Hesperia Garage before opening his station on Route 66. (Courtesy HRPD.)

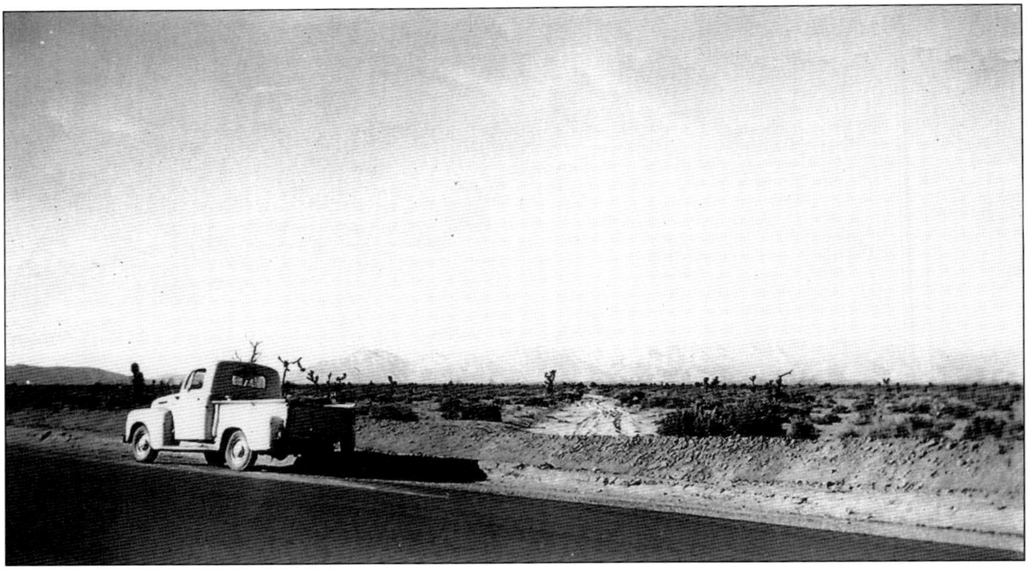

These photographs of the National Trails Highway were taken in the 1950s. The highway as it crossed Hesperia followed today's Hesperia Road. Visitors can view this part of the National Trails Highway, which was excluded from Route 66, by traveling east on Main Street to around Fifth Avenue, where early motorists would have just come off the trail from Cajon Summit. They would have then continued traveling east to Hesperia Road, where they would veer to the northeast. Headed that way, they would have passed Walters Store and the Walters family residence. A block farther on, they would have passed the eye-catching Hesperia Hotel. The route then continued until it reached D Street in Victorville (location of today's Victorville Route 66 Museum) and then on to Oro Grande, Barstow, and the rest of Route 66. (Both, courtesy HF.)

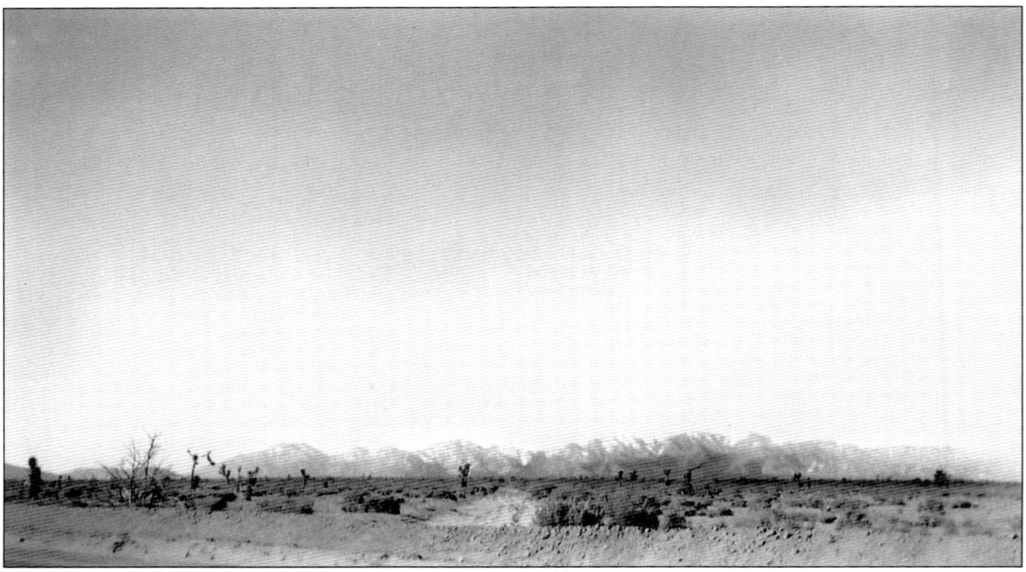

Six

Potatoes and Rodeos

In the mid- to late 1930s, people moved to this quiet town of Hesperia for health reasons and for its rural life. In the early 1940s, the Tatums arrived in Hesperia. The Tatums leased Hesperia to farm the land, raising a variety of crops. The main crop that was noted was the long white rose potato. Other crops included onions and alfalfa hay. The Tatums also ran a herd of cattle, with open range covering from Area 36, now know as Hesperia Lake, to the Phelan area. According to Jim Tatum, it was not unusual to ask the California Highway Patrol to block traffic along Highways 395 and 15 to allow the Tatums to drive their cattle across the two highways to fresh grazing land. During this time, many activities arose; one of the most popular was rodeoing.

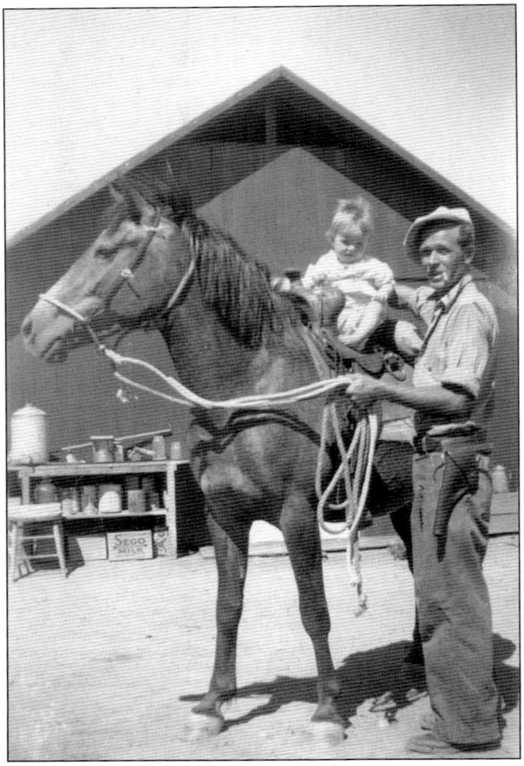

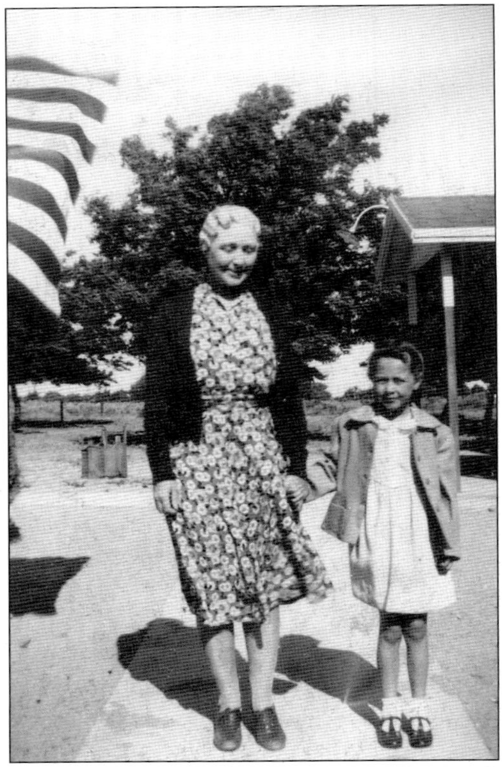

The Creason family moved to Hesperia in 1936 for a drier climate due to Norman Creason's respiratory ailments. The photograph above left of one-year-old Mary Ann Creason, her father Norman, and the family horse was taken in 1937. The 1942 photograph above right shows Mary Ann Creason with her teacher, Miss Schock. In the background is the old schoolyard. (Right photograph by Norman Creason; both courtesy MACR.)

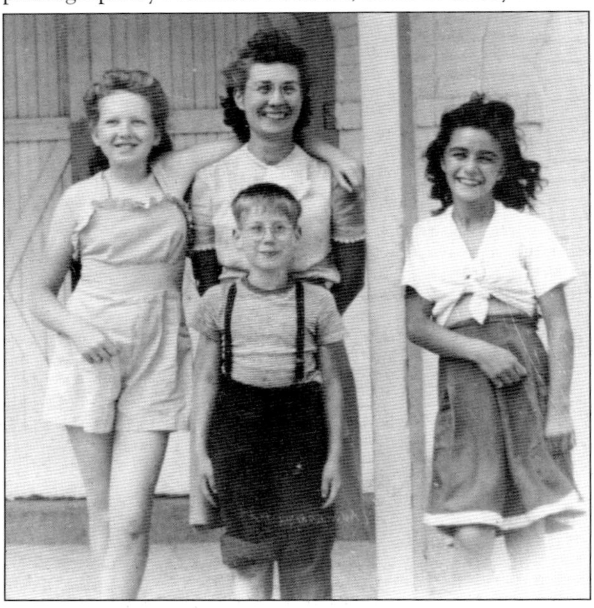

The photograph from the 1945–1946 academic year shows Mrs. Odening in front of the schoolhouse with four of her students. From left to right, they are Lillian Stratton, Walter Odening, and Joyce Phillips. The schoolhouse shown here was Hesperia's second; it was built in 1926 and was used until about 1956, when Joshua Circle was built. When the second schoolhouse was constructed the original was used as a cafeteria. (Courtesy HRPD.)

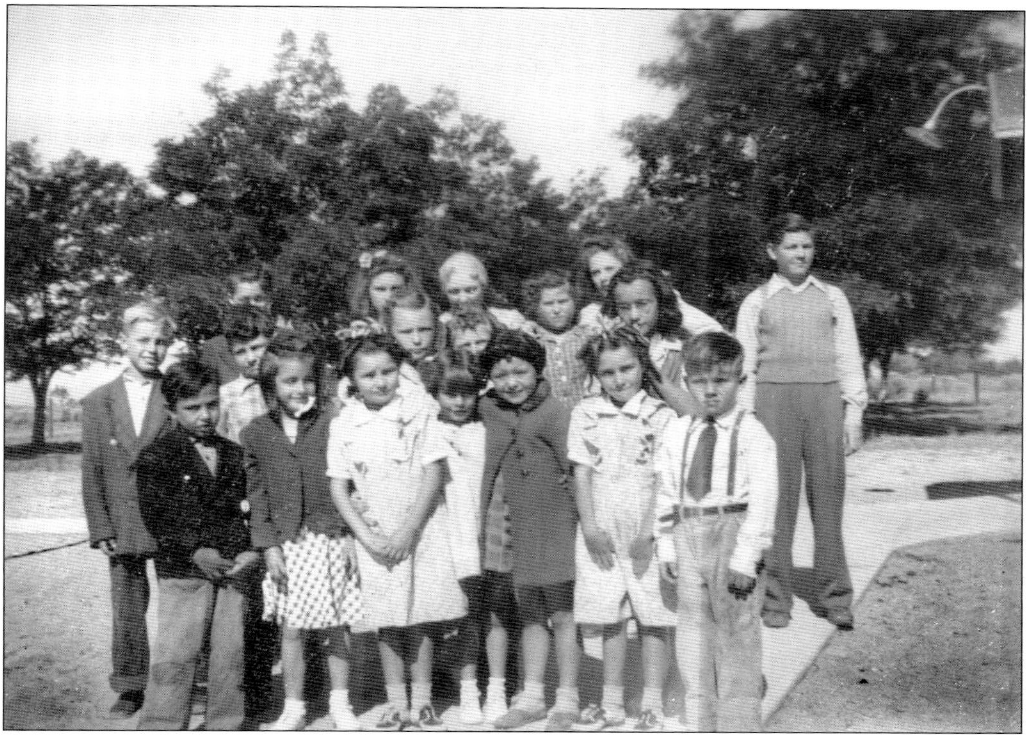

Hesperia School classes of 1942–1943, Grades 1 through 12, are shown here. From left to right are (first row) Harry Armenta, Lee Phillips, Alice Stowell, MaryAnn Creason, Lynda ?, Anna Stowell, and Charles Condis; (second row) Herold Stowell, Billy O'Banion, Catherine Hoehlke, Eleanor Stowell, Bessie Armenta, and Joyce Phillips, (third row) Wally Phillips, Maryann McInnis, teacher Miss Schock, Henrietta Condis, and Lymis Creason. (Courtesy MACR.)

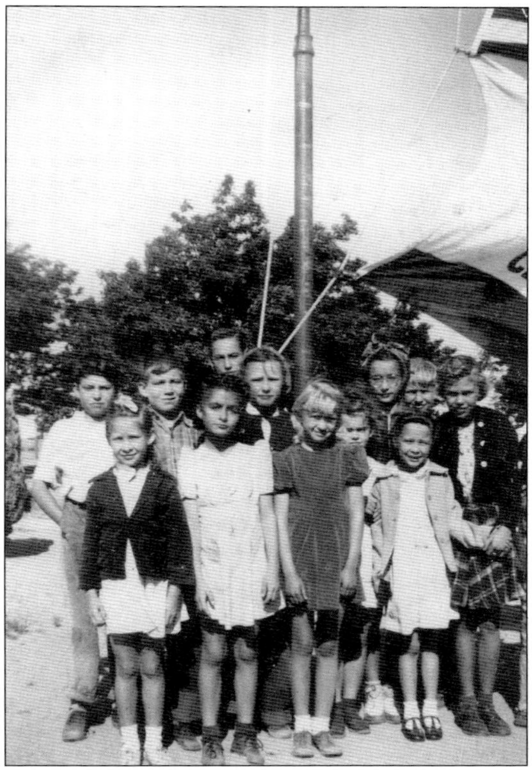

Here are the members of Hesperia School grades one through six from the following year, 1943–1944. Shown from left to right, they are (first row) Shirley Turner, Lee Phillips, Glenna ?, Mary Ann Creason, and Joy Moessner; (second row) Billy O'Banion, Charles York, Catherine Hoelke, and Lois Ann (Sammy) Virgo; (third row) Harry McInnis, Joyce Phillips, and Keith ? Classmates Harry Armenta and Tom Moessner are missing from the photograph. (Courtesy MACR.)

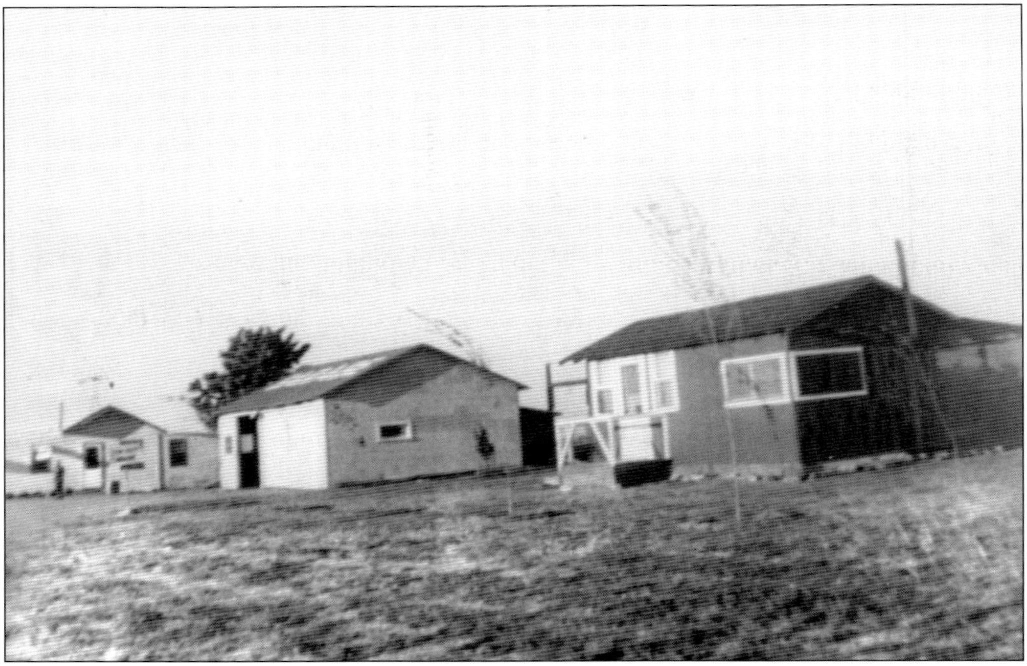

The Rolarses were serious about advertising their business. As seen here, both the front of their gas station and its roof had signage. This photograph of the Rolarses' station was taken in the late 1940s. (Courtesy HRPD.)

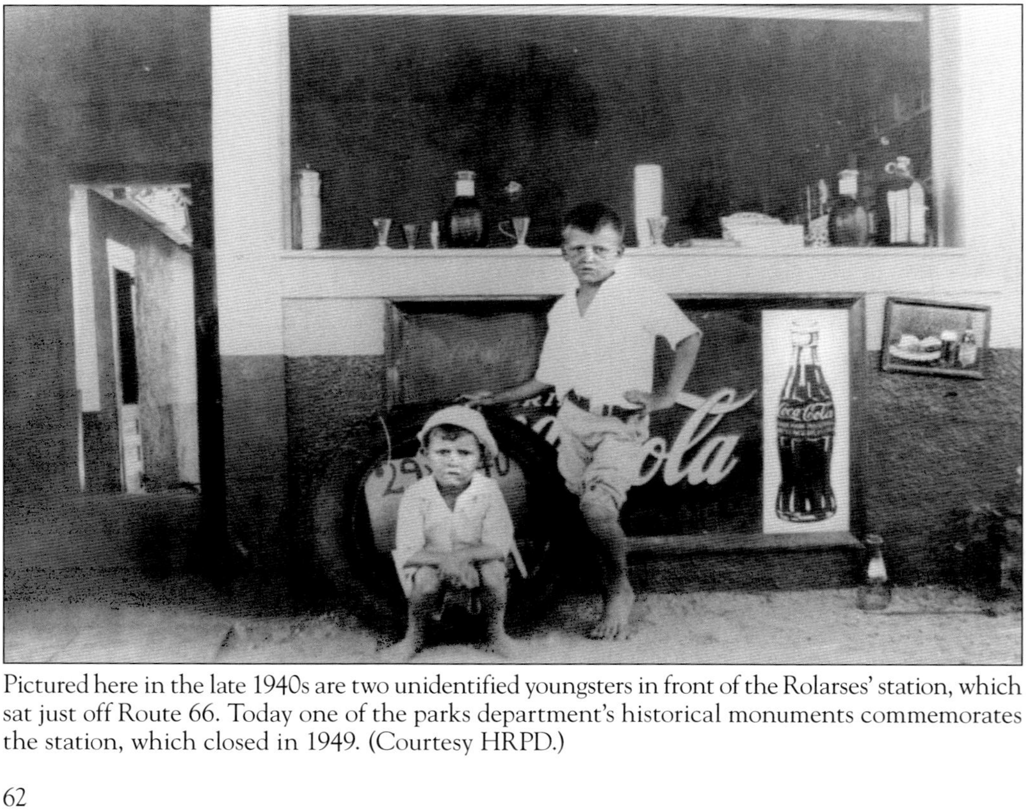

Pictured here in the late 1940s are two unidentified youngsters in front of the Rolarses' station, which sat just off Route 66. Today one of the parks department's historical monuments commemorates the station, which closed in 1949. (Courtesy HRPD.)

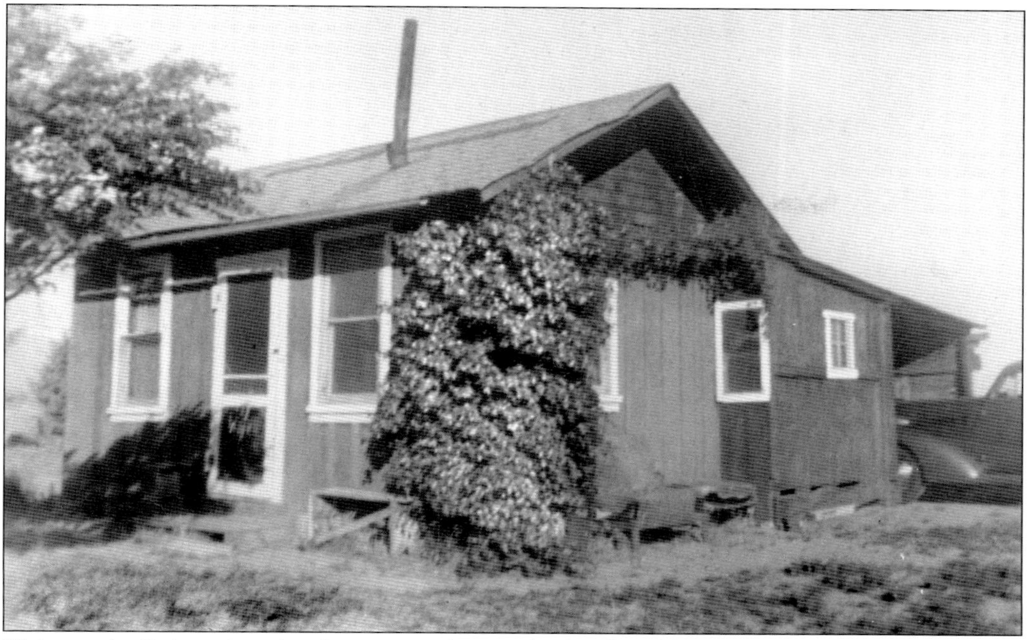

This was the Rolarses' weekend getaway cabin on the family's old homestead land, which lay along Route 66. This photograph was taken in the early to mid-1930s. (Courtesy HRPD.)

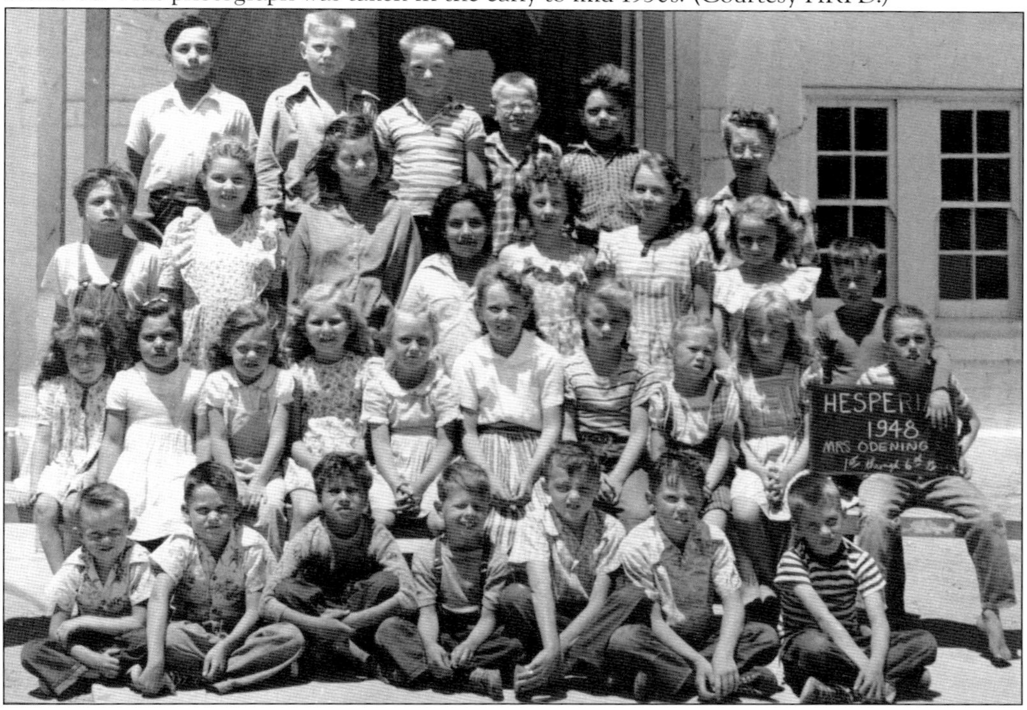

The classes of 1948 pose for their photograph. These 30 students and their teacher, Mrs. Odening, cover grades one through six. Some of the children shown here—and/or their families—still reside in the area and have been a major help with this book, including (in no order) Jim Walker, Mary Ann Creason, Ruth Ann Engle, and Everett Hedrick. (Courtesy MACR.)

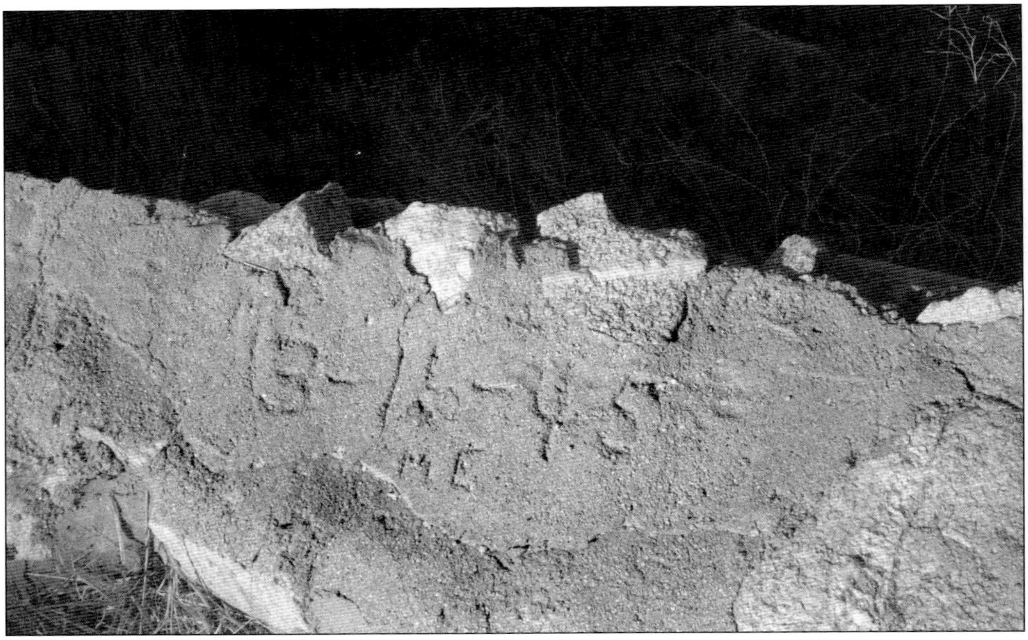

After decades of use, the ditch required constant upkeep and repair. The photograph above shows the spot where someone with the initials "M. E." completed some cement repairs in 1945. The Tatum and Walker families and their farmhands were involved in most of this work, as the ditch provided the water for the potatoes and other crops they raised on the mesa. The lower photograph shows the end of the flume where it connected with the 14-inch and 30-inch pipes to continue the water's journey to the reservoir at Lime Street and Hesperia Road. The manifold area shown here tended to get clogged, causing overflows that scarred the side of the hill. (Both, courtesy HOTM.)

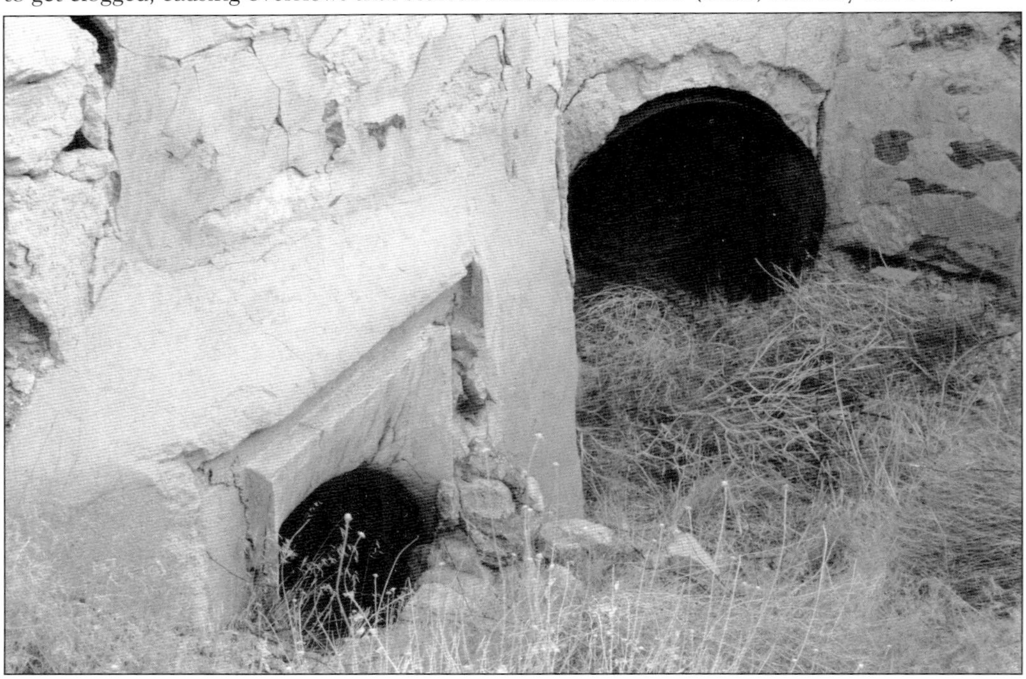

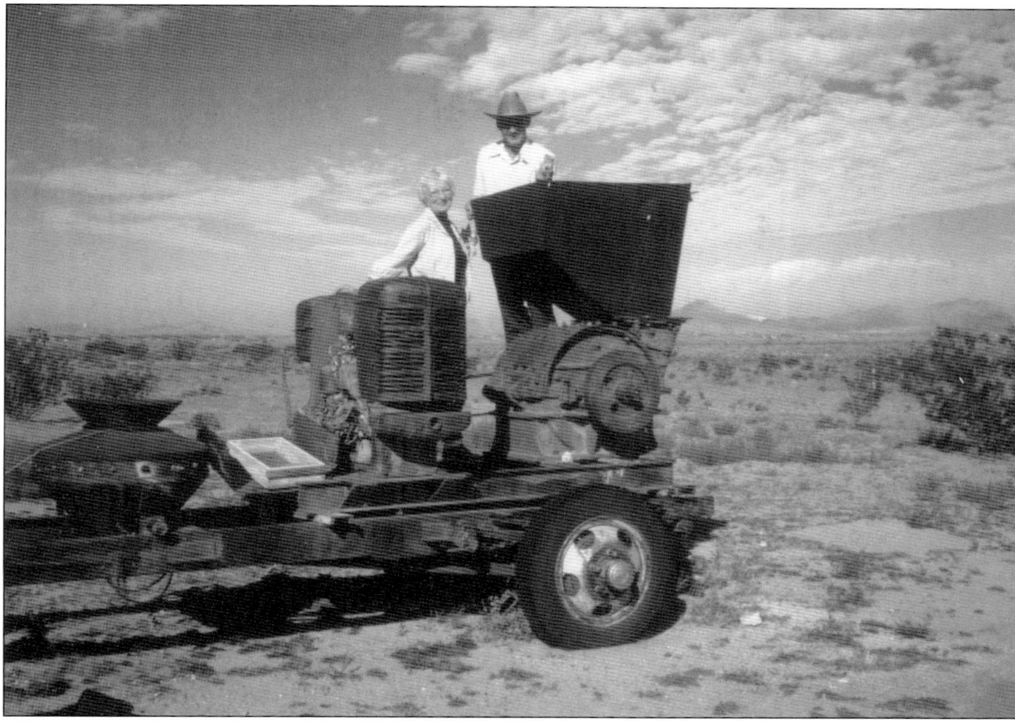

This machine was built by a Mr. Dunagan, one of Clyde Tatum's relatives. It was used to replant the potato fields. Workers would cut the eyes out of some of the potatoes and put them into the hopper. The equipment would then be run up and down the rows, seeding them with the potato eyes. (Courtesy TF.)

In this 1940s photograph, it is harvest time for the Tatums' white rose potatoes. The Tatums farmed 600-plus acres up on the mesa with a variety of crops. Though the field-workers shown here are busily sorting out the potatoes in the troughs, a look in the background reveals that many more potatoes are on their way, all in need of sorting. (Courtesy TF.)

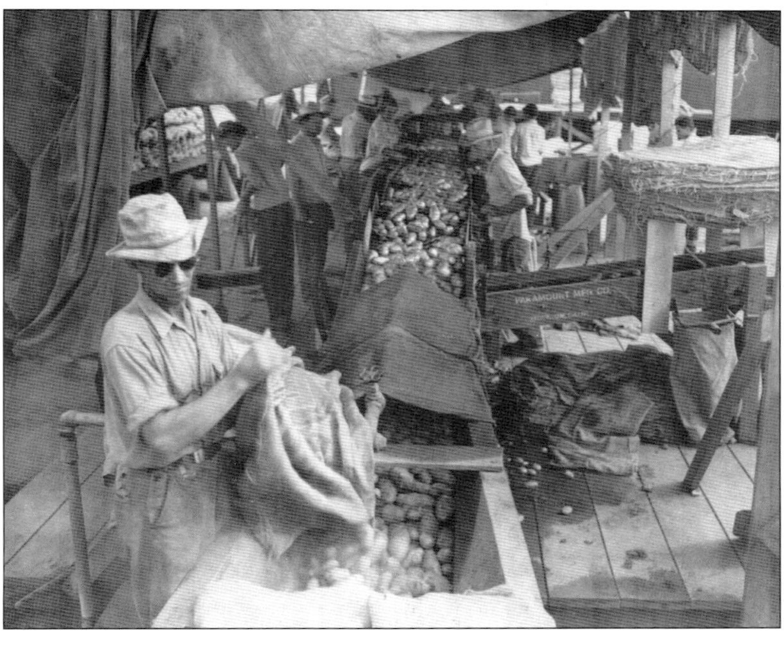

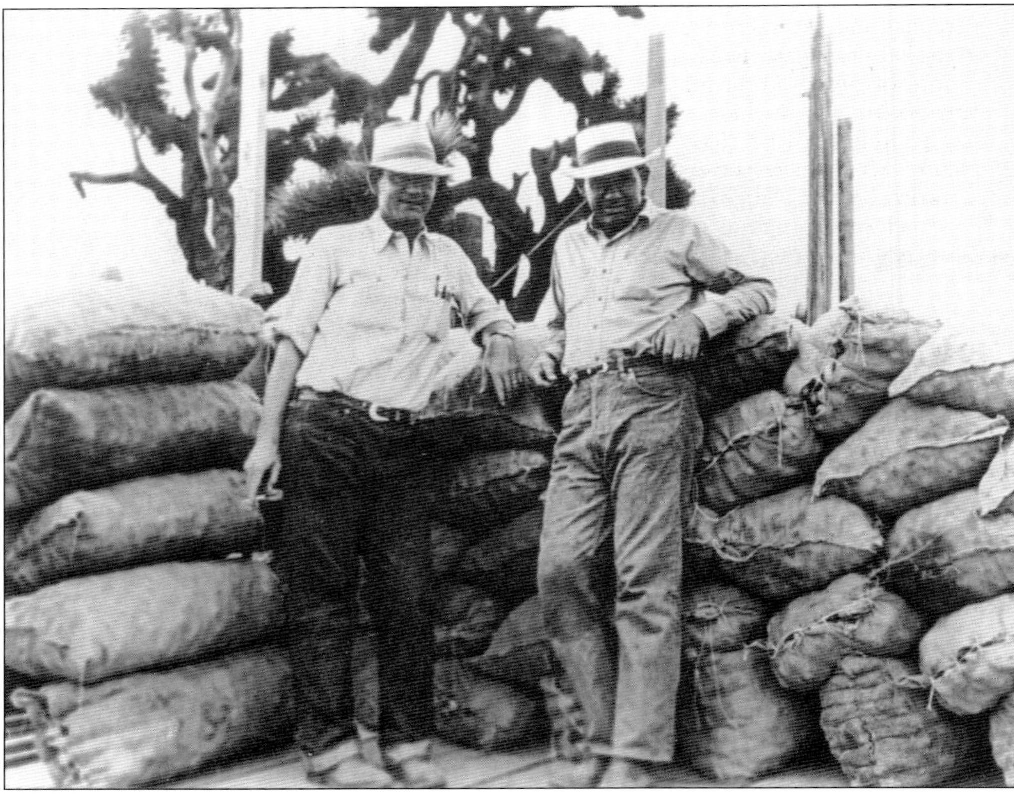

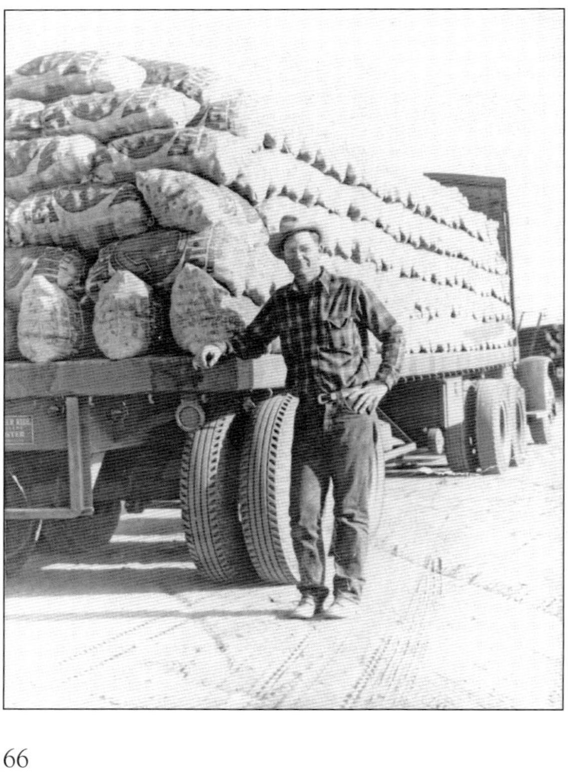

Clyde (left) and Harry Tatum have piled up a mound of full potato sacks ready for loading. The field-workers would use a belt with two chains on the front, which connected with a board just above the worker's knees. The board had two hooks on it, to which the worker would attach a sack. The workers would then push the boards with their thighs, dragging their sacks as they filled them. (Courtesy TF.)

Clyde Tatum stands by one of his trucks loaded with the family's T Brand white rose potatoes. The "T Brand White Rose" was shipped all over Southern California. White rose potatoes remained very popular until the early 1960s, when russets surpassed them. (Courtesy TF.)

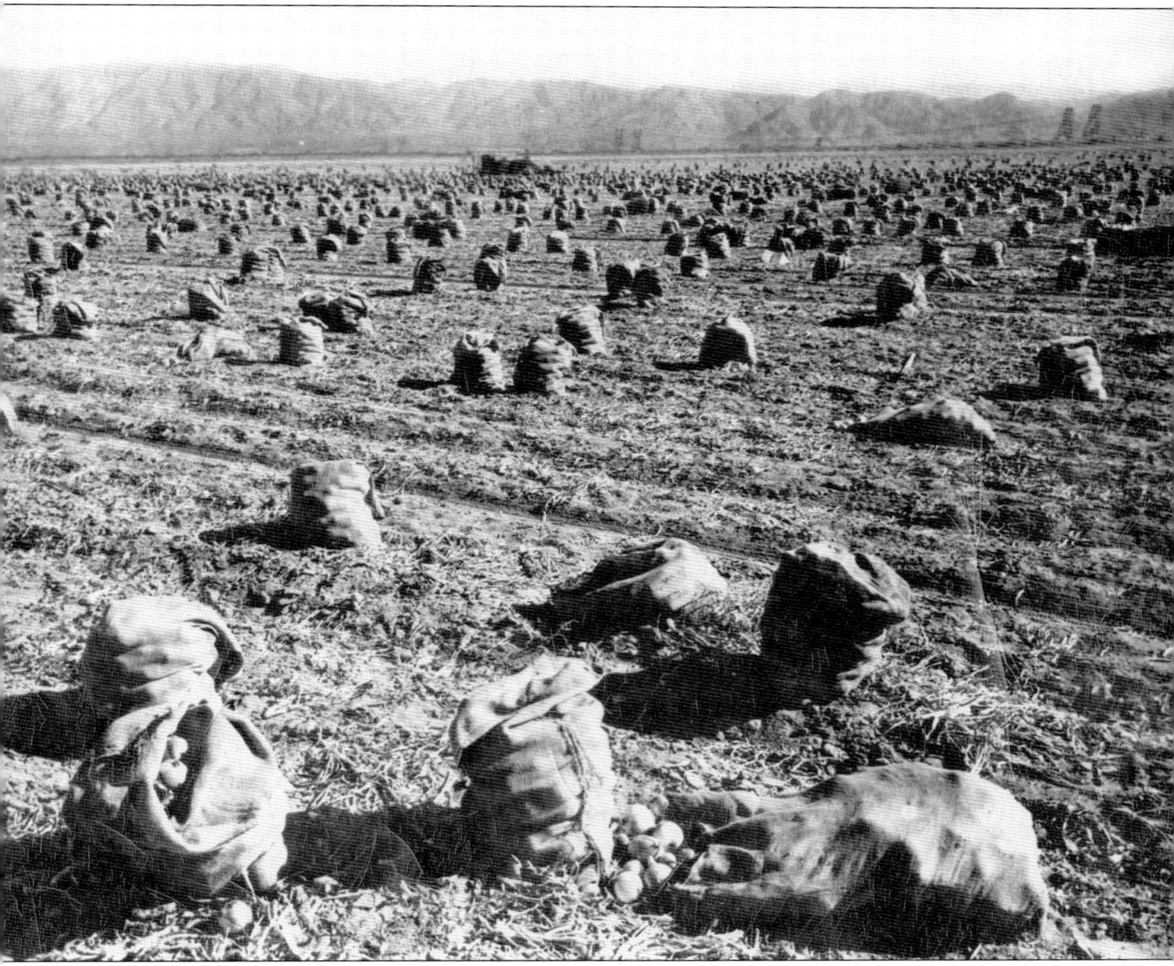

This photograph shows the national-record onion crop harvested out on the mesa by the Tatums and Walkers one year in the late 1940s. The families hoped that their bumper crop was going to generate a tremendous amount of money for them, but the timing was off, the tops turned, and Hesperia's national-record onion crop became feed for livestock. (Courtesy HOTM.)

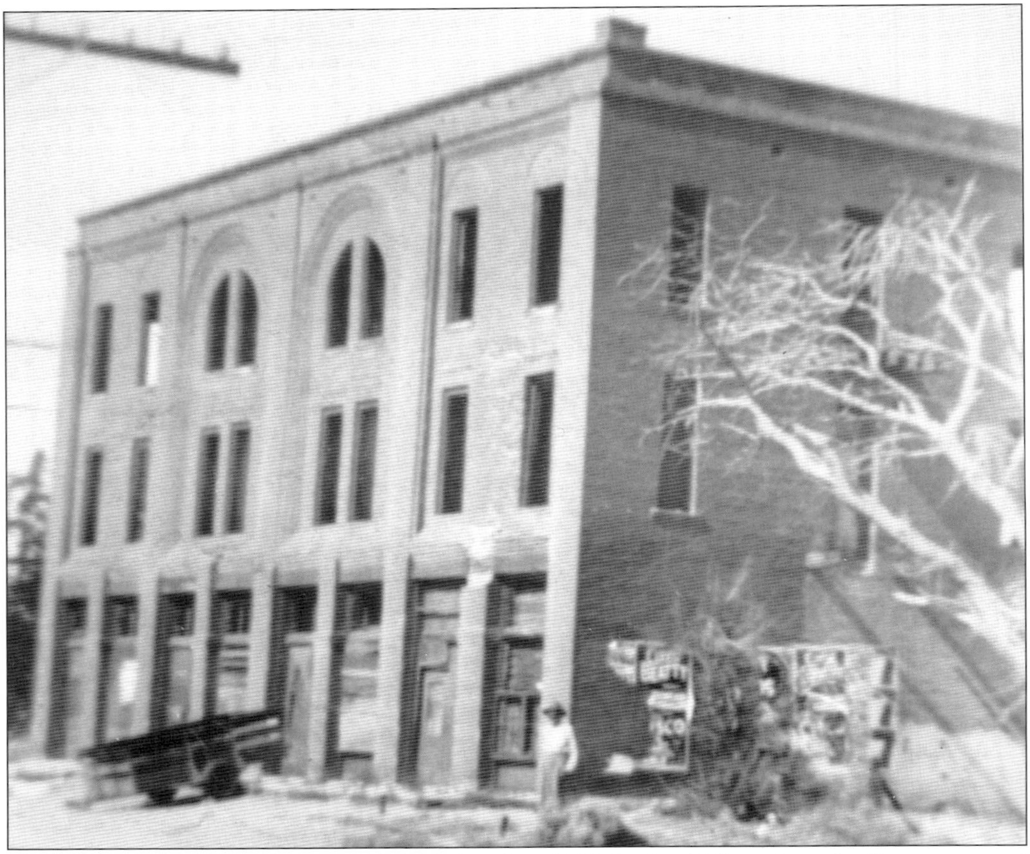

The Hesperia Hotel lay dormant after it closed in 1926. In the 1940s, when the Tatums started their farming and ranching venture in Hesperia, the former hotel was used for storage and as a place to feed the farmhands. (Courtesy HOTM.)

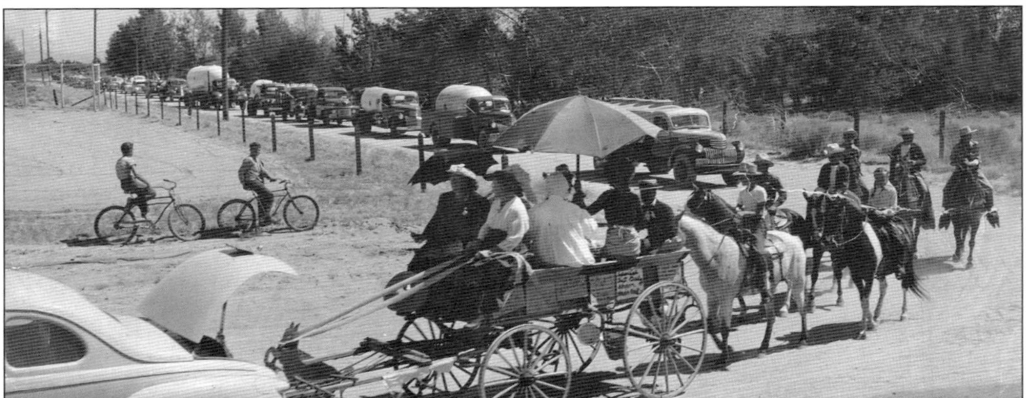

This 1946 photograph was taken at C Avenue and Main Street. Some of the participants seen here (in no order) are Val and Anita Shear, Elizabeth Harris, and Libby and Audrey Ellis. According to longtime residents, the pretext for this particular parade was to celebrate the town's acquisition of a new electrical source. One suspects, however, that the real reason behind this celebration was the same that underlay all the others: Hesperians simply liked to have fun. (Courtesy HRPD.)

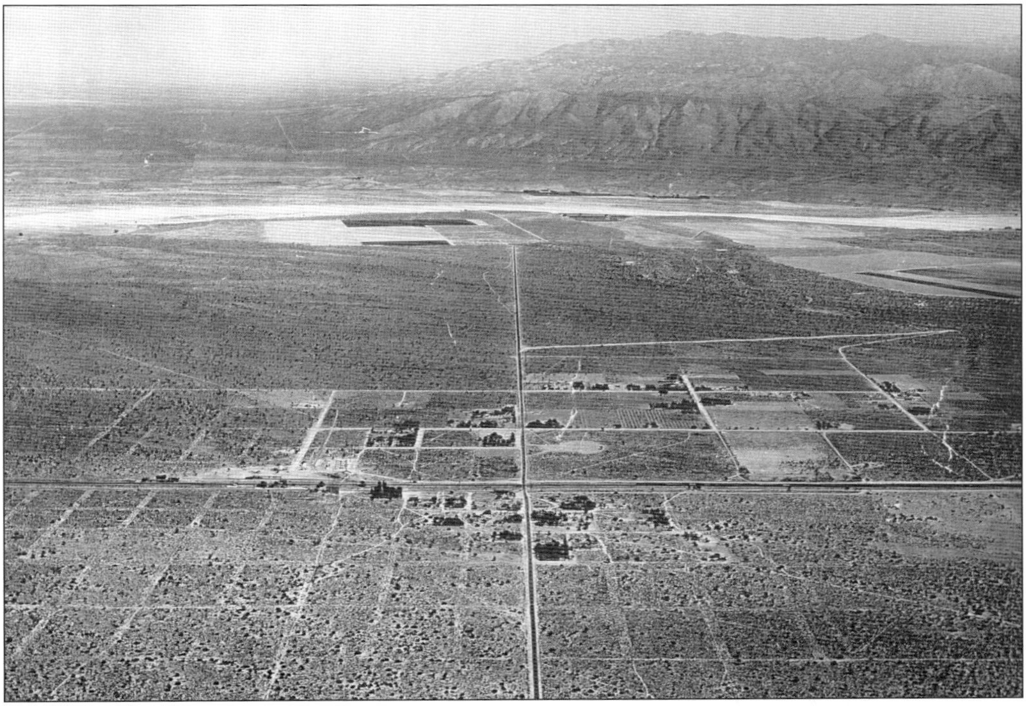

This late-1940s aerial photograph looks east from around Eleventh Street. The Hesperia Hotel and Walters Store stand to the left of the intersection of Main Street and Hesperia Road, just below the center of the photograph. The old schoolhouse is just above that same intersection, one block to the left. (Courtesy JW.)

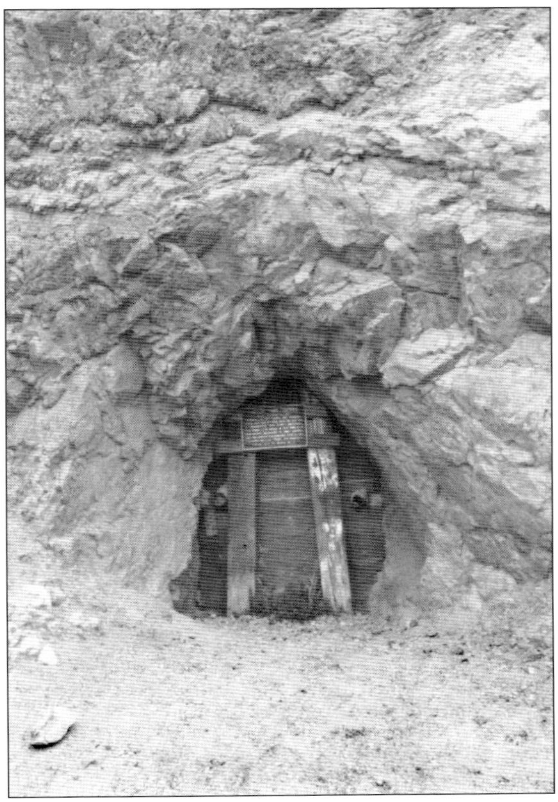

Mining and spelunking have long been popular with High Desert residents. The Mojave is home to numerous old mines dating back 100 to 200 years. One of Hesperia's pioneers, George Dewey Hedrick, was a prominent miner of his era. (Courtesy HRPD.)

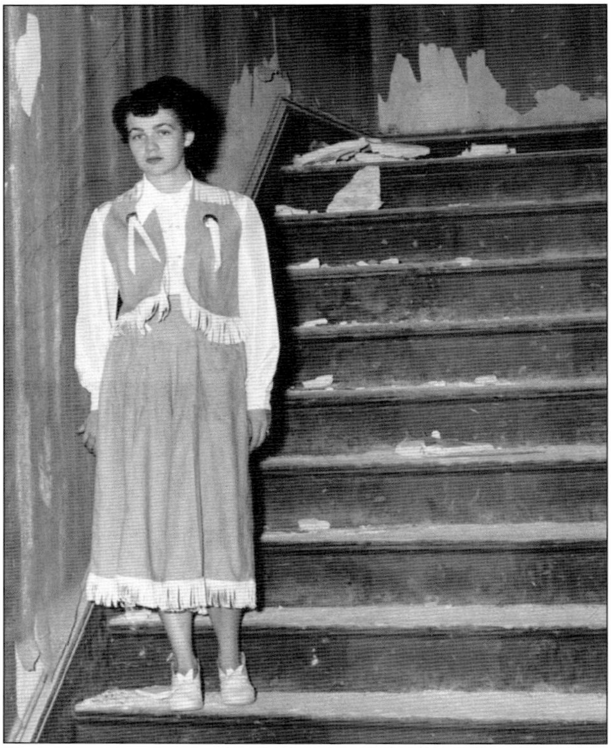

The woman standing on the stairway of the Hesperia Hotel in 1952 is Lorraine Cottrell Moffat. These images were taken by a friend of Lorraine's who enjoyed taking photographs of unique places but insisted on having people in the picture. This is the hotel's central stairway, which provided access to the three aboveground floors. Lorraine still resides in Hesperia. (Courtesy LCM.)

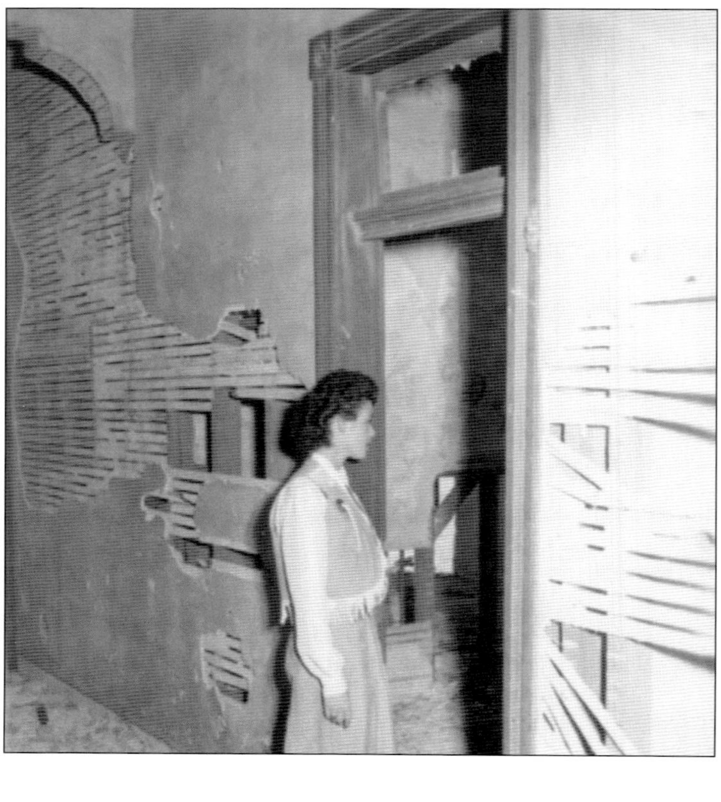

Lorraine looks into one of the Hesperia Hotel's guest rooms. The outside walls of the hotel were made of sun-dried adobe bricks, but the inside walls were constructed of lumber and lath and plaster. Seen in the upper-left corner of this photograph is one of the arches that the hotel's architect incorporated into the hallways. (Courtesy LCM.)

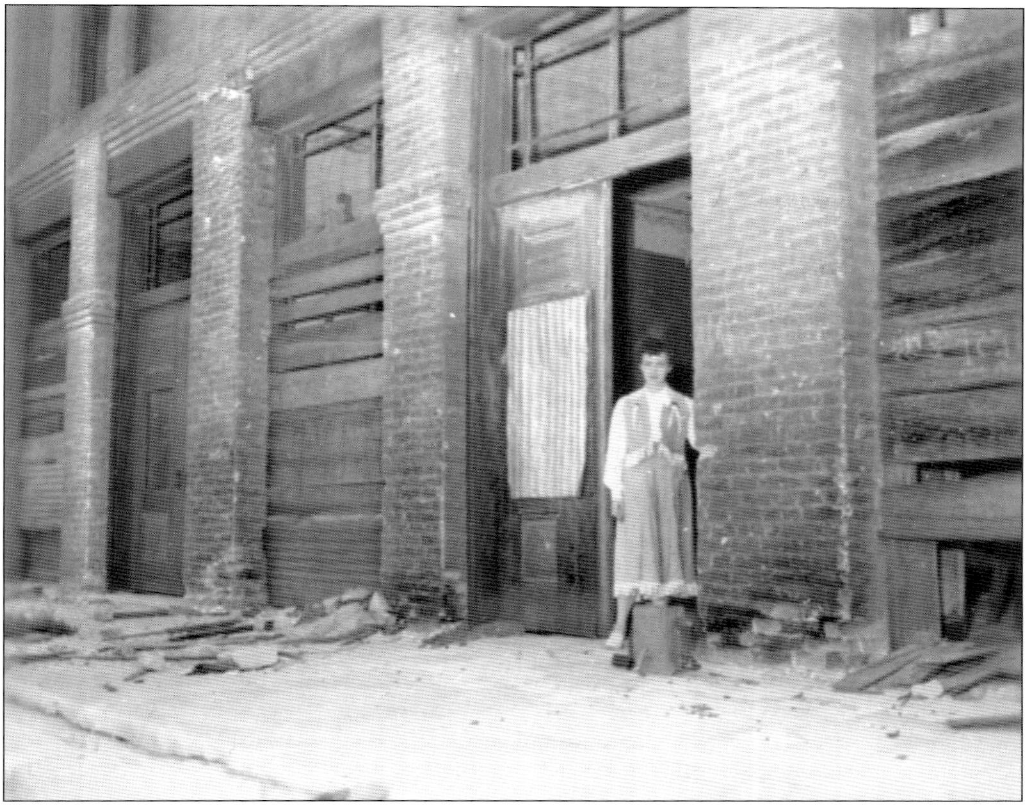

With Lorraine Cottrell Moffat standing at one of the doorways of the Hesperia Hotel, it is possible to get an idea of the hotel's scale. The first floor appears to have featured ceilings that were at least 10 feet high. Even as seen here in its dilapidated 1952 condition, it is easy to imagine how majestically the Hesperia Hotel must have towered over the High Desert at the turn of the century. (Courtesy LCM.)

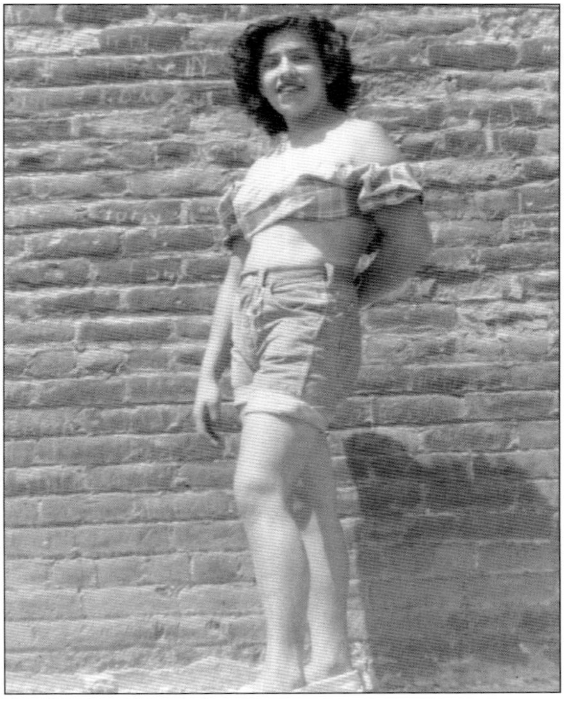

Mary Armenta is shown standing alongside the Hesperia Hotel in 1953. A closer look at the bricks reveals that by this time, vandals had carved their names into some of the old bricks. In later years, when the hotel was torn down, many of its bricks were used to build fireplace hearths or other decorative accents for people's homes. (Courtesy MACR.)

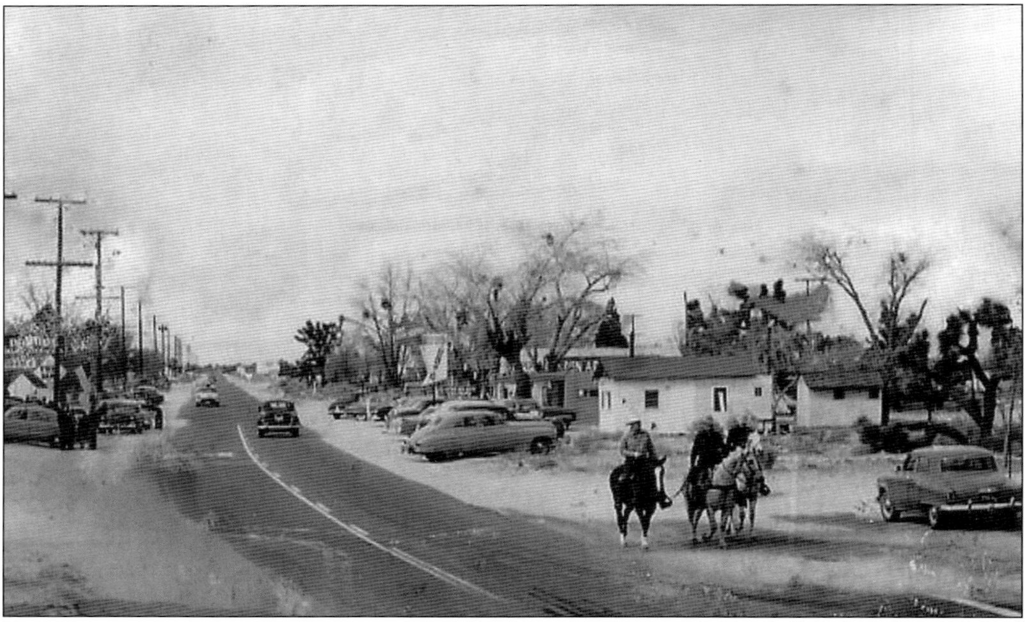

Here is Main Street, Hesperia, as it appeared in the 1940s. In this era, Hesperia's streets were still traveled by as many horses as cars. Even into the mid-1980s, it was not uncommon for someone to ride rather than drive to a store or shop in some parts of Hesperia. (Courtesy HOTM.)

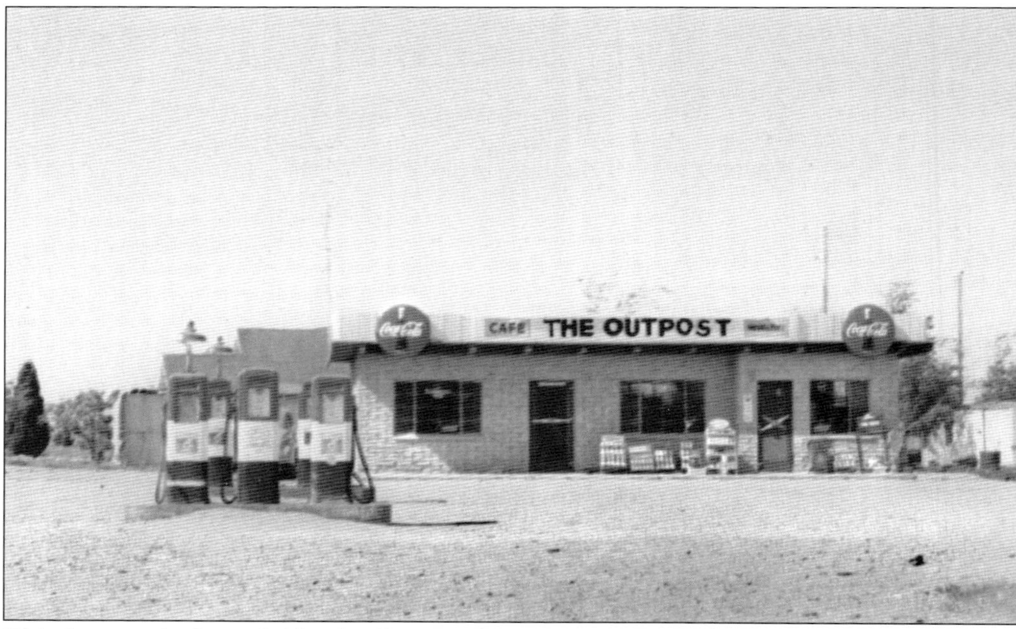

This does not look much like the Outpost that most Hesperians know today, and, as a matter of fact, this is not the same Outpost. The original Outpost seen here, owned by the Moessners, stood south of today's Outpost. When I-395 and Route 66 were widened, the Outpost was moved north. (Courtesy VVR66M.)

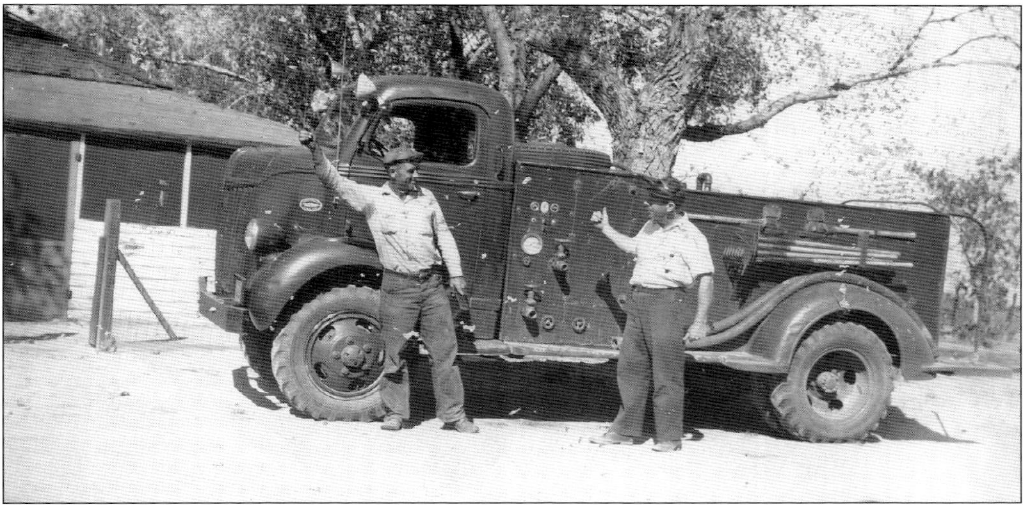

Older firefighters around Hesperia can remember the early days of the Hesperia Volunteer Fire Department, which started in 1954 after Bill Coe's house burned down. Hesperia's first pumper truck was a 1942 Chevrolet fire engine purchased from George Air Force Base for $100. An additional $250 was raised to put a working engine into it. Pictured here on the right is Hank Inskeep. (Courtesy HRPD.)

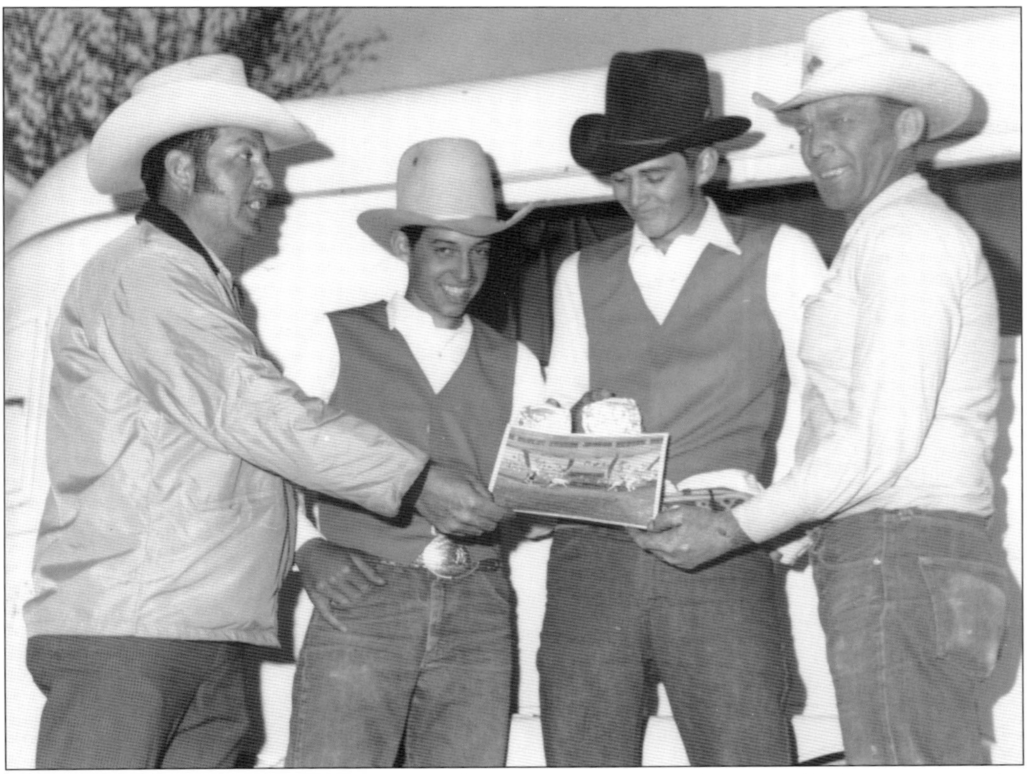

Pictured here are four cowboys after the Hesperia Days Rodeo showing off their prize buckles and a photograph of one of them roping a calf. Pictured from left to right are Marion and Billy Garlick and Bobby and Charlie York. (Courtesy HRPD.)

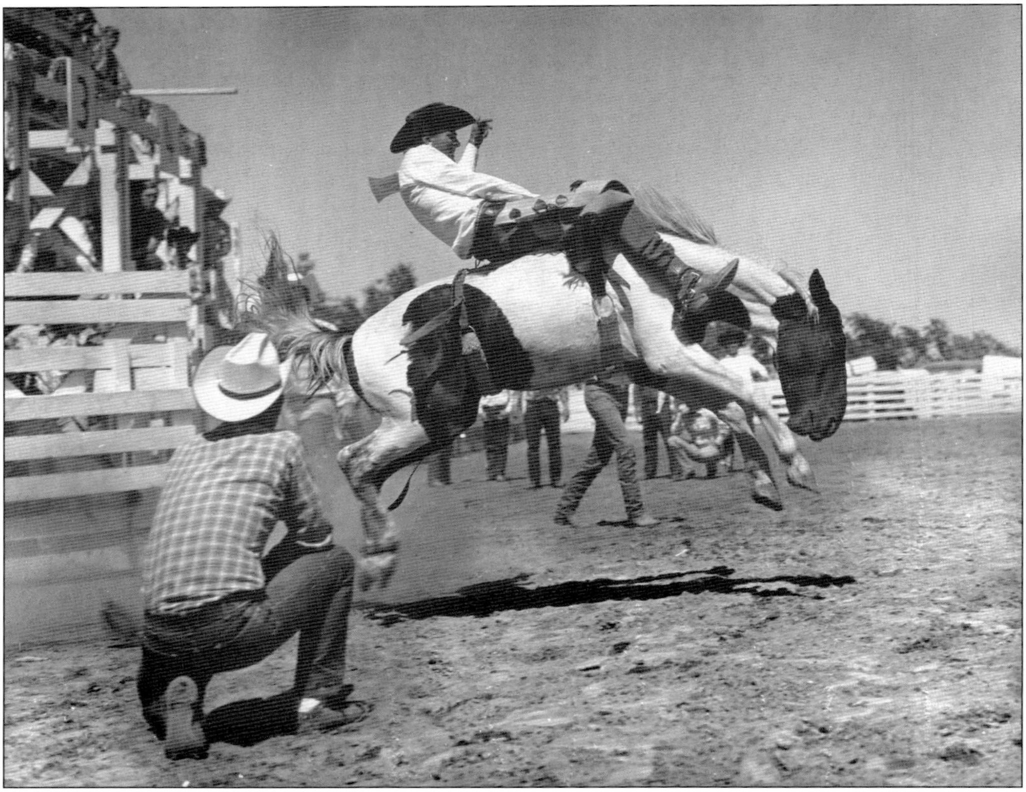

Rodeos have been part of Hesperia since the late 1940s, when Hesperia Days emerged as an annual event. (Courtesy HRPD.)

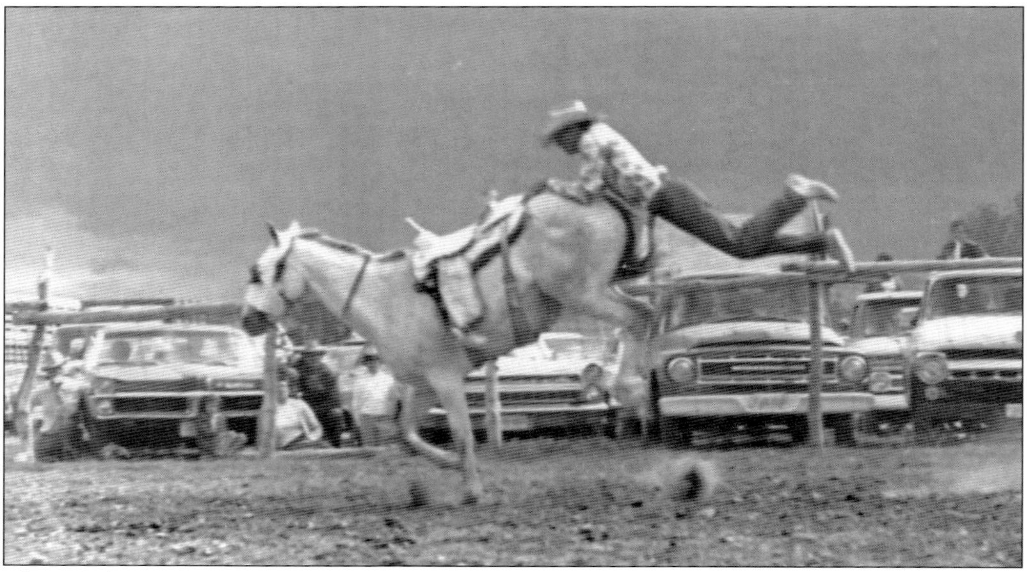

The exhibitions at the Hesperia Days Rodeos featured some great talent. Here Billy Bascom performs a trick called the Crupper Vault. Like his uncle Earl before him, Billy traveled the country making a name for himself as a top trick/stunt rider. (Courtesy BF.)

Charlie York was a well-known face at the Hesperia Days Rodeo. Here he is in the late 1950s sizing up his next roping challenge. (Courtesy HRPD.)

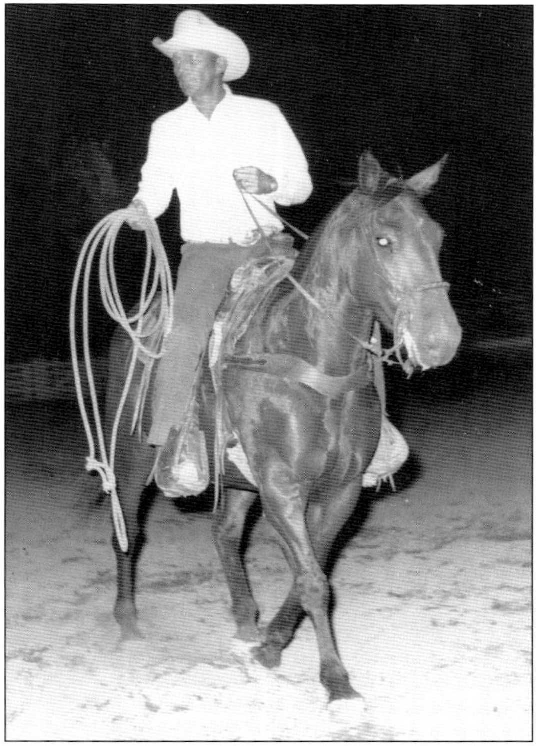

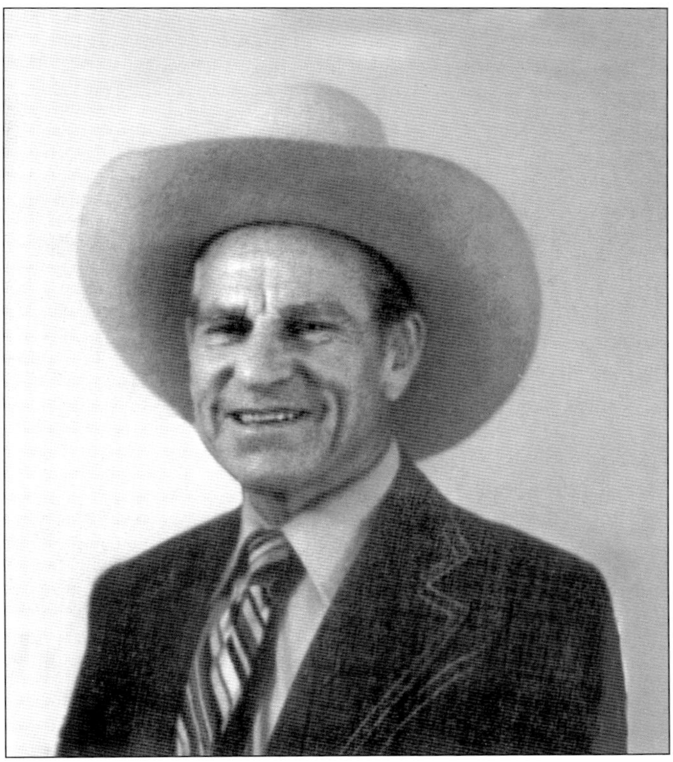

Earl Bascom was a well-known sculptor as well as being inducted into five different halls of fame—the Canadian Rodeo Hall of Fame; California Hall of Fame; Utah Sports Hall of Fame; Marion County, Mississippi, Cattlemen's Hall of Fame; and Raymond Sports Hall of Fame in Alberta, Canada. Earl Bascom had numerous prestigious awards bestowed upon him during his career. During the 1950s, the Bascom family called Hesperia home. (Courtesy BF.)

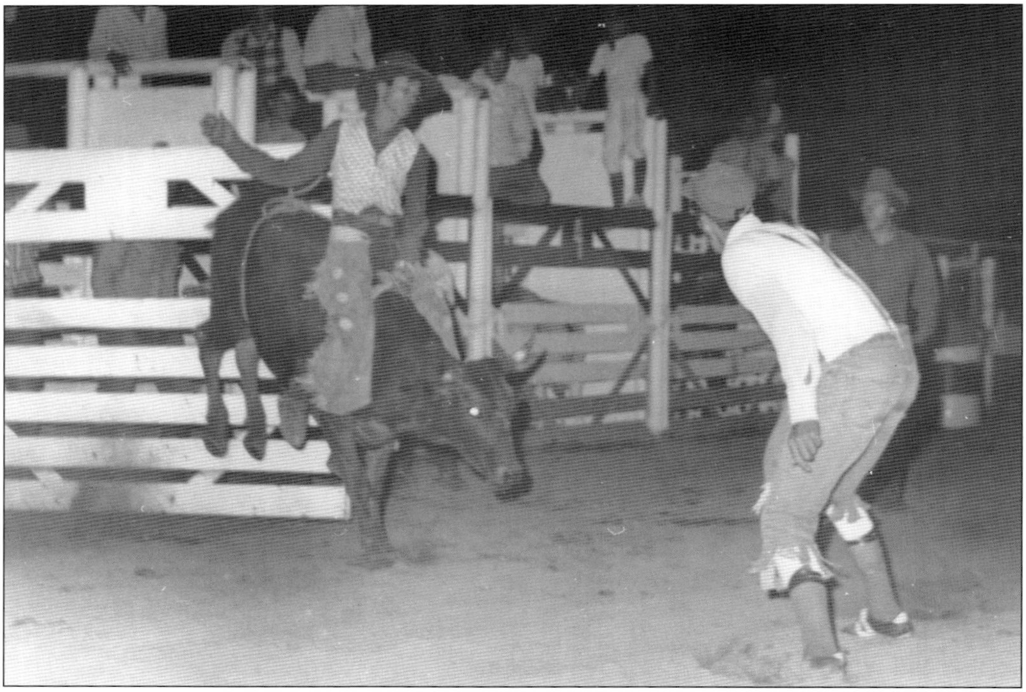

With the bull's eyes blazing and the clowns ready, here comes a rider out of the chute. Local athletes and professional riders came to the Hesperia Days Rodeos, which used stock suppliers including Gene Autry. (Courtesy HRPD.)

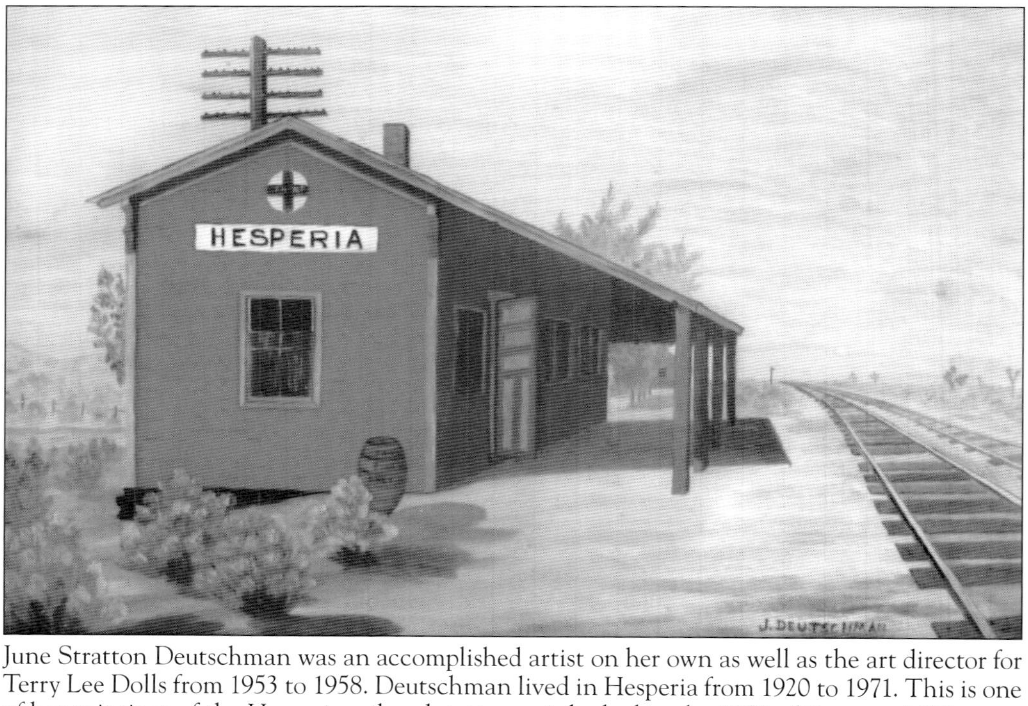

June Stratton Deutschman was an accomplished artist on her own as well as the art director for Terry Lee Dolls from 1953 to 1958. Deutschman lived in Hesperia from 1920 to 1971. This is one of her paintings of the Hesperia railroad station as it looked in the 1950s. (Courtesy LSP.)

Seven

The New Era

In the 1950s, a series of events jump-started Hesperia's growth. F. X. McDonald remembers when he first saw the area in 1946 at the age of 17. His father brought him and his brother up to Hesperia to learn how to handle a shotgun and hunt rabbits. Little did he know that he would be involved in Hesperia's new growth in the 1950s. Just a few years later, F. X. and his brother built a shack on the outskirts of Hesperia with spare lumber from a building their father had built in Los Angeles. The shack had no water or electricity. McDonald remembers cold nights around the campfire doing what he loved, singing folk songs with a group of friends.

When McDonald heard that M. Penn Phillips planned to start a large development in Hesperia, he took his real estate license in hand and headed for the sales office. Phillips's purchase was said to be the second-largest land purchase in the western United States since the William Wrigley family had purchased Catalina Island.

The first day's property sales were very slow. McDonald had an opportunity to appear on the *Arthur Godfrey Talent Scouts* show, so he flew to New York. When asked where he was from, McDonald proudly told Godfrey and his 3 million viewers that he was from Hesperia, California—the "New Frontier," where a major land boom was happening. McDonald won the contest and spent the following week in New York. When he returned to Hesperia, people were heading into town to look and buy property. His father, Dr. F. X. McDonald Sr., who had no musical talent, wrote the song, "Headin' for Hesperia," sung to the tune of the "Battle Hymn of the Republic." M. Penn Phillips liked the song and asked F. X. Jr. to record it. Four thousand copies of the single were pressed, to be given to property buyers. Over the years, many have told McDonald that either his mentioning Hesperia as the "New Frontier" on *Arthur Godfrey Talent Scouts* or hearing his recording of "Headin' for Hesperia" had helped spark their interest in the town. And so began the new era.

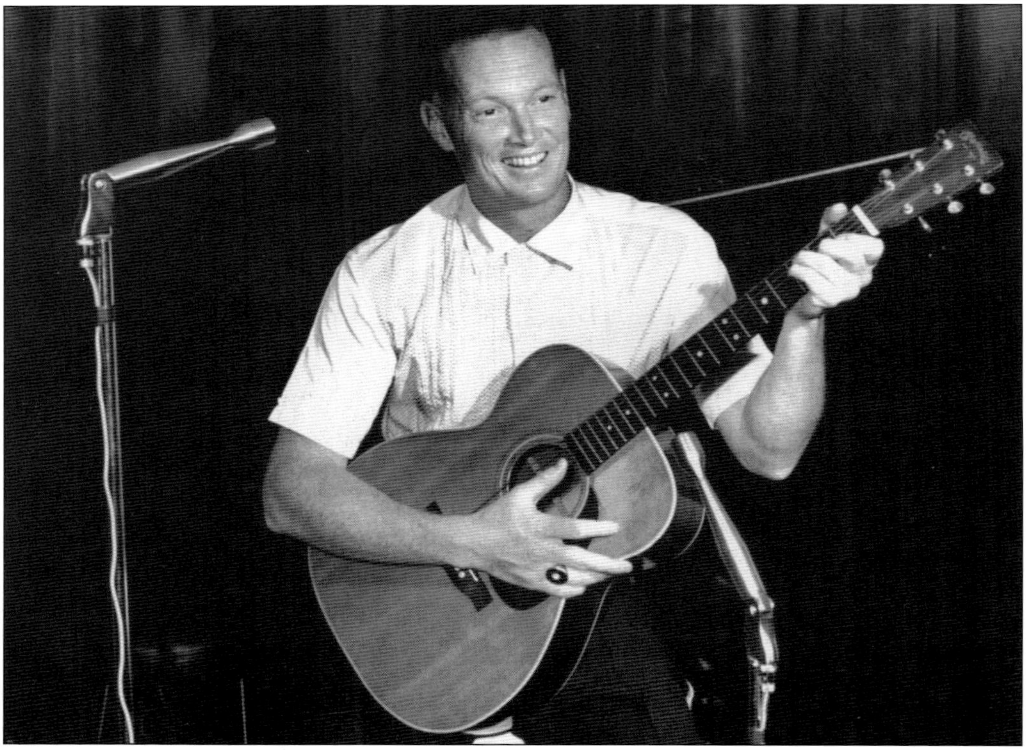

F. X. McDonald, shown here in the early 1950s, says, "Today at the age of 81, I look up at the photograph of the shack on my bedroom wall before retiring, and I can go right back into the shack in my mind's eye and remember everything—the bat-and-board walls with no insulation, the potbelly stove, the old carpet and furniture. It was like a shack in an old Roy Rogers Western movie." (Courtesy FXM.)

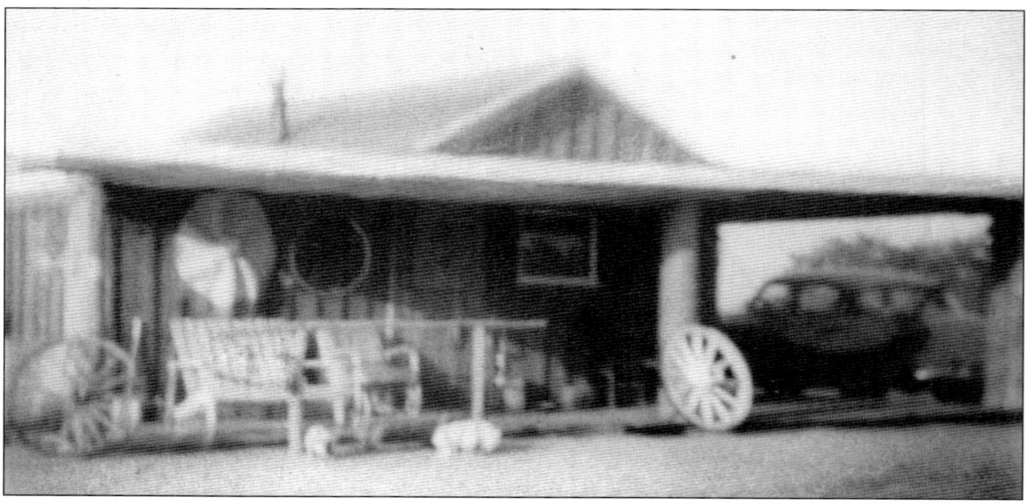

This was the shack that F. X. and his brother Chad built about 1.5 miles east of old Route 66 and 2.5 miles south of Main Street. In some ways, F. X. says, he felt that he had nothing at that time, but he realizes now that he had everything. A peaceful home under the beautiful star-filled skies of Hesperia, the shack was burned down by high school students in the 1980s. (Courtesy FXM.)

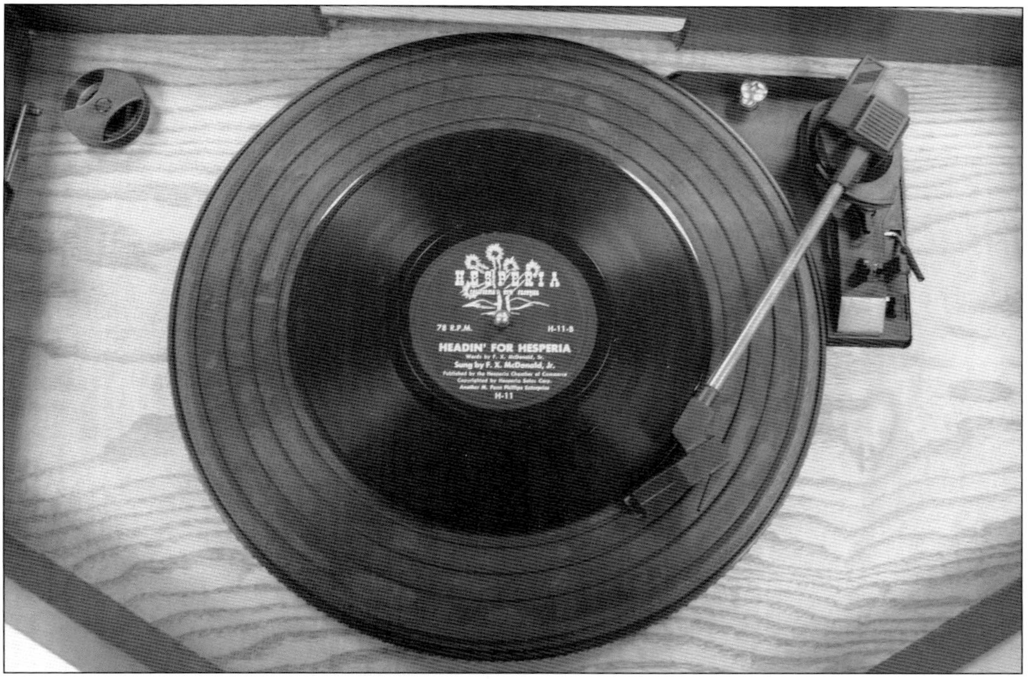

Headin' for Hesperia (lyrics by Dr. F. X. McDonald)

He was a huffin' and puffin', comin' fast along the trail
With a snort'n sneeze, he cut the breeze, his shirt tail was a sail
As he passed me I asked him why, he hollered, "I can't hear ya."
But there's not a doubt, I heard him shout, "I'm "Headin' for Hesperia."

(chorus) Headin' for Hesperia, I'm gettin' out of here
I'm leavin' my gout and headin' for California's new frontier
Where there's no smog, no smoke, no noise, and freedom from hysteria
I'm tellin' ya Mac, I'm ballin' the jack. I'm headin' for Hesperia.

Out where common things are handy, sold in the general store
Calico eggs and candy, the post office behind the door
Out where the air is fresh and clean, there is no smog or smoke
Out where you're held in high esteem and the undertaker's broke

(repeat chorus above)

If you're hiring a psychiatrist whose treatin' your hysteria
Jump off his couch and shout out loud, I'm "Headin' for Hesperia"
Then tell old Mac you won't be back, now pack your sack and call a hack
Get off the rack and make a track, and on the way be "ballin' the jack."

(repeat chorus above)

(Courtesy FXM.)

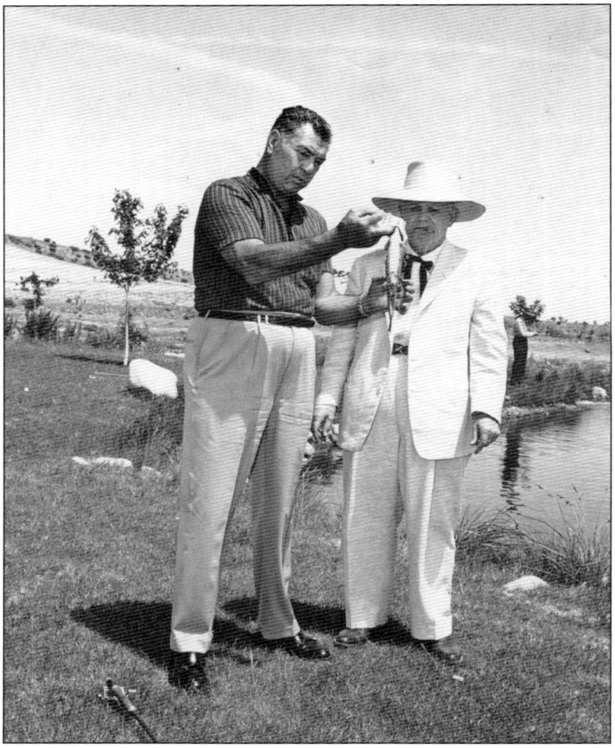

M. Penn Phillips (right) is pictured here with the former heavyweight boxing champion of the world, Jack Dempsey, holding a fish from the Lake RoToBo Trout Farm—later to become Hesperia Lake. Dempsey also played a role in the getting Hesperia noticed and in continuing its development. (Courtesy HRPD.)

The trout farm is shown here in its early years with three young women standing at the bridge as water flows over the inlaid rocks. The trout farm's water was supplied by the ditch; the Tatums had installed a pump in the 1940s to continue the water flow up onto the mesa. (Courtesy HRPD.)

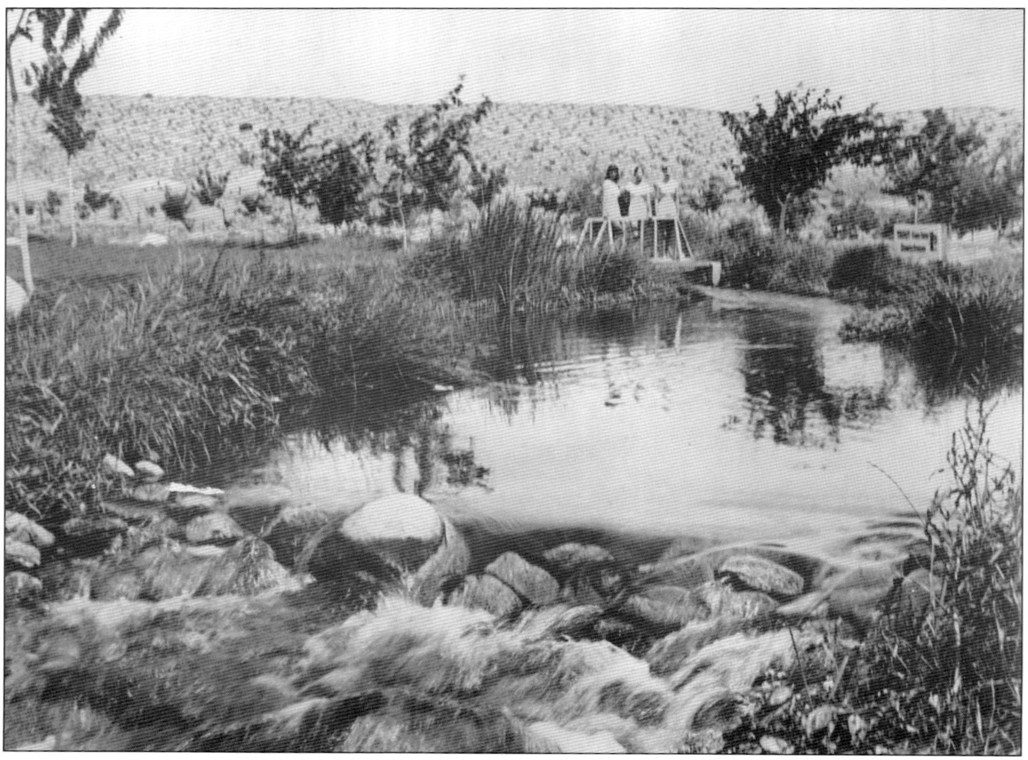

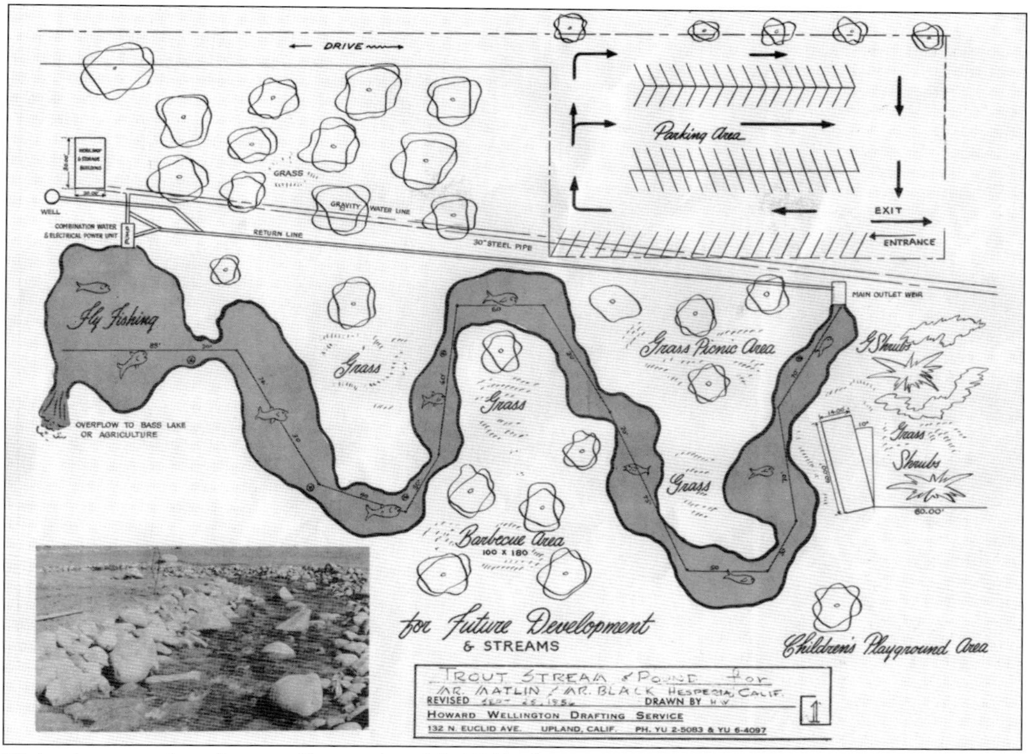

This photograph, taken on September 25, 1956, shows a revision to the trout stream and pond. The lake was filled by the 30-inch gravity-fed pipe installed by Columbus Frank Hedrick in 1911. Lake RoToBo was named for the three sons of its owner, Mary Emery: Ron, Tom, and Bob Emery. (Courtesy HOTM.)

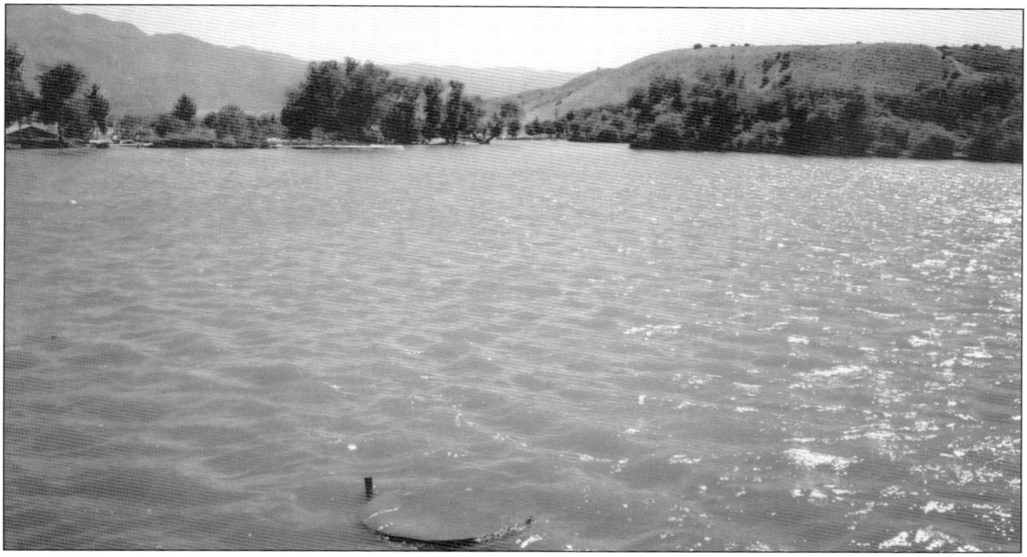

Visible in the lower part of this photograph is the inlet pipe that fed the lake. This system was all gravity-fed. The Tatums installed a booster pump in the 1940s to supply water for the potato fields on the mesa. (Courtesy HOTM.)

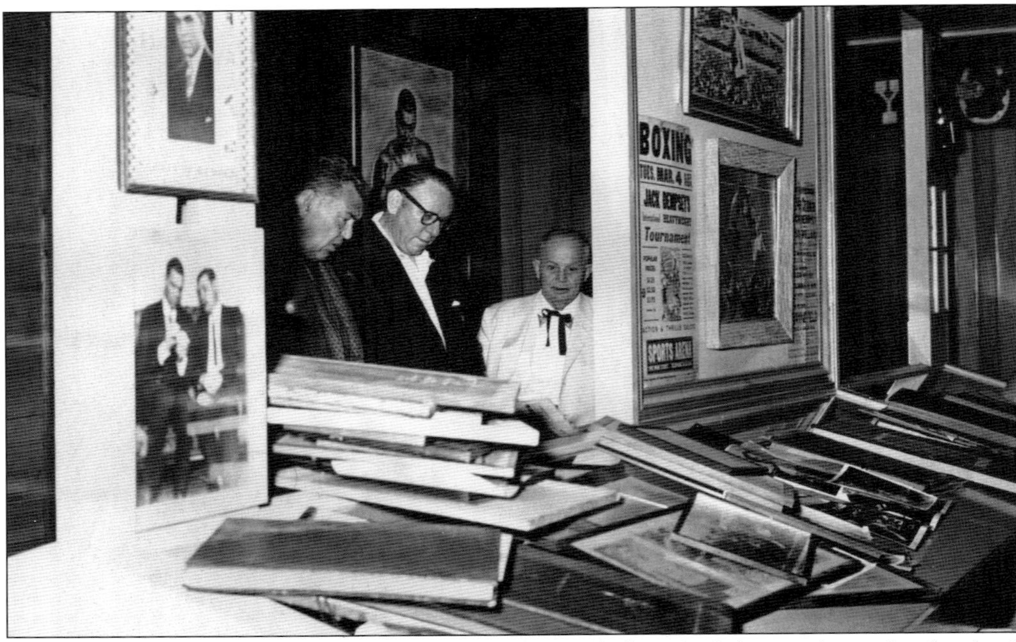

Pictured here are Jack Dempsey (left) and M. Penn Phillips (right), to either side of a third, unidentified man. The three of them are sorting out Jack Dempsey's memorabilia to put on display at the new Jack Dempsey Museum. (Courtesy HRPD.)

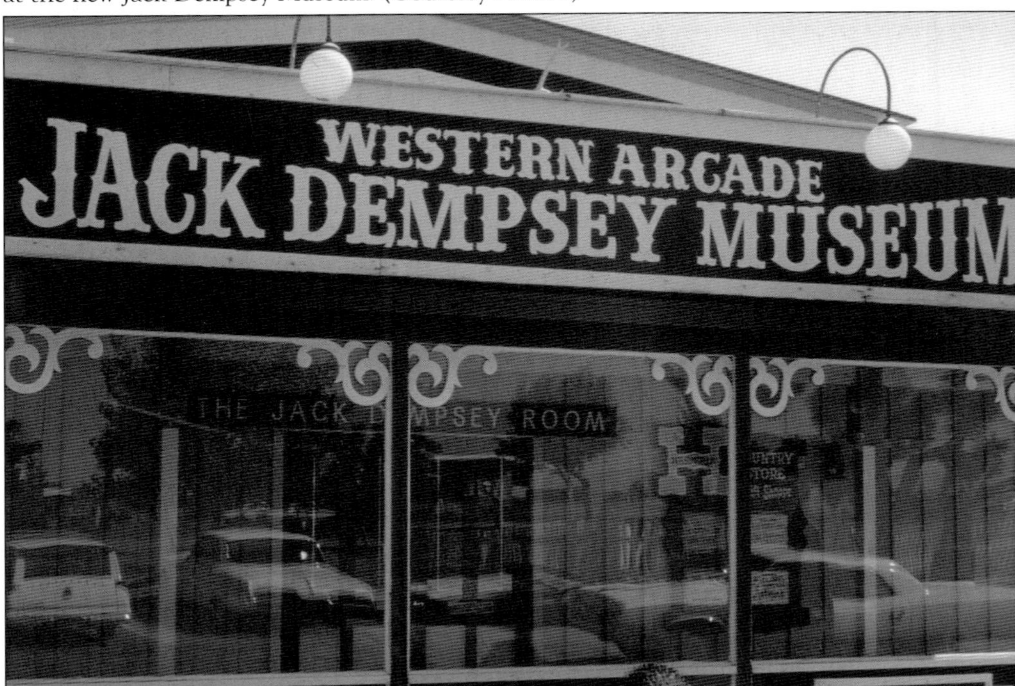

The Jack Dempsey Museum in Hesperia is believed to be the first museum dedicated to the fighter, even predating the museum in his birthplace in Manassa, Colorado. Jack Dempsey, the "Manassa Mauler," held the world heavyweight title from 1919 to 1926. (Courtesy HRPD.)

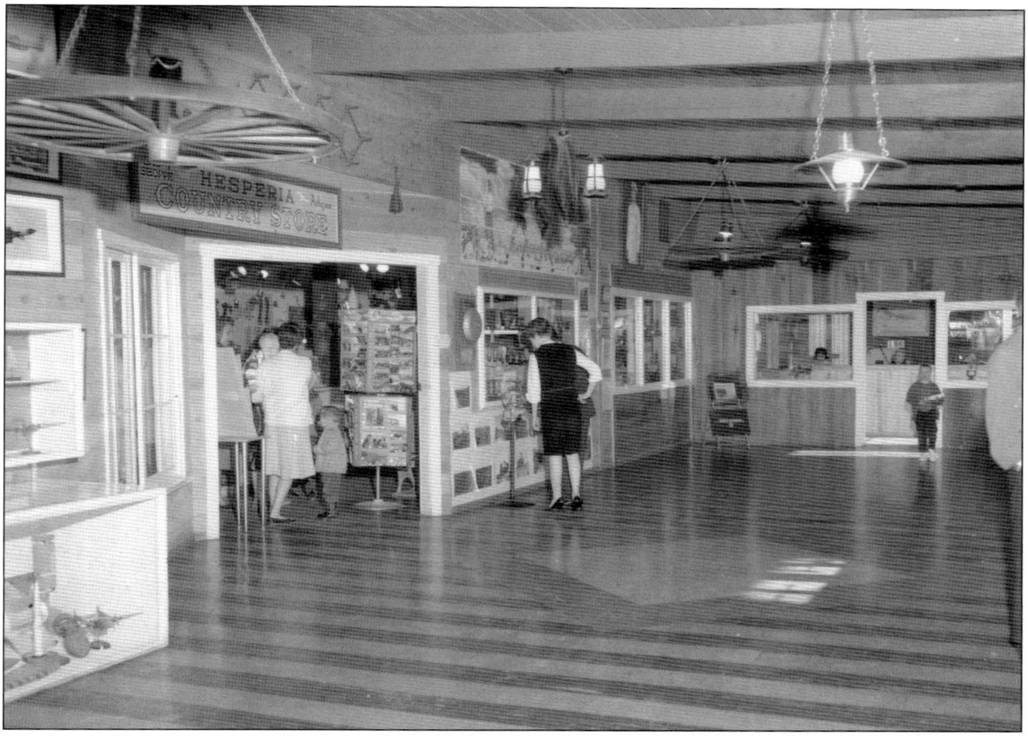

Inside of the Western Arcade was a country store decorated with wagon wheels and lantern light fixtures. This area later became known as Old Town Hesperia and housed a number of different businesses, including barbershops, art studios, and a variety of restaurants. (Courtesy HOTM.)

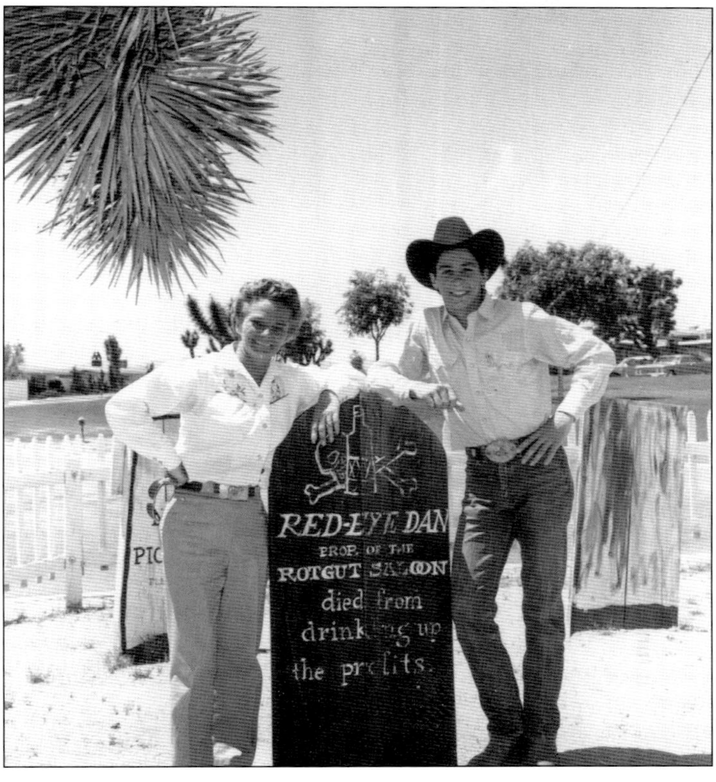

Standing in this graveyard are Myra McGinnis and an unidentified young man in 1965. They seem to be pretty happy to be there. This was a mock graveyard just behind the Western Arcade that housed the Dempsey Museum. (Courtesy HRPD.)

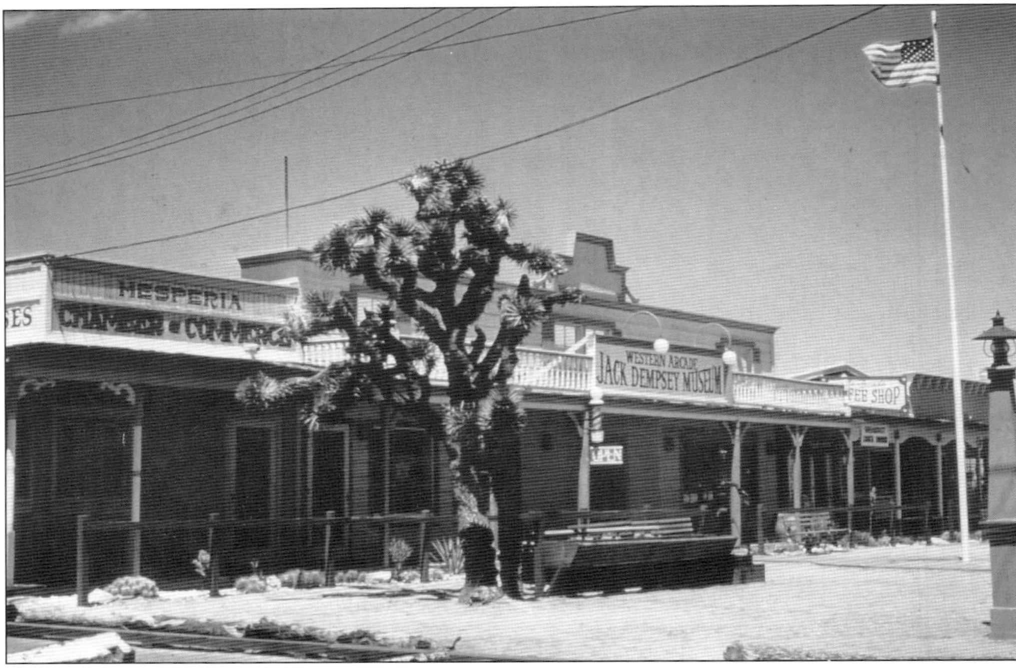

The Western Arcade was also the first home of the Hesperia Chamber of Commerce. The chamber was run by Loren Pratt under the direction of M. Penn Phillips. This remained the chamber's location until the early 1960s, when it moved out to Main Street. (Courtesy HOTM.)

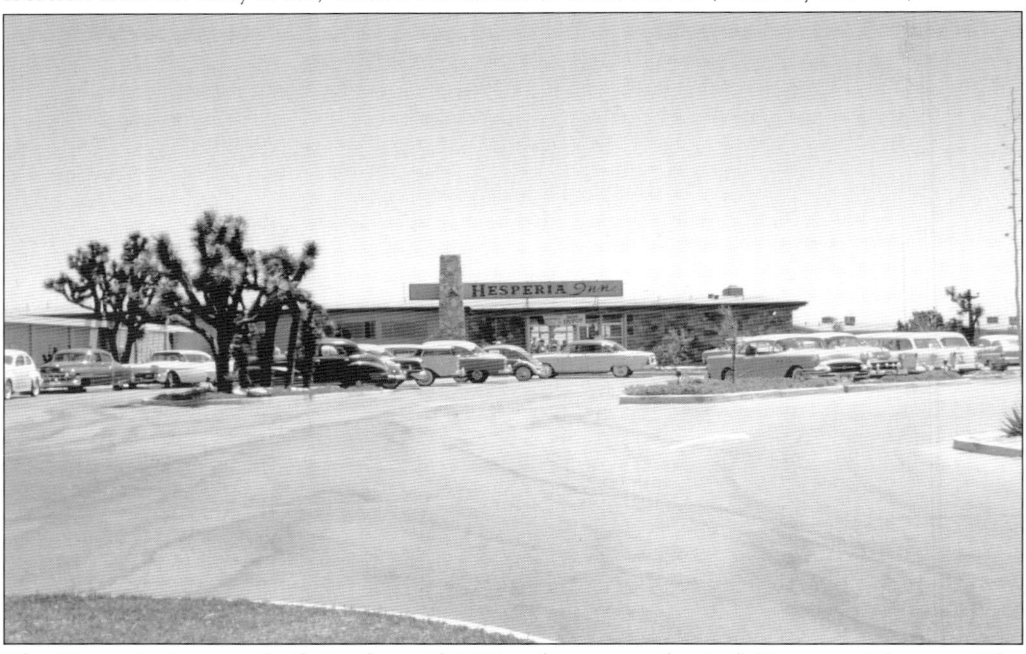

The Hesperia Inn was built in the mid-1950s adjacent to the Jack Dempsey Museum. The grounds contained a swimming pool and a variety of other amenities. The Hesperia Inn was the hub of all the new attractions that were developed during the late 1950s by M. Penn Phillips. (Courtesy HOTM.)

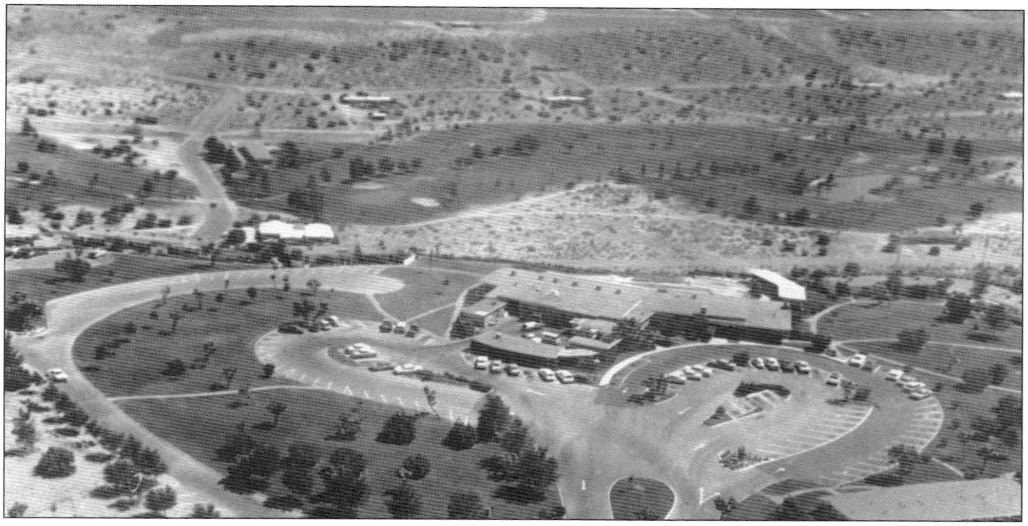

The aerial of the Hesperia Inn was taken in the early 1960s. The grounds have everything that a visitor might want for a relaxing vacation, such as tennis courts, a golf course, and the restaurants available at the inn, the Western Arcade, and the golf course. The grounds featured multiroom apartments and some larger units nicknamed "Holi-Houses." Many top entertainers performed at the Hesperia Inn, including Sammy Davis Jr., Donald O'Connor, Rudy Vallee, Eddie Peabody, Dorothy Dandridge, Mel Torme, the Marx Brothers, Pinky Lee, Marie Wilson, Alan Mowbray, the Wiere Brothers, and Tommy Noonan. (Both, courtesy HOTM.)

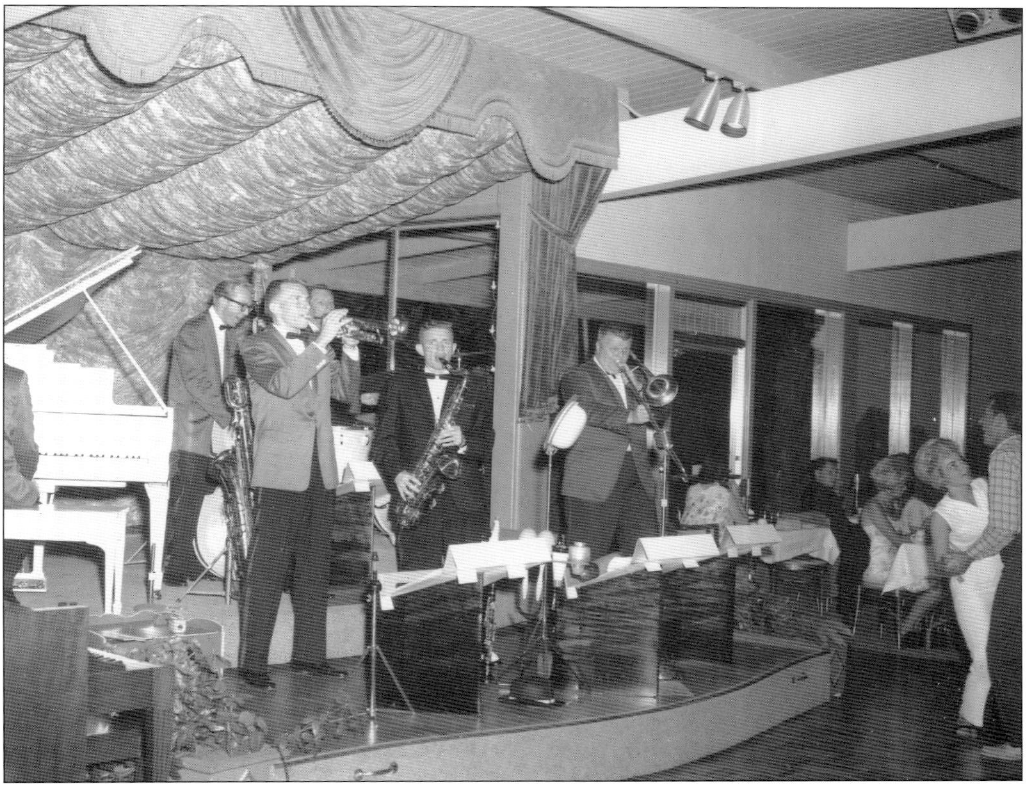

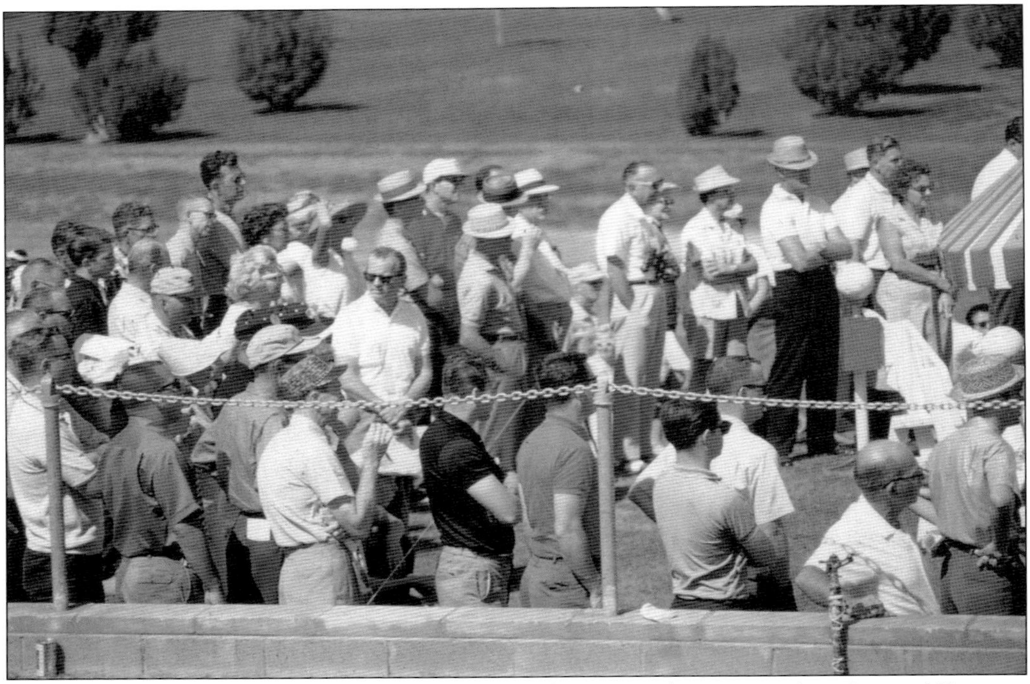

This was the fourth annual PGA golf tournament in the 1960s. The Roy Bearden–designed Hesperia Golf Course was the only course in the High Desert on the PGA tour. (Courtesy HOTM.)

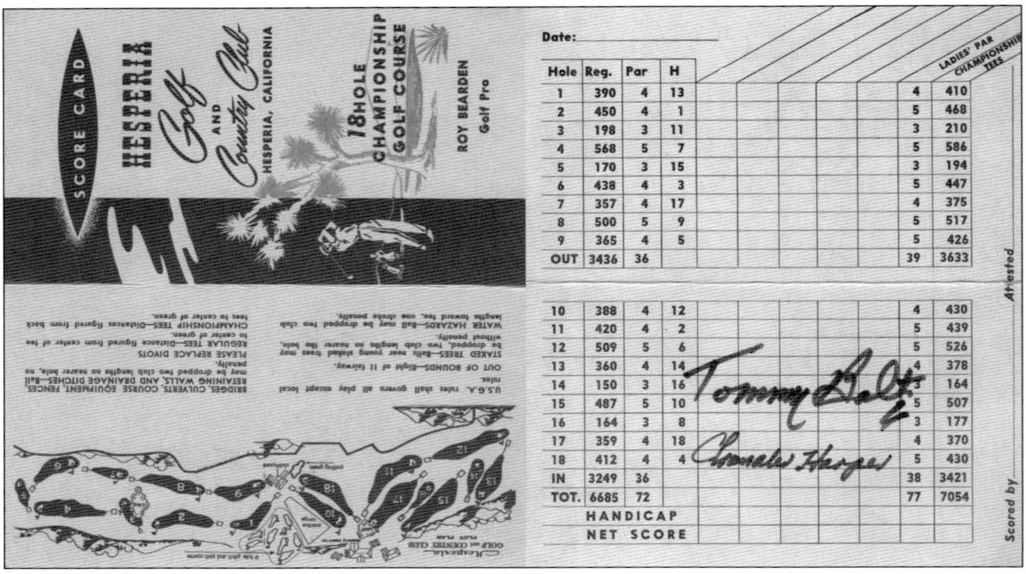

SCORE CARD

HESPERIA Golf and Country Club

HESPERIA, CALIFORNIA

18 HOLE CHAMPIONSHIP GOLF COURSE

ROY BEARDEN Golf Pro

Date:

Hole	Reg.	Par	H	Ladies' Par	Championship Tees
1	390	4	13	4	410
2	450	4	1	5	468
3	198	3	11	3	210
4	568	5	7	5	586
5	170	3	15	3	194
6	438	4	3	5	447
7	357	4	17	4	375
8	500	5	9	5	517
9	365	4	5	5	426
OUT	3436	36		39	3633
10	388	4	12	4	430
11	420	4	2	5	439
12	509	5	6	5	526
13	360	4	14	4	378
14	150	3	16	3	164
15	487	5	10	5	507
16	164	3	8	3	177
17	359	4	18	4	370
18	412	4	4	5	430
IN	3249	36		38	3421
TOT.	6685	72		77	7054
HANDICAP					
NET SCORE					

Attested

Scored by

This Hesperia Golf Course scorecard was autographed by noted golf professionals Chandler Harper and Tommy Bolt in the late 1950s or early 1960s. (Courtesy HOTM.)

Golf professional Tommy Bolt played the Hesperia Golf Course on several occasions. He was inducted to the PGA Hall of Fame in 2002 and won 15 PGA Tours. Tommy's temper earned him the nickname of "Terrible Tommy." He later wrote a book on how to control one's temper on the golf course. (Courtesy HOTM.)

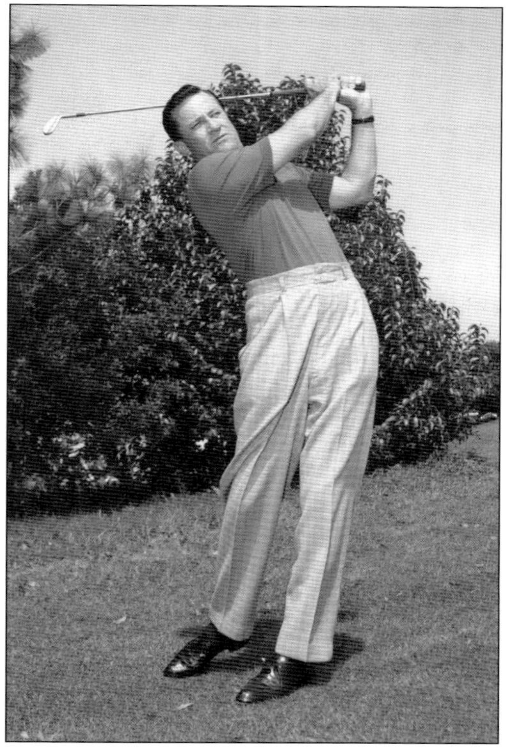

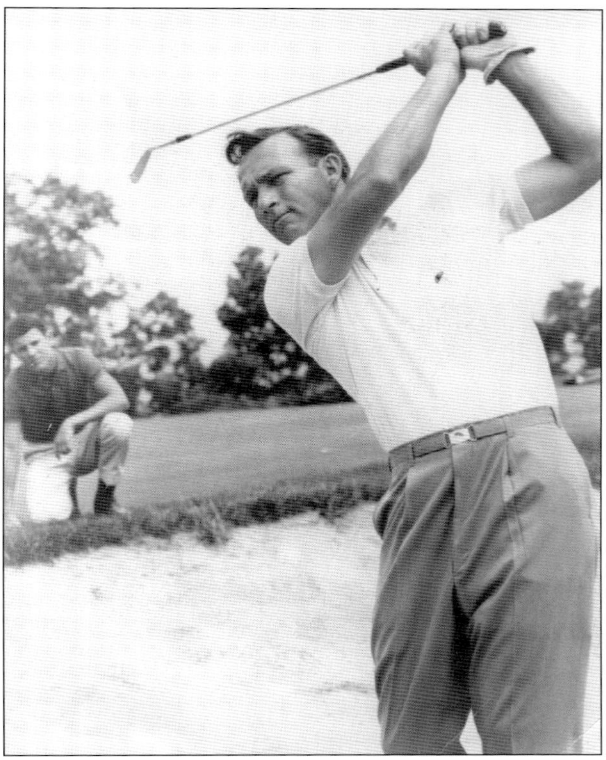

Arnold Palmer is shown here playing a PGA tournament at the Hesperia Golf Course. Although he never won any of the five PGA tournaments he played in Hesperia, his presence was always known. The photograph was taken by Hesperian Myra McGinnis. (Courtesy HRPD.)

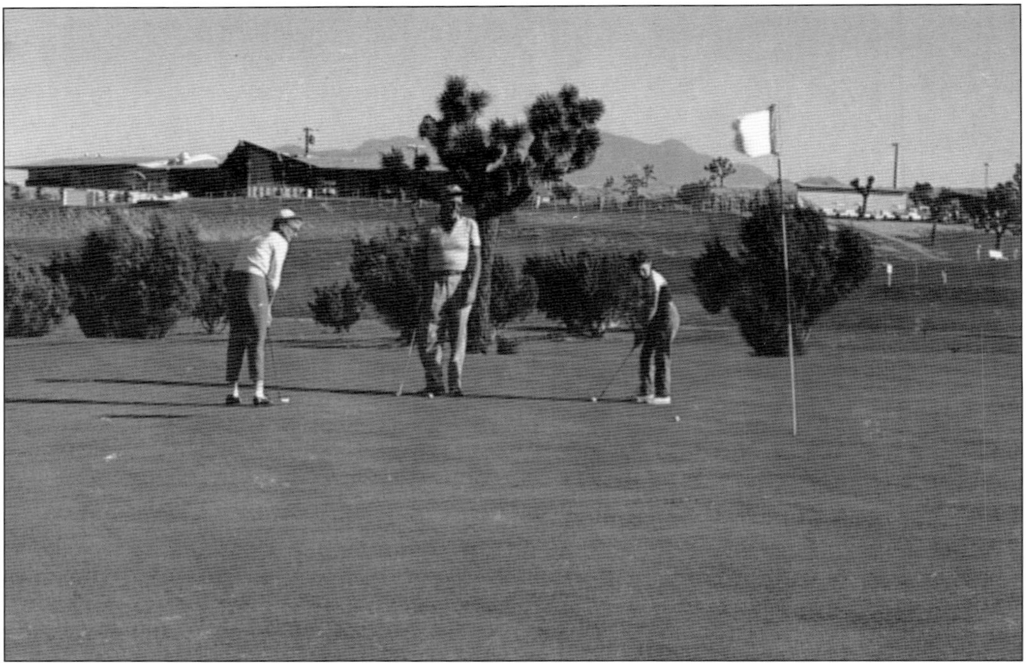

High Desert golf enthusiasts of all ages have found great joy at the Hesperia Golf Course since its creation. In this early 1960s image, a young man goes for the final putt. (Courtesy HRPD.)

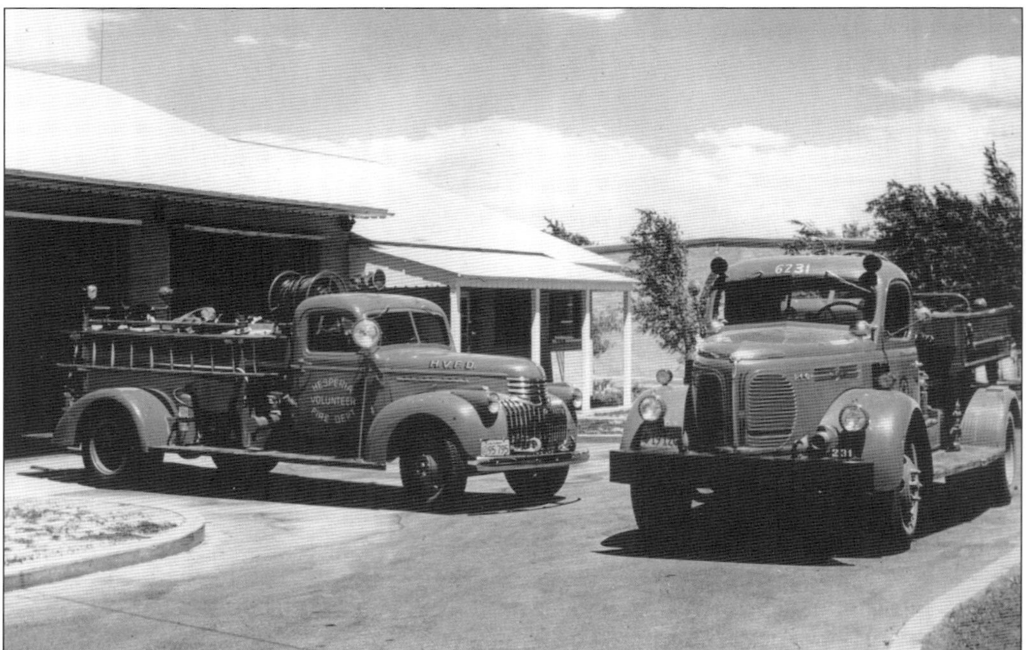

Since its founding, the Hesperia Volunteer Fire Department has stood ready to protect Hesperia from any type of fire. Pictured here are the department's engine No. 30 (left) and California Department of Forestry (CDF) engine No. 6731. The photograph was taken at the CDF station on Main Street next to the Hesperia Grange Hall in the early 1950s. (Courtesy HRPD.)

This landing strip developed into one of 600 airparks in the nation and the third-oldest airpark in the state. Lodging was built at the airstrip, along with a restaurant and a maintenance hangar. One very unique feature of the airpark is its airplane-shaped swimming pool, easily identifiable from the air. In later years, homes with runway access were built around the landing strip; this trait is what makes Hesperia's facility an airpark instead of an airport. Hesperia Airpark is strategically located along the flight corridor used by those flying over the Cajon Pass, as was Miller's Corner in its day. (Left, courtesy HOTM; below, courtesy HRPD.)

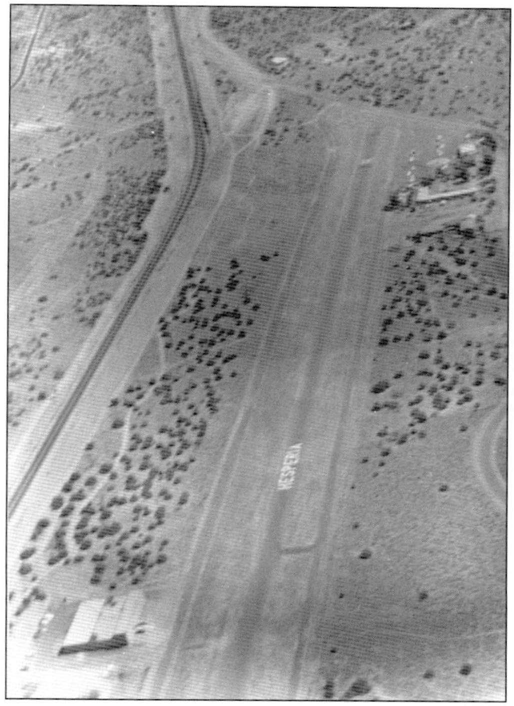

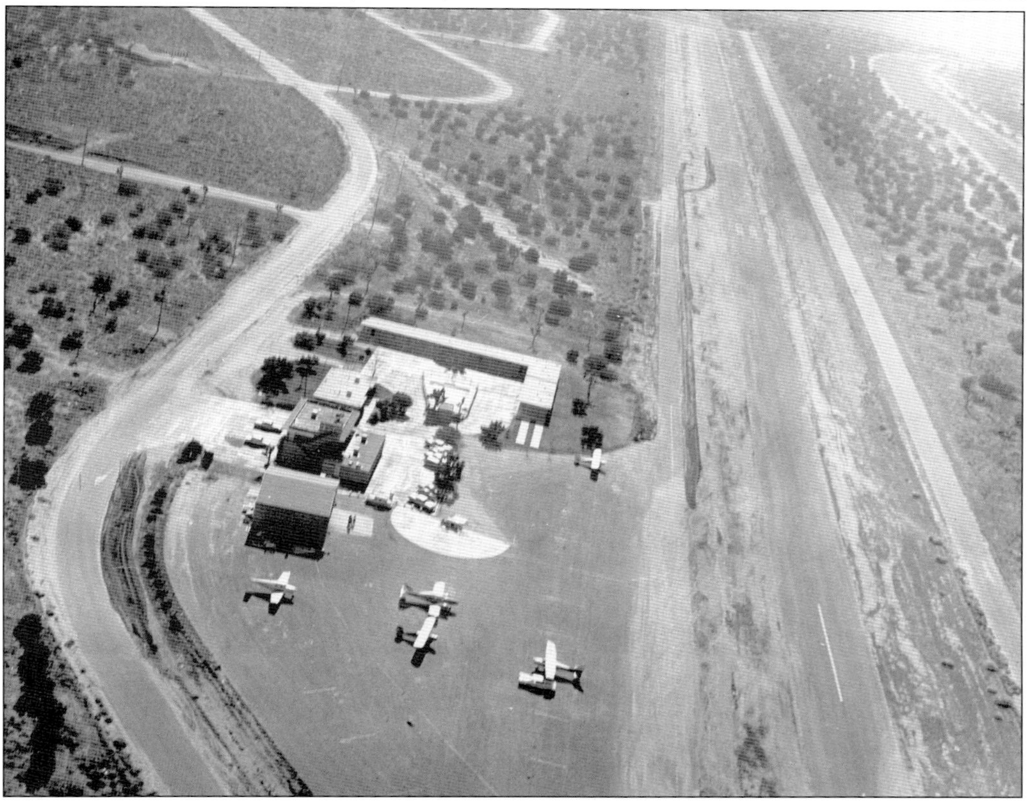

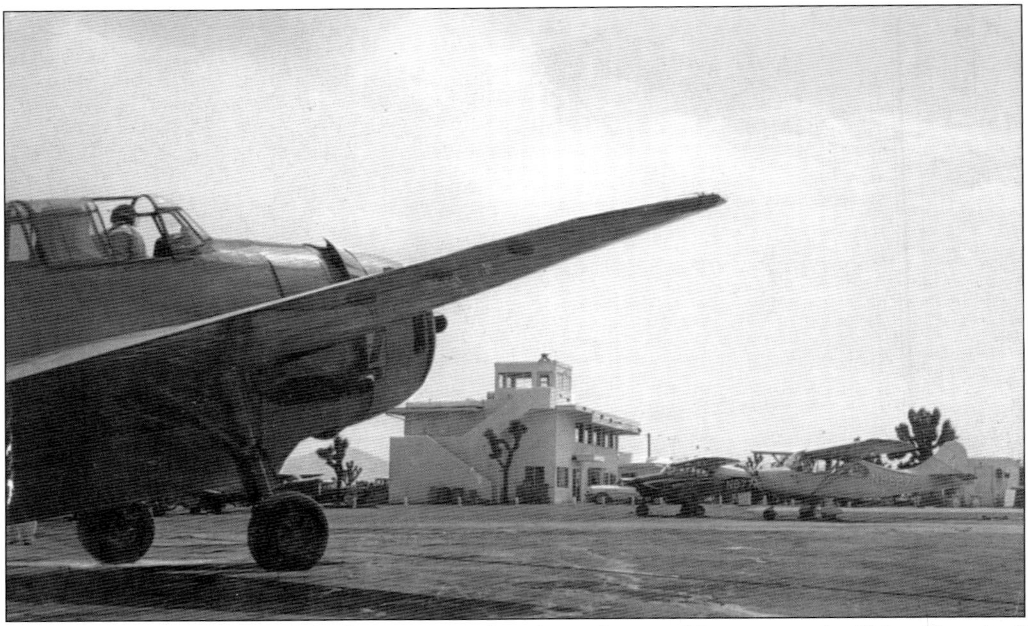

This is one of many postcards that were produced to advertise Hesperia as the "New Frontier." Pictured on the left is a military aircraft using the airpark in the early 1960s. M. Penn Phillips used the airfield to fly in prospective buyers and name entertainers. (Courtesy HOTM.)

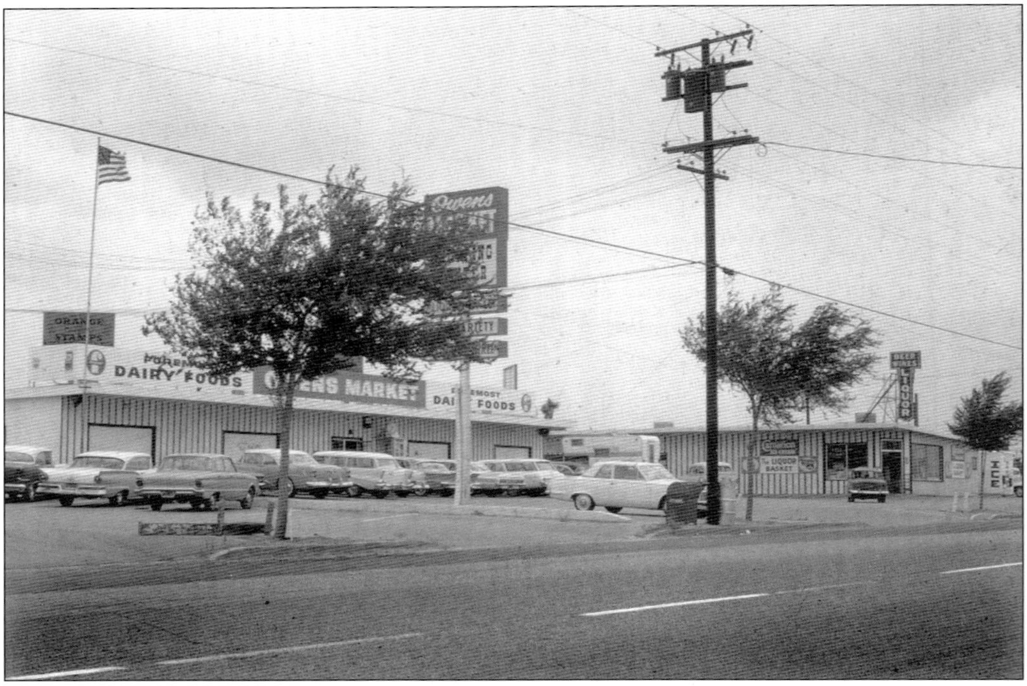

After nearly 45 years of Walters Store being the main venue, Hesperia received a new, larger grocery outlet when Owen's Market opened. Owen's quickly became a new stopping point for the San Bernardino County Bookmobile. Joan Brown made regular stops at the new Owen's Market, which removed the need for the small library in the Walters Store. (Courtesy HOTM.)

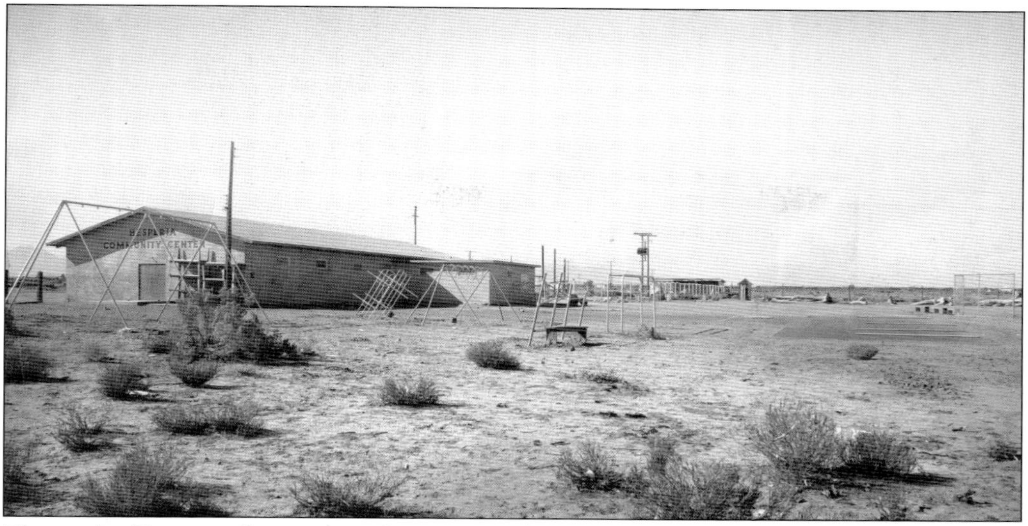

This is the Hesperia Community Center in its humble beginnings around 1955. In 1957, the Hesperia Recreation and Parks District was founded. It was a major benefit to the community to have a district that could respond to Hesperia's growth and needs. Within a few years, Lime Street Park has grown to include baseball diamonds and additional facilities. The aerial photograph of Lime Street Park below was taken by Myra McGinnis in the early 1960s. According to the original maps, the reservoir for the ditch was just north of Lime Street and just south of Muscatel Street. (Both, courtesy HRPD.)

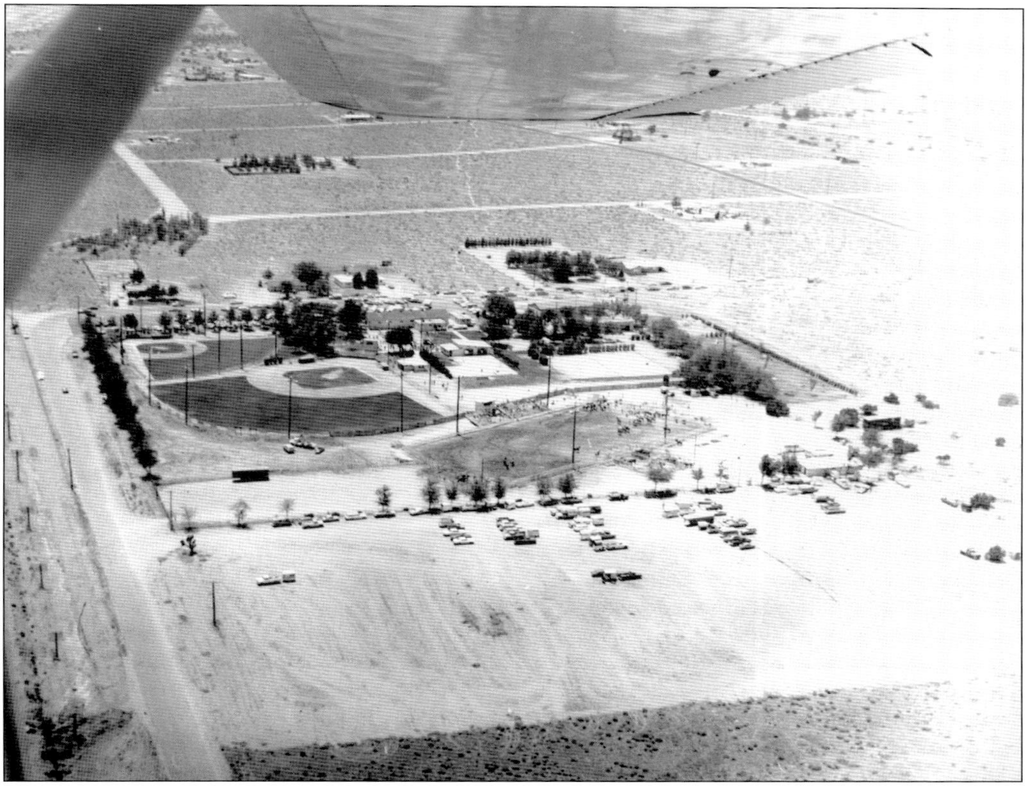

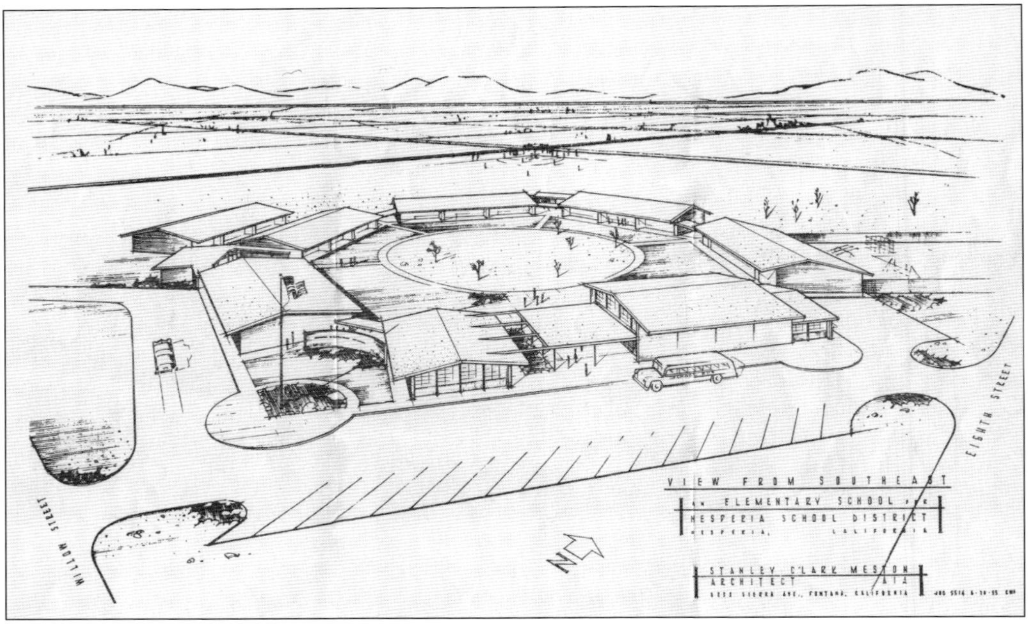

This architectural drawing is dated May 28, 1955. Hesperia Elementary was built in 1957 and is now known as Joshua Circle Elementary. The original schoolhouse bell, seen below, had sat behind its former building since it was removed from the tower in 1930. It was moved to the new elementary school, which was renamed Joshua Circle Elementary after a contest was held among the students for a new name. The winning entry came from student Carol Munger. (Both, courtesy HOTM.)

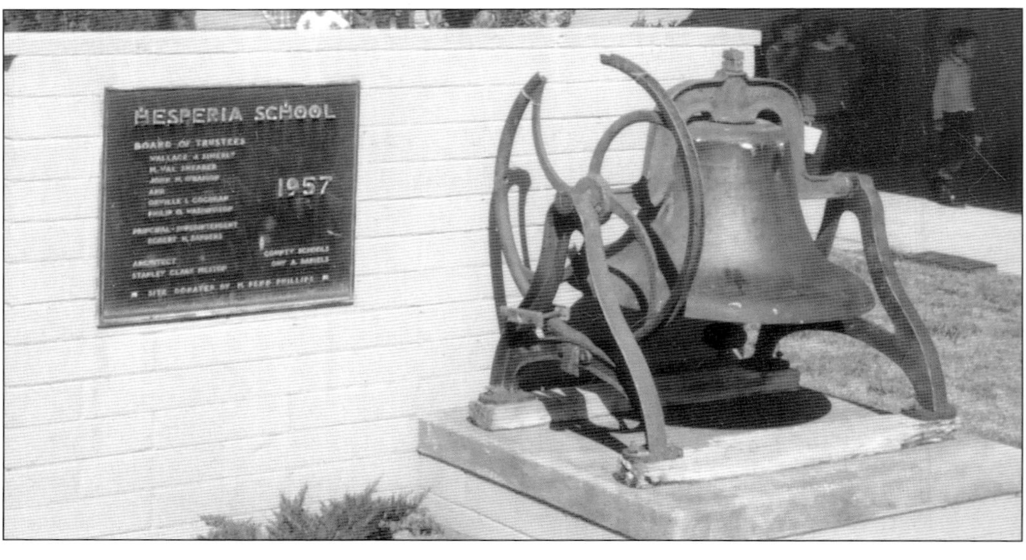

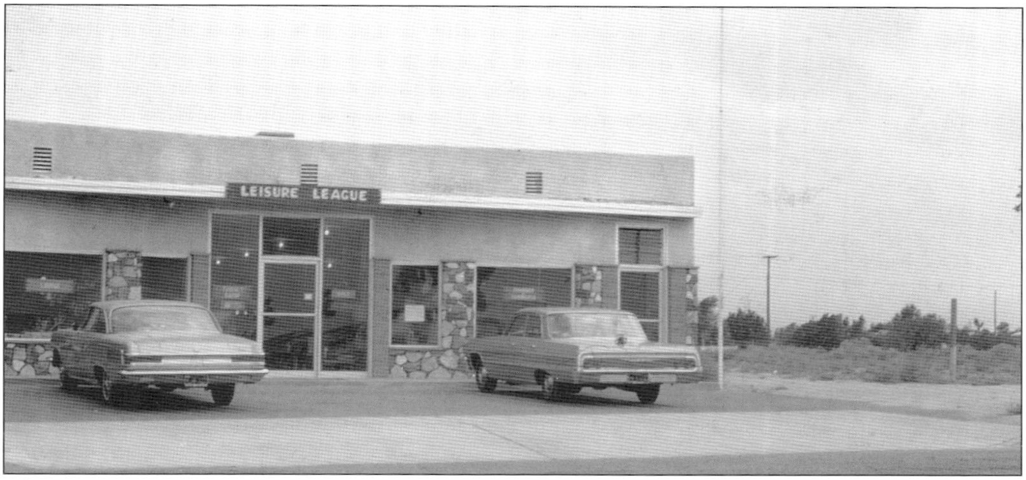

The Hesperia Leisure League came into being in 1961. Shortly after the league was formed, it was offered the opportunity to take over a thrift store. Within a year, the Hesperia Leisure League was erecting its own thrift store, complete with an office for the Hesperia Chamber of Commerce. When the Hesperia Senior Center was built on Third Avenue in 1971, the average age of those doing the construction was 72. This energetic group has been serving the community ever since. Considering all that they do and have done for Hesperia, their leisure time must truly be labors of love. (Both, courtesy HRPD.)

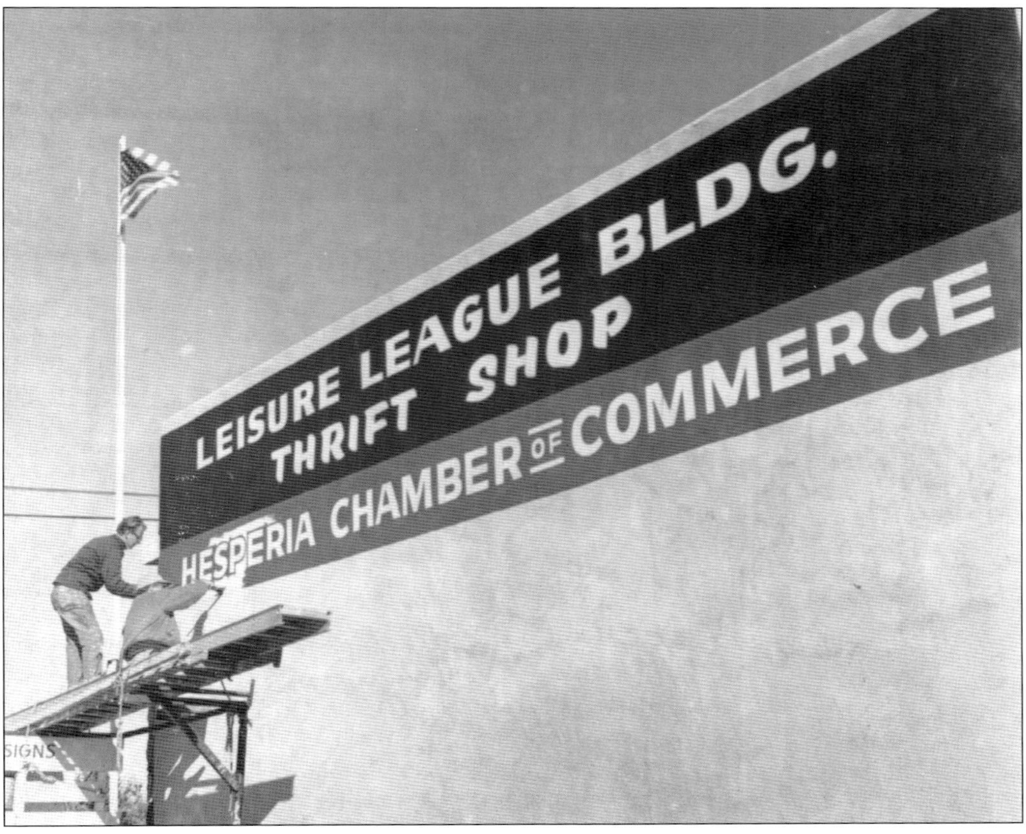

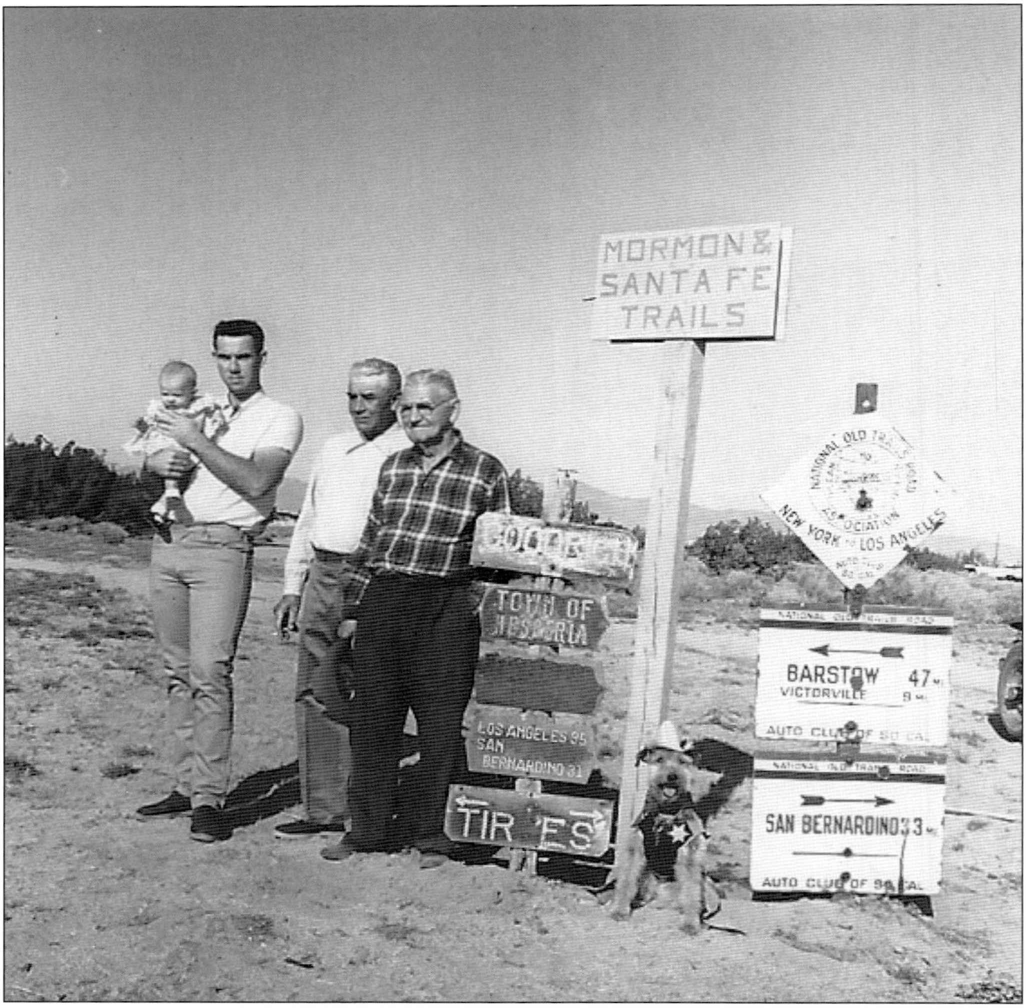

This four-generation photograph of the Hedrick family was taken in 1964. Seen here from left to right are Juli Ann Hedrick and her father, George Everett Hedrick, grandfather George Dewey Hedrick, and great-grandfather Columbus Frank Hedrick. The photograph was taken at Eleventh Street and National Old Trails Highway. The signs were from George Dewey's collection and date back to the 1920s. Columbus Frank Hedrick arrived in Hesperia in 1900 and married Charlotte Dewitt in 1902. Their Sycamore Dell Ranch lay along the Mojave River and Arrowhead Road, and the Hedrick home stood just south of today's Hesperia Lake. George Dewey grew up on the Sycamore Dell Ranch and rode his horse 10 miles each way to and from the Summit Valley School. George Dewey lived in Hesperia all his life; he worked as a surveyor and helped M. Penn Phillips to subdivide his 1950s land development. George Dewey was also a historian; these photographs of the Hedrick family come from George Dewey's collection. George Everett and his family lived in the Old Town area until around 1995. (Courtesy HF.)

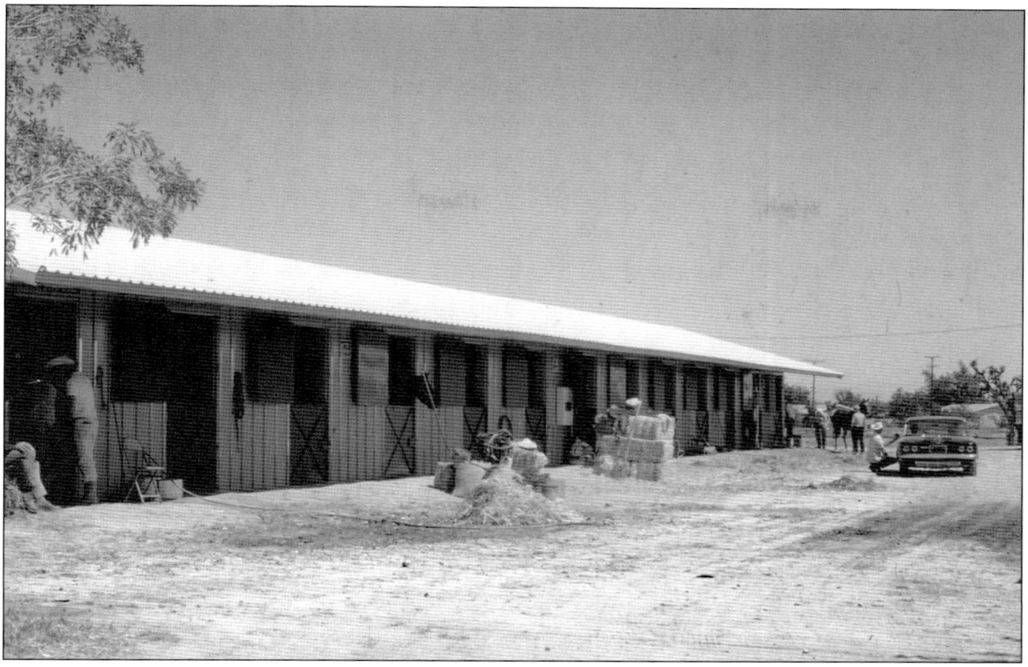

The Hesperia Dude Ranch opened in 1957 and was owned and run by Texas-born Mabel "Big Mama" and James R. "Big Daddy" Akridge, parents of Edward Henry "Eddy" Akridge, who earned four world championship titles in 1953, 1954, 1955, and 1961 and was inducted into the Professional Rodeo Hall of Fame in 1979. Many celebrities frequented the Akridges' ranch, including screen cowboys Roy Rogers and Clayton Moore. The facility also offered horse boarding, a restaurant, and a swimming pool. Ranch guests could take riding lessons or enjoy a trip on the Mojave River. In late 1958, fire consumed the ranch, and Eddy Akridge returned to the rodeo circuit. The ranch was not rebuilt. (Both, courtesy HOTM.)

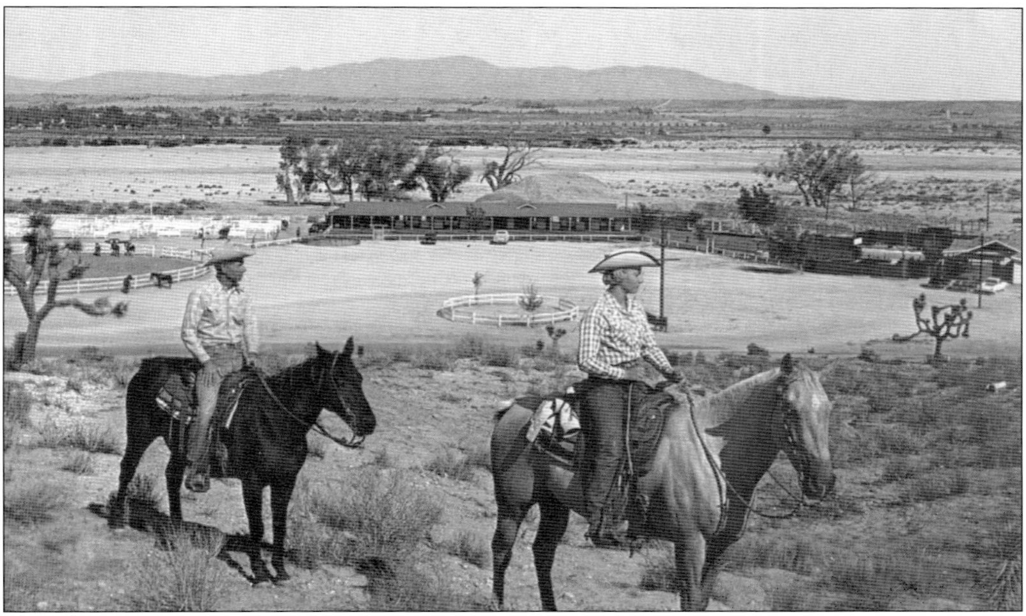

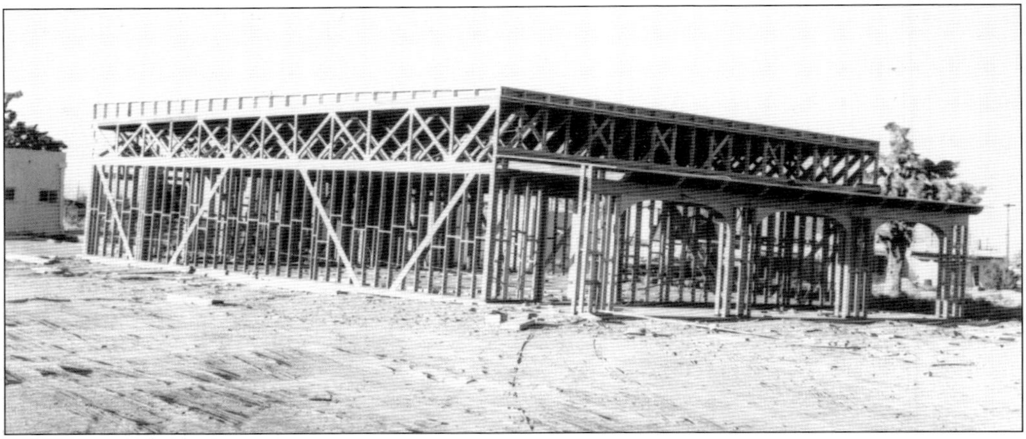

Hesperians have enjoyed library services of one type or another since the early 1950s, when a small collection of San Bernardino County Library books was housed in the Walters Store, overseen by Laura Walters. From 1956 through 1970, Joan Brown would regularly bring the San Bernardino County Library Bookmobile to Owen's Market. Marjorie Bakker also operated a one-room library in Juniper Elementary School. In 1970, Bakker became the assistant librarian in Hesperia's first county library branch at 16170 Walnut Street, built by Jim Pipla. In 1988, the library moved to a rented facility at 9565 Seventh Avenue, just north of Main Street. Bakker retired in 1991; Ann Marie Wentworth has managed the Hesperia library branch since 1972. The photograph below shows Hesperia's newest library building at 9560 Seventh Avenue, which opened in 2006 next to city hall. (Both, courtesy HOTM.)

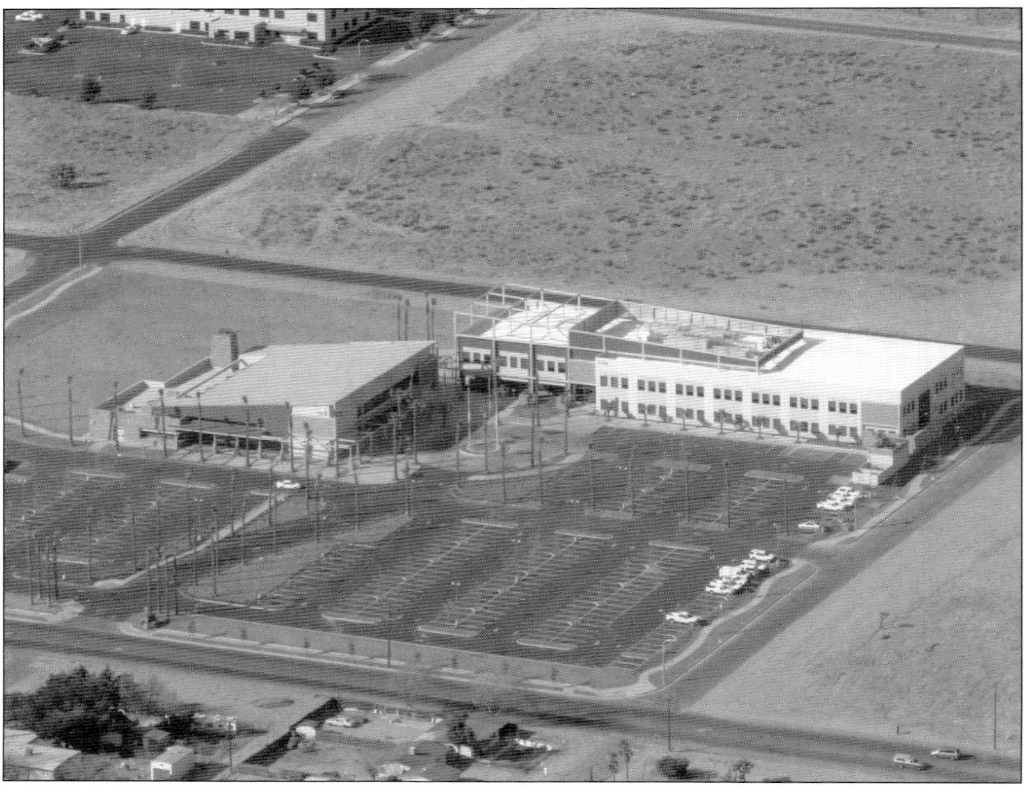

Hesperia has seen several newspaper reporters, but photographer Myra McGinnis was always in the middle of things looking for the best vantage point from which to get her picture. Myra was responsible for capturing on film a large part of Hesperia history from the 1950s, 1960s, and 1970s. (Courtesy HRPD.)

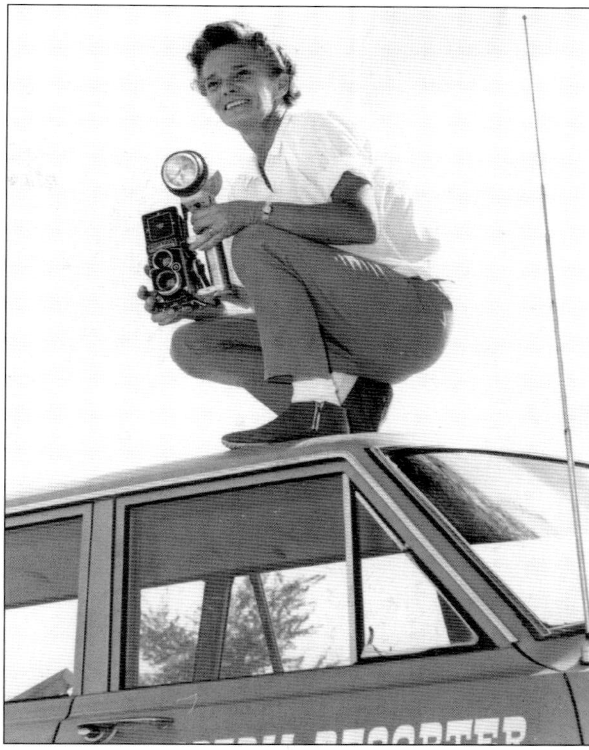

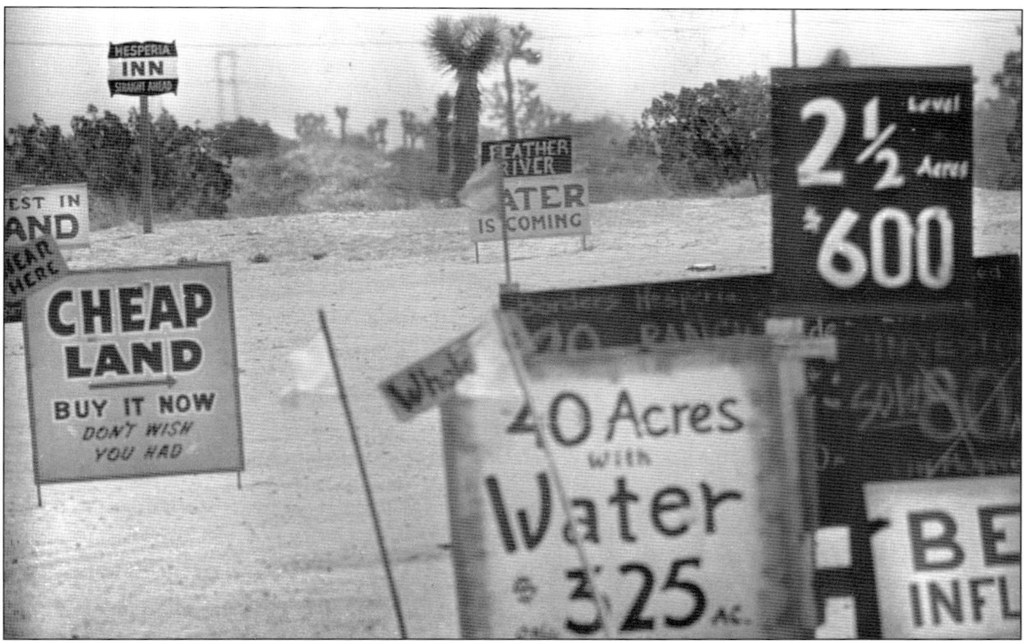

During the late 1950s and early 1960s, land was for sale everywhere in Hesperia. There were signs on nearly every corner: a sign pointing to the Hesperia Inn, an informational sign about the Feather River Project, and a real estate sign advertising 40-acre parcels for $325 an acre (and $600 for 2.5 acres). (Courtesy HOTM.)

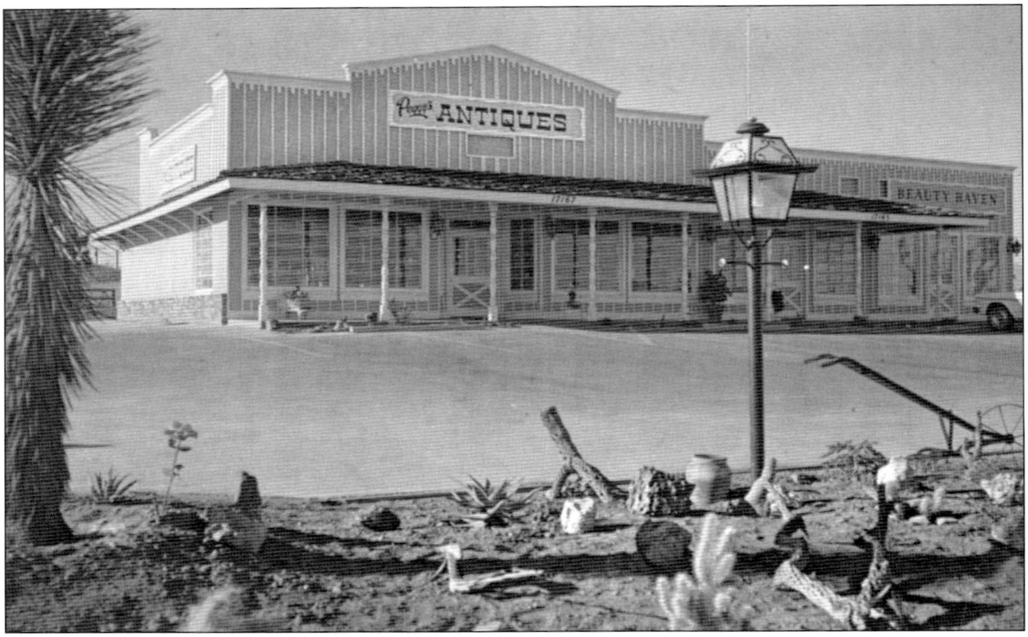

Peggy's Antiques was built in the early 1960s and painted pink. It remained pink and white for over 40 years. Although the small desert scene in this photograph is now gone, the lamp seen here in its midst is still in place in the sidewalk today. (Courtesy HOTM.)

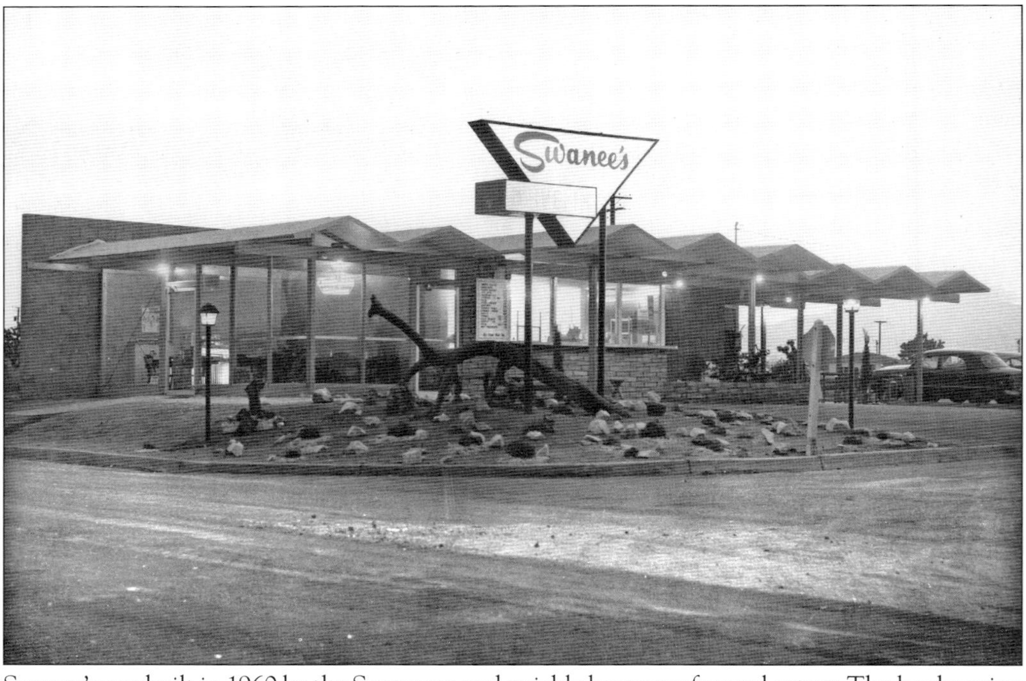

Swanee's was built in 1960 by the Swansons and quickly became a favored eatery. The landscaping out front was a desert scene that featured a fallen Joshua tree lovingly called Emma. The building still stands, but Emma was retired some years back. (Courtesy SF.)

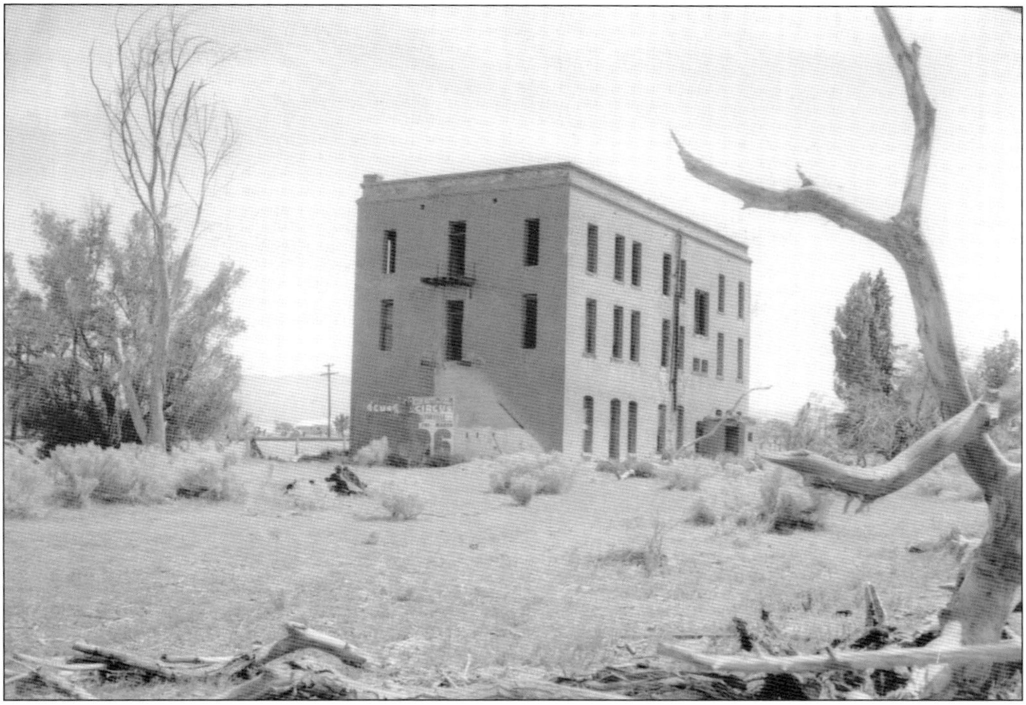

In the late 1950s, the Hesperia Hotel stood in solitude as a remembrance of its once-glorious past. In 1922, due to a landslide in the Cajon Pass, the train was delayed in Hesperia. After the Walterses moved a piano from the store over to the hotel, Hesperia residents were delighted by an impromptu recital by the world-renowned pianist Ignacy Paderewski. The hotel closed its doors in 1926, when traffic was rerouted with the opening of the new Route 66. (Above, courtesy HOTM; below, photograph by George Dewey Hedrick, courtesy HF.)

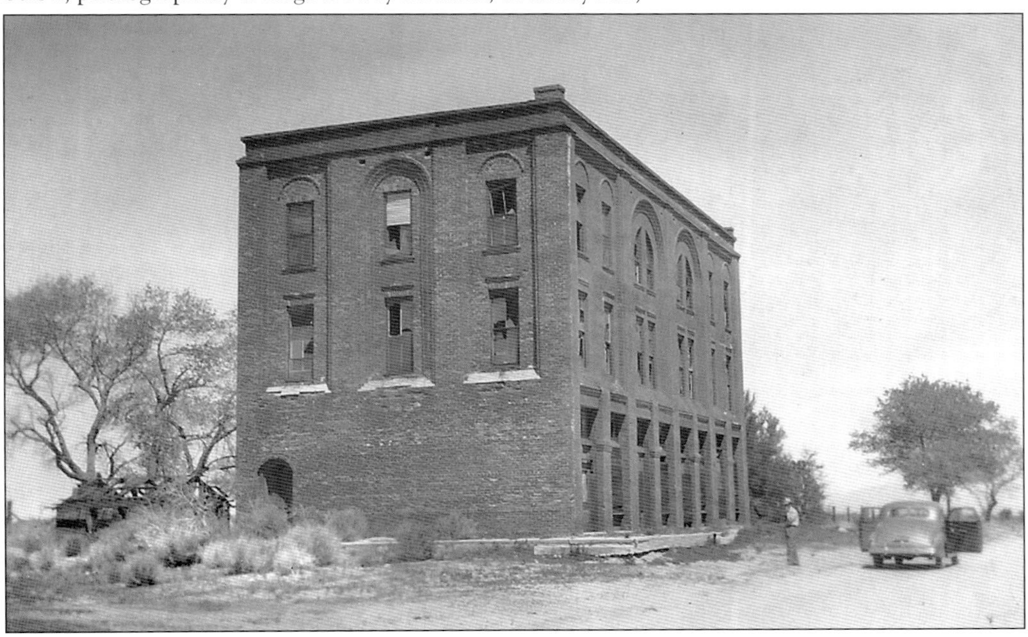

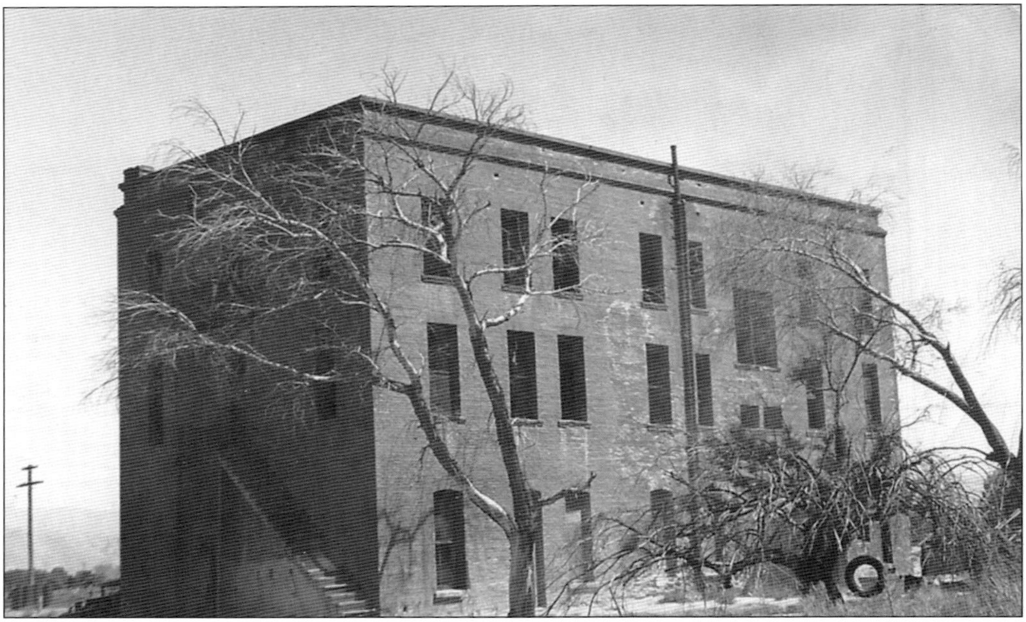

This photograph and the one at the bottom of the preceding page were taken by George Dewey Hedrick in the mid- to late 1950s. These are two of the most detailed photographs of the hotel known to exist. As a surveyor and local historian, Hedrick found himself in many places where he was able to photograph remnants of Hesperia's history. (Courtesy HF.)

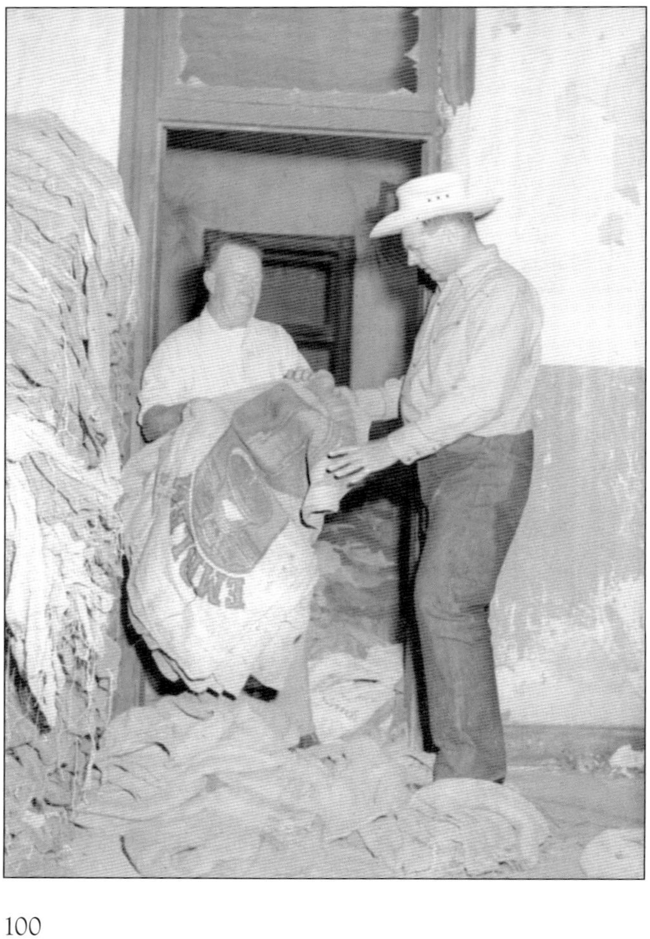

This 1950s photograph captures Roy Walters displaying some of the old potato sacks used by the Tatums during the 1940s and early 1950s. (Courtesy UCLA.)

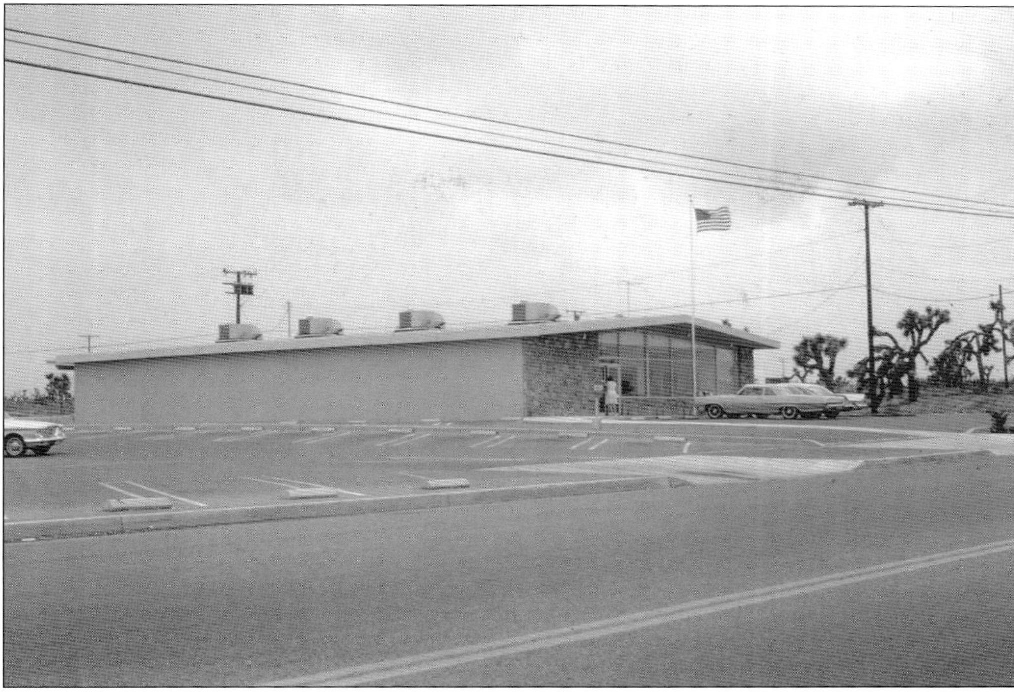

Hesperia's original post office was in Mrs. Ferrell's Stationery Store just south of the Hesperia Hotel. Shortly after the Walters Store opened in 1915, the post office was relocated there. As postmaster and postmistress, the Walterses sorted mail using the old pigeonhole slots. The Walters Store was the center of information during those times, serving as the town's post office, library, and general store. It continued to serve as the town's post office until the 1960s. (Both, courtesy HRPD.)

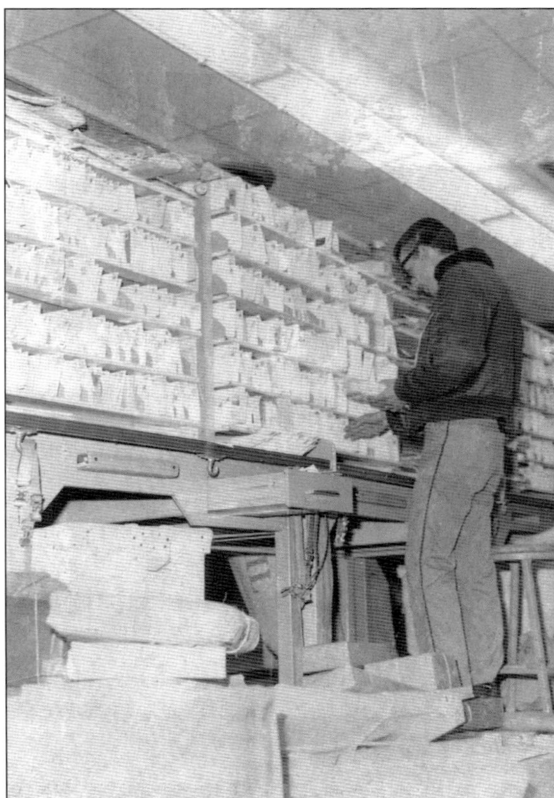

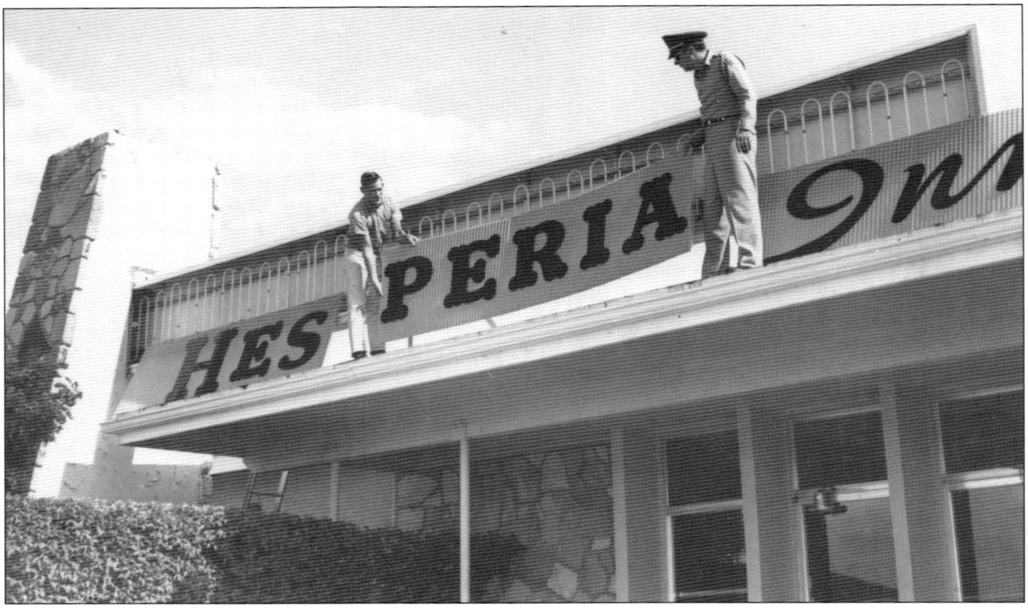

After the Hesperia Inn closed, the M. Penn Phillips Military Academy opened in its place. The academy provided a highly structured learning environment for young men. The photograph below shows a changing-of-command ceremony. (Above, courtesy HRPD; below, courtesy HOTM.)

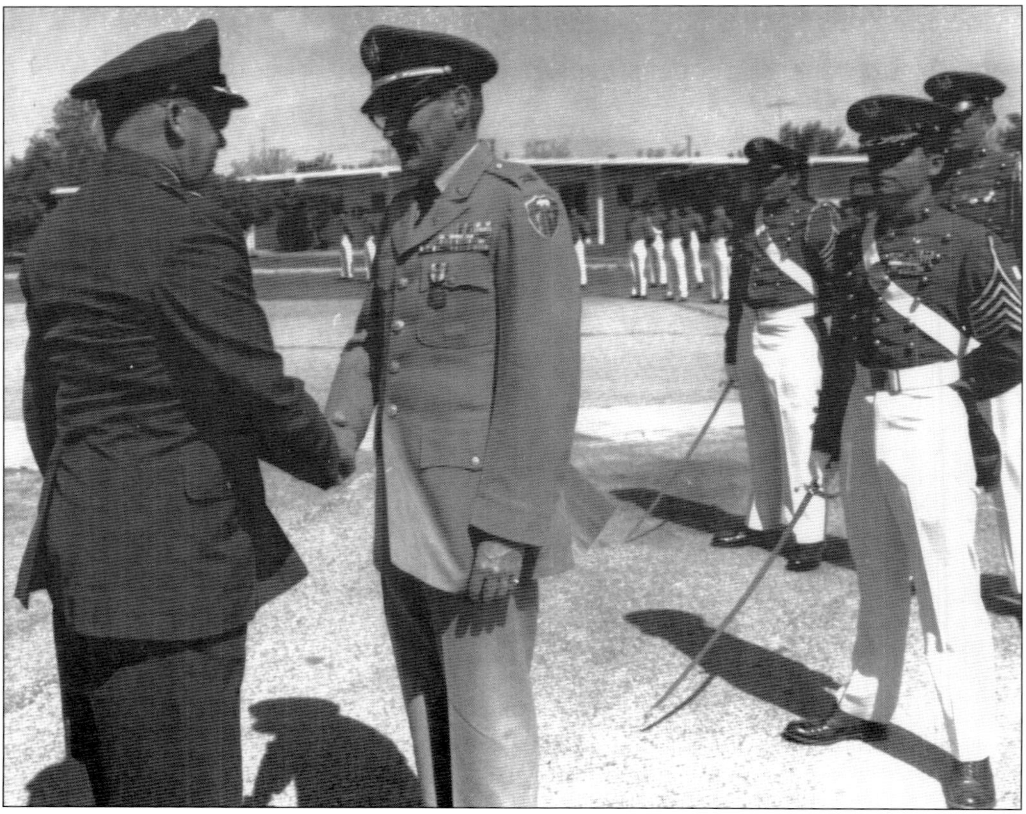

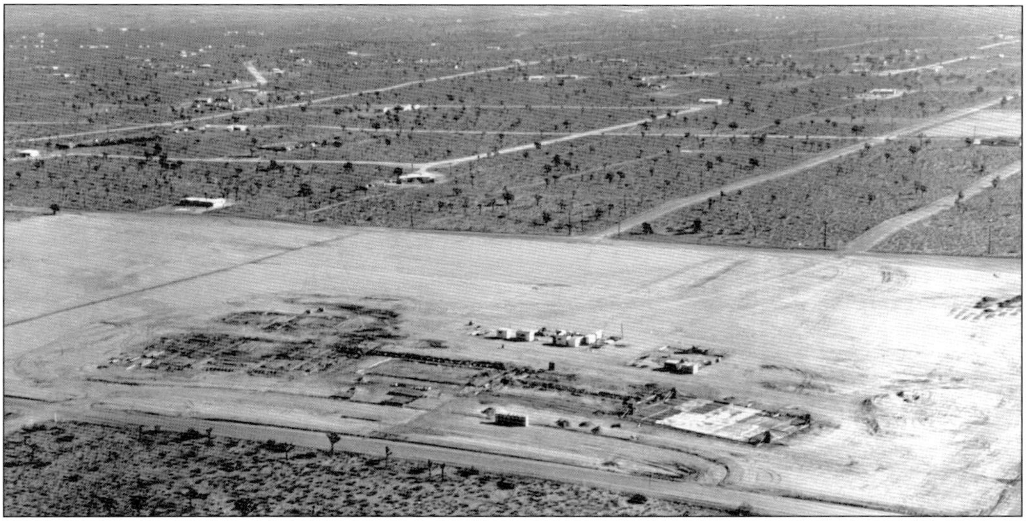

The Hesperia Unified School District was founded in 1986. There were seven public schools in the district, including Hesperia Junior High (shown here), built in 1962. By 2006, Hesperia was home to 21 schools serving more than 20,000 students. The schools in Hesperia, from the time of the first schoolhouse on Main Street, have built a reputation for quality education ranging from academics to vocational training. There are 27 schools in the district as of 2010. (Courtesy HRPD.)

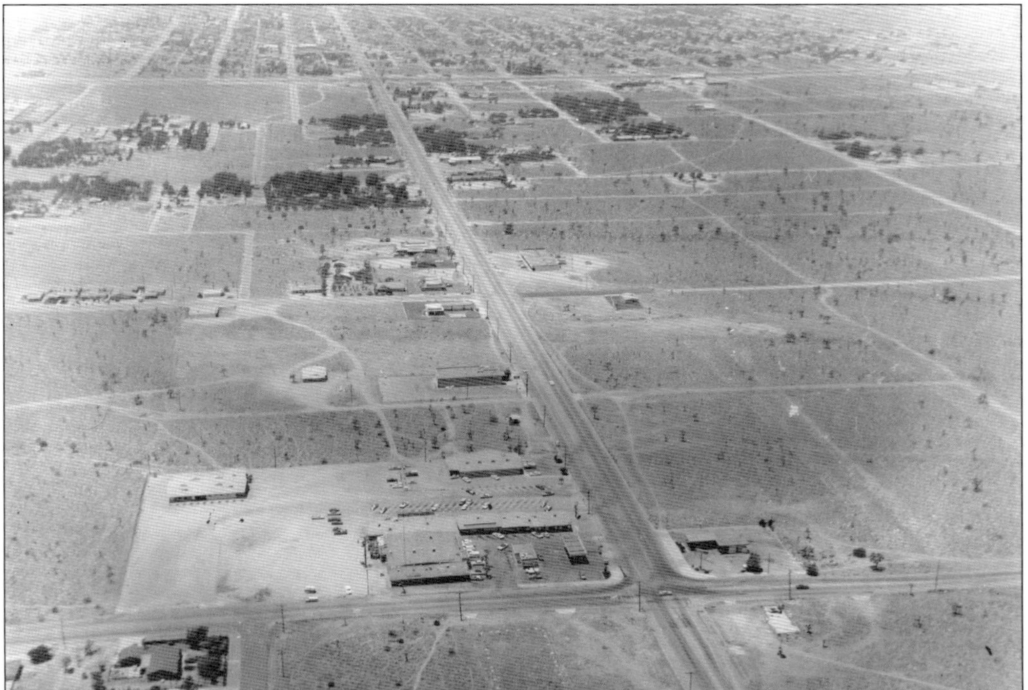

This photograph appears to have been taken around the time the Hesperia Hotel was being demolished in the early 1960s. In the background is a stand of trees around the Walters Store and possibly the remnants of the Hesperia Hotel. In the foreground is the new post office just west of I Avenue. (Courtesy HRPD.)

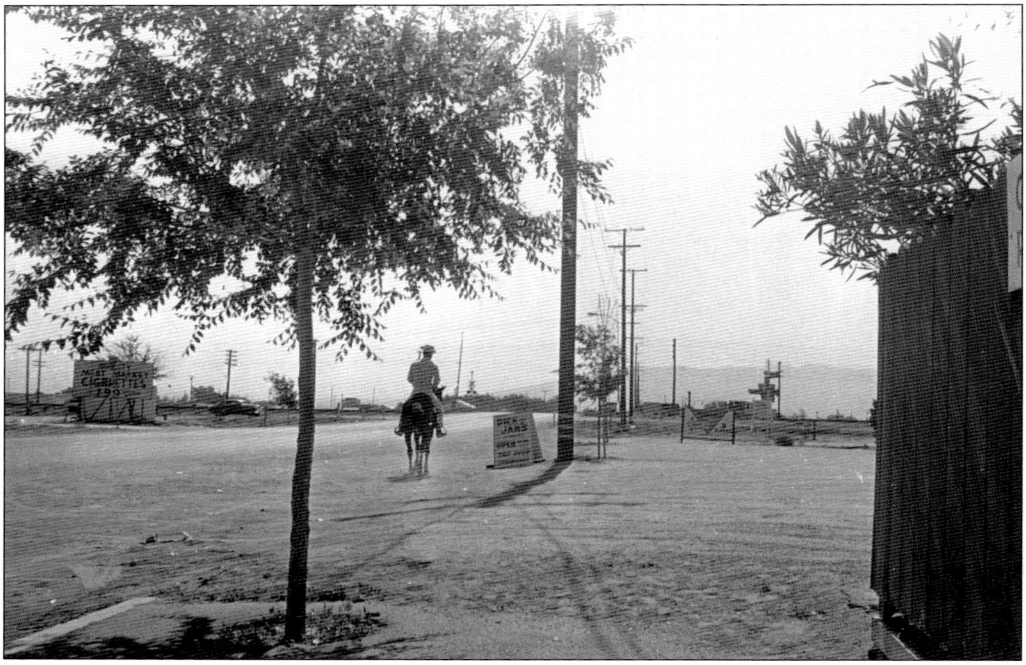

Taken at the intersection of Main Street, Hesperia Road, and Santa Fe Avenue, these two photographs from the late 1950s or early 1960s show traffic heading both east and west. The cars are heading west and waiting for the train to pass. On the right side of the photograph above, between the telephone poles and the fence, is the sign pointing south to the airpark. In later years, the sign was moved to the airpark. The photograph shows a lone horseman traveling east on Main Street. On the right side of the photograph below is the airpark sign on the opposite side of the street. The sign was switched from side to side in the years prior to its final destination at the airpark. (Both, courtesy HOTM.)

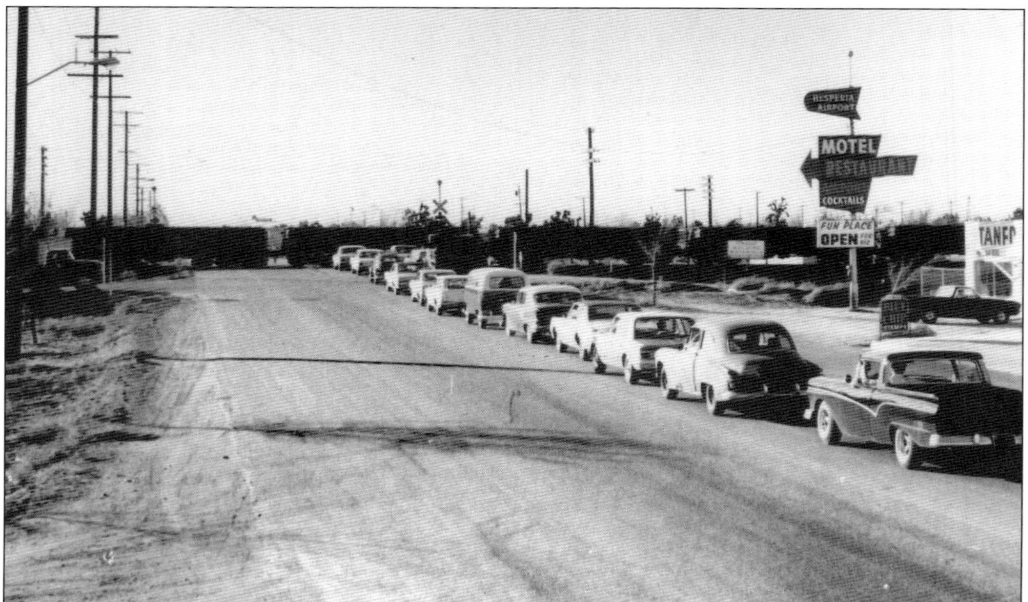

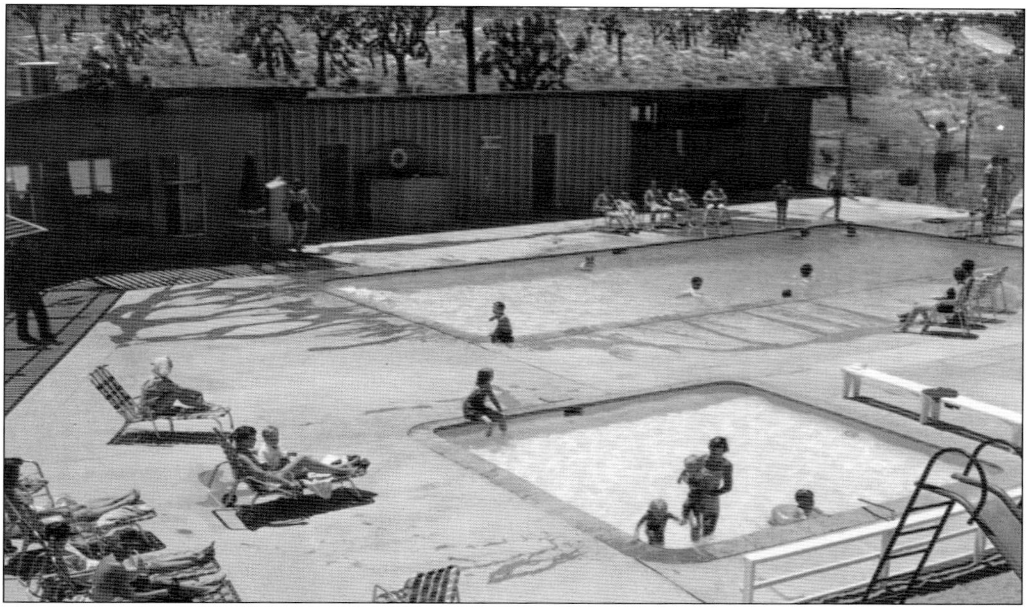

Hesperia Recreation Club provided many activities for the general public and families with pools and a clubhouse. The recreation club later became Timber Lane Park, and the pools were removed. The venue, run by the Hesperia Recreation and Park District, still provides a quality park for the local residents. (Courtesy HOTM.)

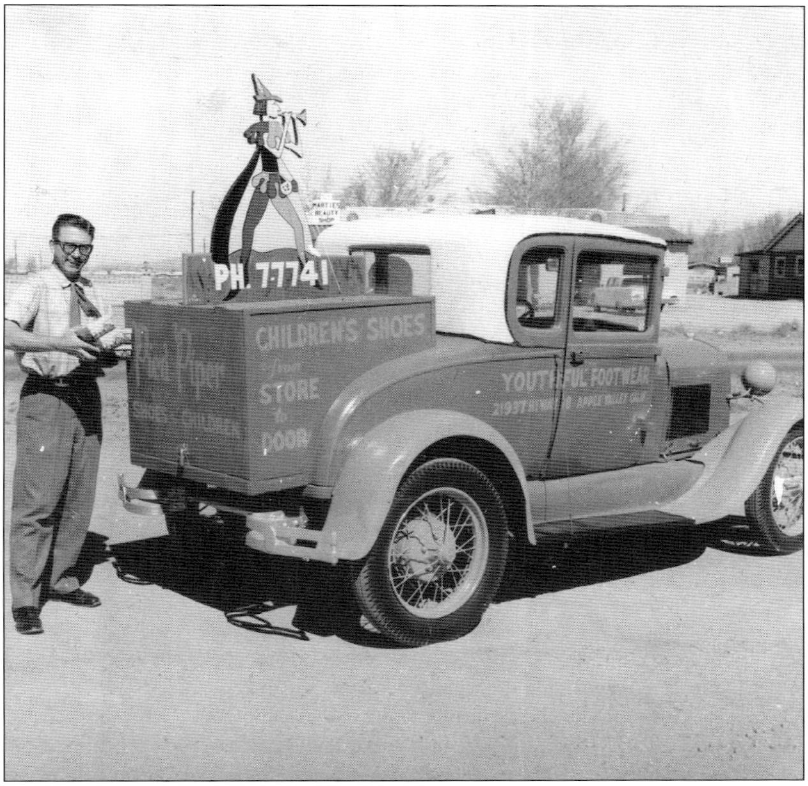

Back in the 1950s and 1960s, it was not unusual to have home delivery of milk and eggs, but here is something more unique. This man traveled the High Desert going from home to home selling shoes. With just one call, the store drove up to one's door. (Courtesy HRPD.)

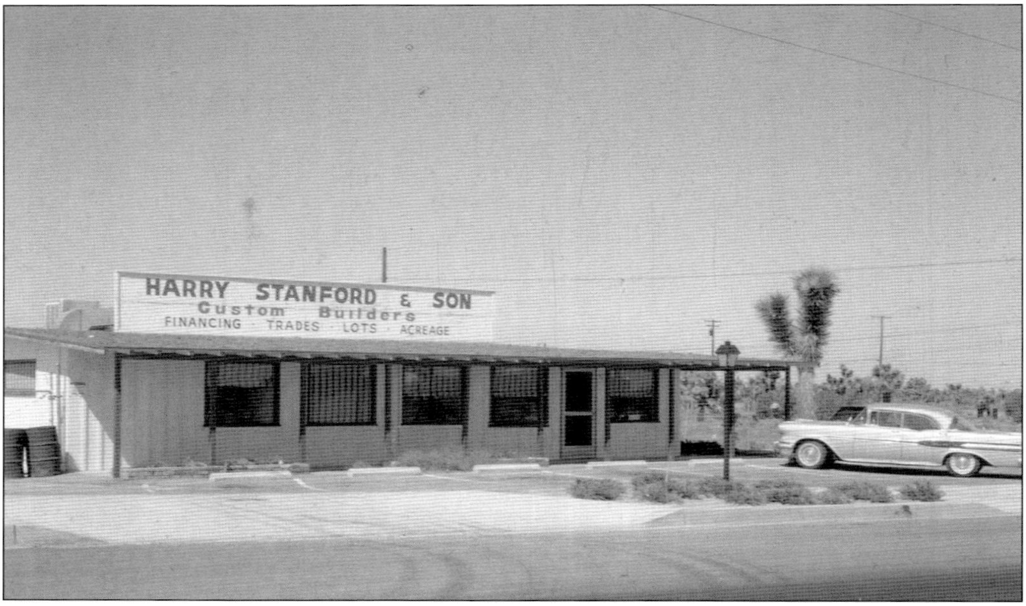

Stanford Construction was heavily involved in the building of the several areas during the 1950s development by M. Penn Phillips. Stanford and Son built the structures at the new airpark as well as the Hesperia Inn and the Western Arcade/Jack Dempsey Museum building. Harry Stanford built many of the homes of that era. (Courtesy HRPD.)

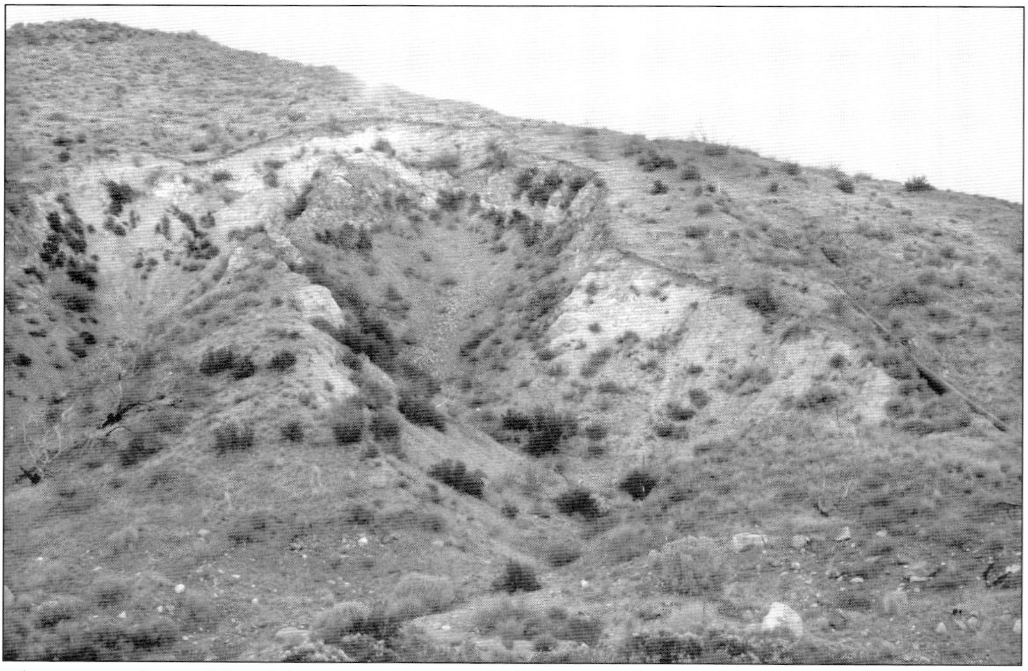

The area in the middle of this picture looks as though someone had started to hydraulically mine it, but the scarring actually occurred after the ditch plugged up at the 14-inch and 30-inch pipes. Just to the right of the large gouge in the hillside lie the two pipes that delivered the water from Deep Creek to the reservoir at Lime Street and Hesperia Road. (Courtesy HOTM.)

Eight

Vanishing History, Time Travelers, and Visionaries

In any given moment, people are usually involved in one of three thought processes. Some are living in the moment (the Actives); some research, ponder, or document times gone by (the Historians); and a third group dreams of how the future will be or could be (the Visionaries). People can move from group to group even within a single day, but their response to these three thought processes shapes their lives in the present, which shapes their lives in the future—all of which will become their history. Throughout Hesperia's history, there have been people and events that illustrate these thought processes. Within this chapter is a reflection of the past and a look at present-day efforts to archive history for future generations.

Change is inevitable, but remembering the past is worth the effort, for it can help shape the future.

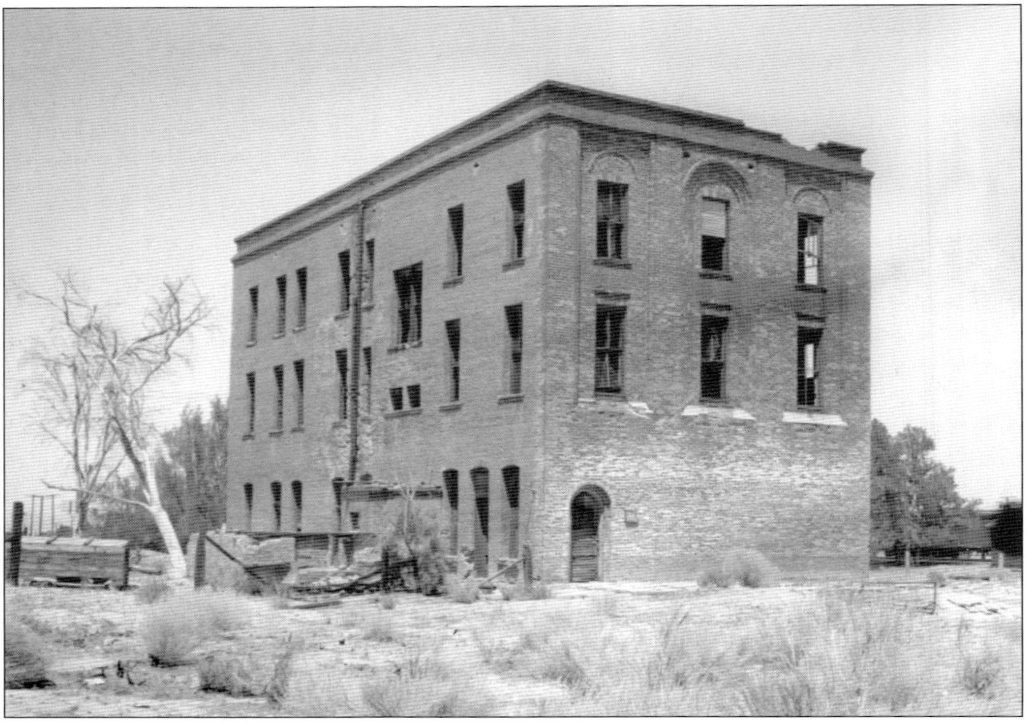

The Hesperia Hotel operated from about 1887 to 1926 and stood second to none in the area. The Tatums used the abandoned building for a storage facility and commissary in the 1940s, but afterwards, preservationists considered restoring the old hotel as a museum. It was found to be structurally unsound, however, and the plans were abandoned. (Courtesy UCLA.)

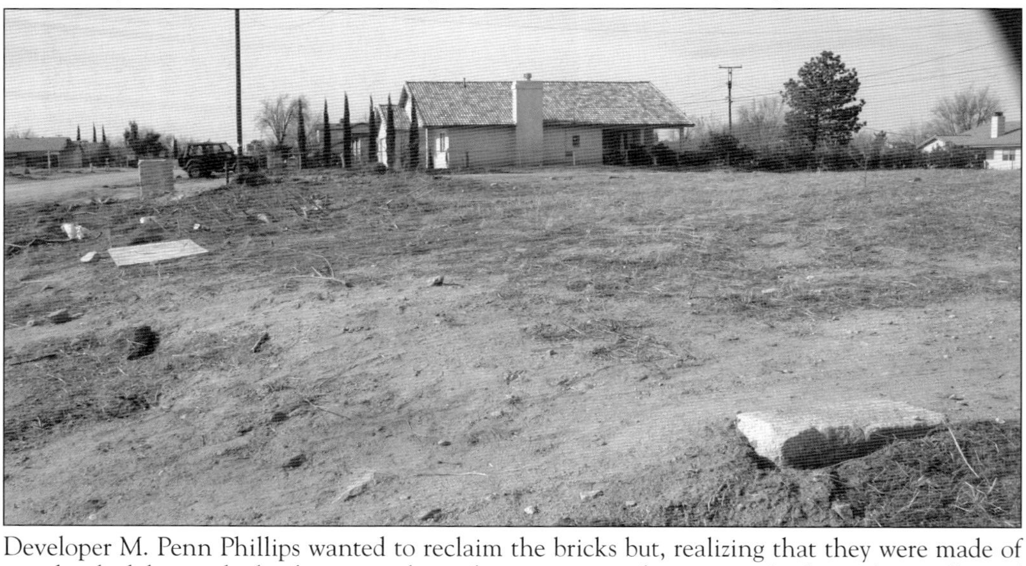

Developer M. Penn Phillips wanted to reclaim the bricks but, realizing that they were made of sun-dried adobe, made the decision to burn the interior wood structure. As the timbers collapsed so did the walls of the once magnificent hotel. The remnants were bulldozed in to the basement. All that remains of the hotel is a pile of rubble and the monument telling of the glory that was the Hesperia Hotel. (Courtesy HOTM.)

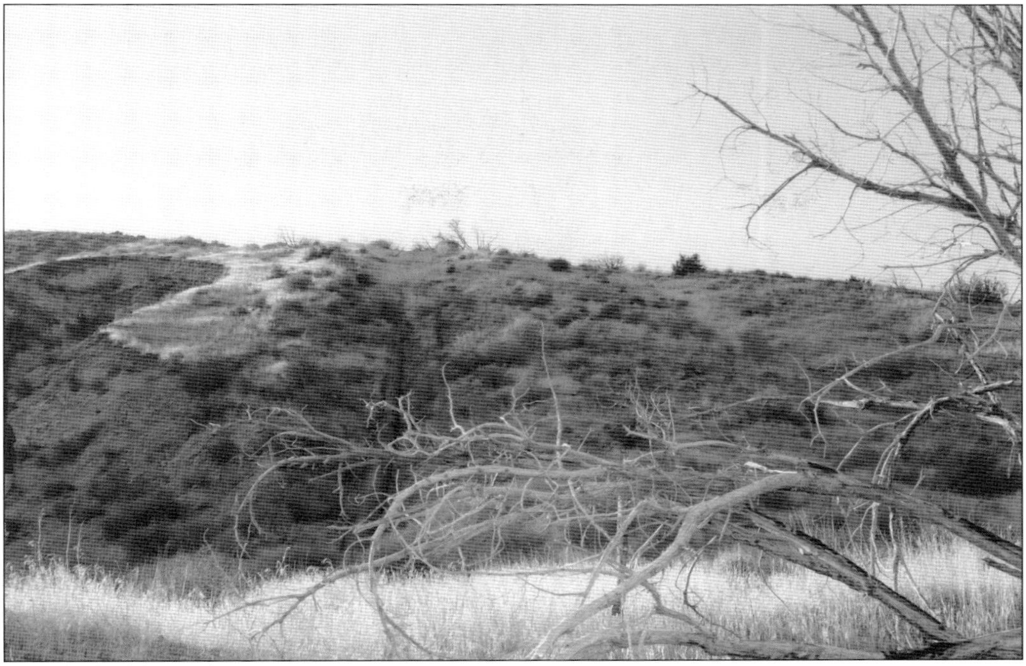

The ditch delivered water to Hesperia from the late 1880s up into the early 1950s. This water source fed not only Hesperia but also many others, as farmers used it to irrigate their crops, much of which was sold and shipped off to many areas. There is no marker to remind future generations of this water system's location, but many people have walked its path. (Courtesy HOTM.)

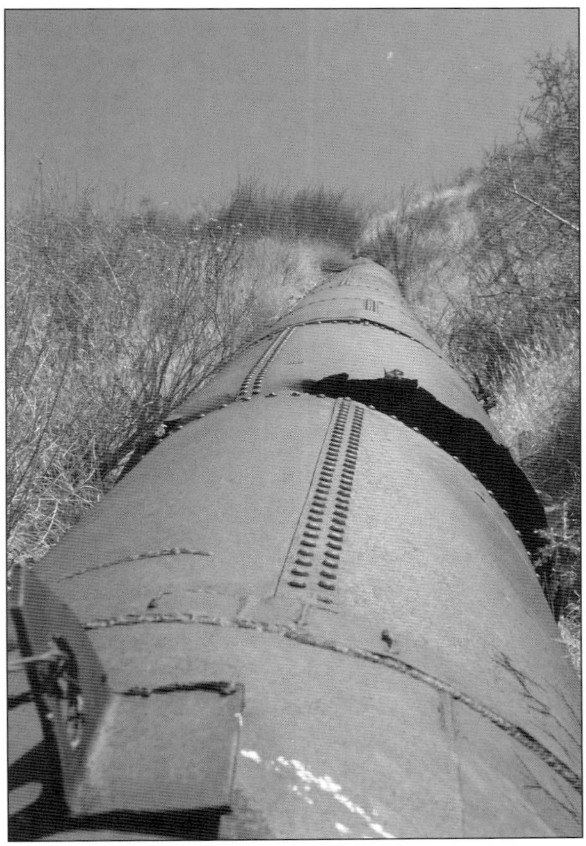

This 30-inch pipe was installed in 1911 with Columbus Frank Hedrick as foreman. It was assembled with rivets and cork to seal the joints. As time went by, the pipe rusted, and the normal way to repair a hole was to insert a redwood spike. The redwood would swell and seal the leak. This method is still used for temporary fixes until more permanent repairs can be made. (Courtesy HOTM.)

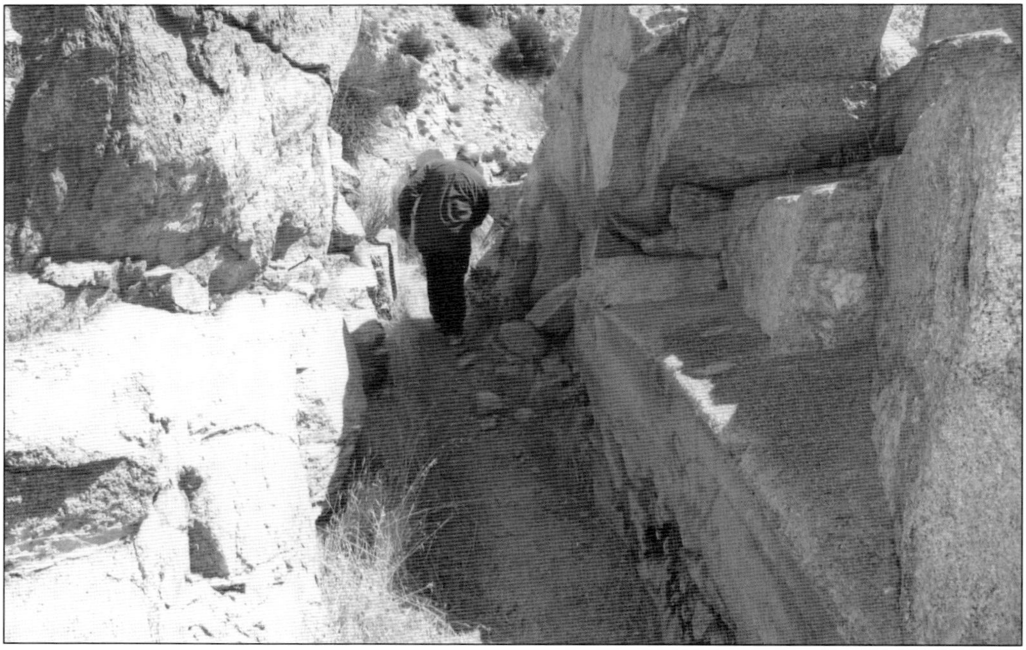

People can still hike the ditch. Many hikers from outside the area know they are hiking a portion of the Pacific Crest Trail towards the Deep Creek Hot Springs. Little do they realize, however, that each step they take is another step back in history. (Courtesy HOTM.)

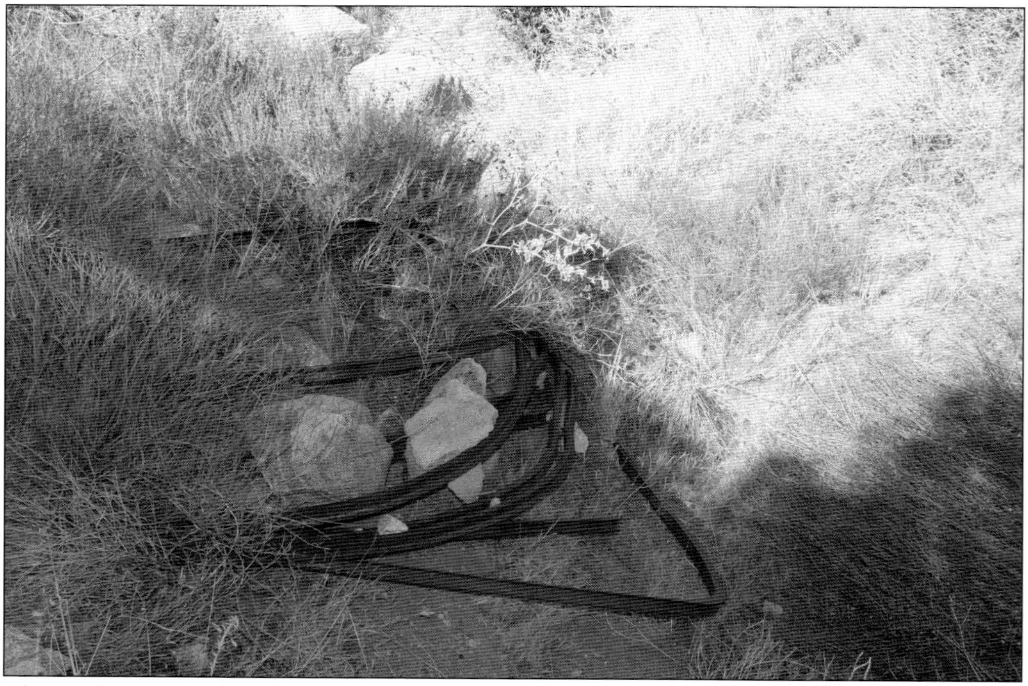

This is all that remains of the trolley that crossed Deep Creek and gave additional access to the ditch. This tangled mess is part of the rail the trolley car traveled on. It was pulled by hand above the creek. (Courtesy HOTM.)

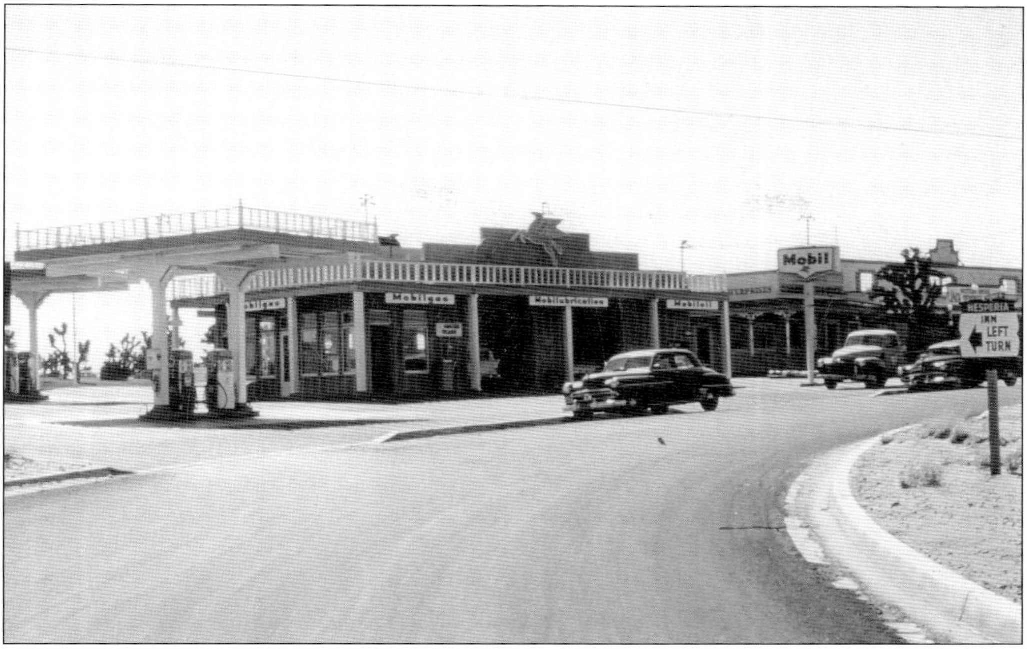

This *c.* 1989 photograph shows the Mobil gas station that stood in the middle of a soon-to-be-residential area, and it was also next to the Hesperia Inn and the Western Arcade building—home to the Jack Dempsey Museum. The gas station is now gone, as is the museum. The Western Arcade building served as home to Iron Horse Hobbies, Shelly's Place Restaurant, the Hesperia Chamber of Commerce, art studios, antiquaries, and many other businesses until the second half of the 1990s. (Both, courtesy HOTM.)

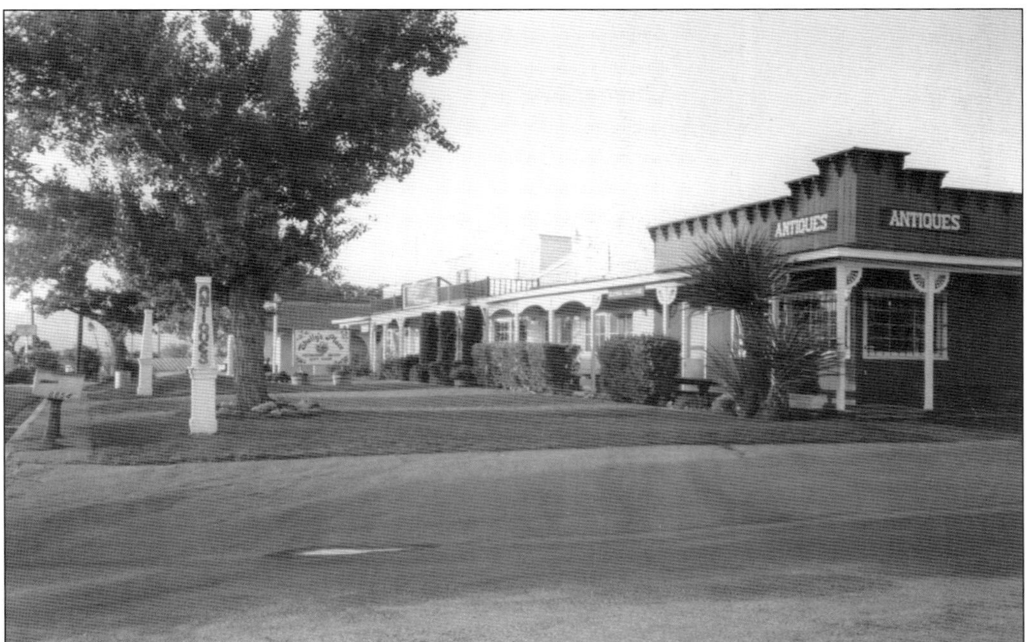

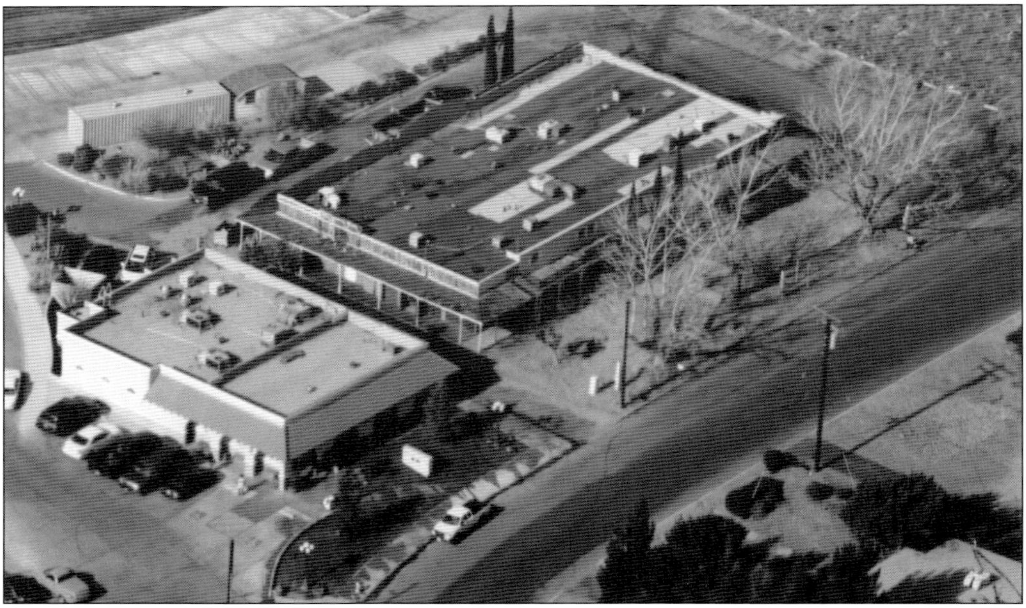

Here are two photographs of Old Town today. This business district sits hidden in the middle of the residential area built in the late 1950s. The large building on the right is the original Western Arcade building, which has sat dormant since about 1996. Since this photograph was taken, the building has had a facelift, but it remains vacant. The Mobil gas station once stood in the lower left area shown here. In its place stands a modern building that is home to Mary Ann's Restaurant, formerly Shelly's Place Old Town Restaurant. The aerial photograph below shows the Foremost Health Care Facility. In the late 1990s, Old Town was purchased, and the old Hesperia Inn was replaced with this new facility, which was built on a footprint similar to the Hesperia Inn. (Both, courtesy HOTM.)

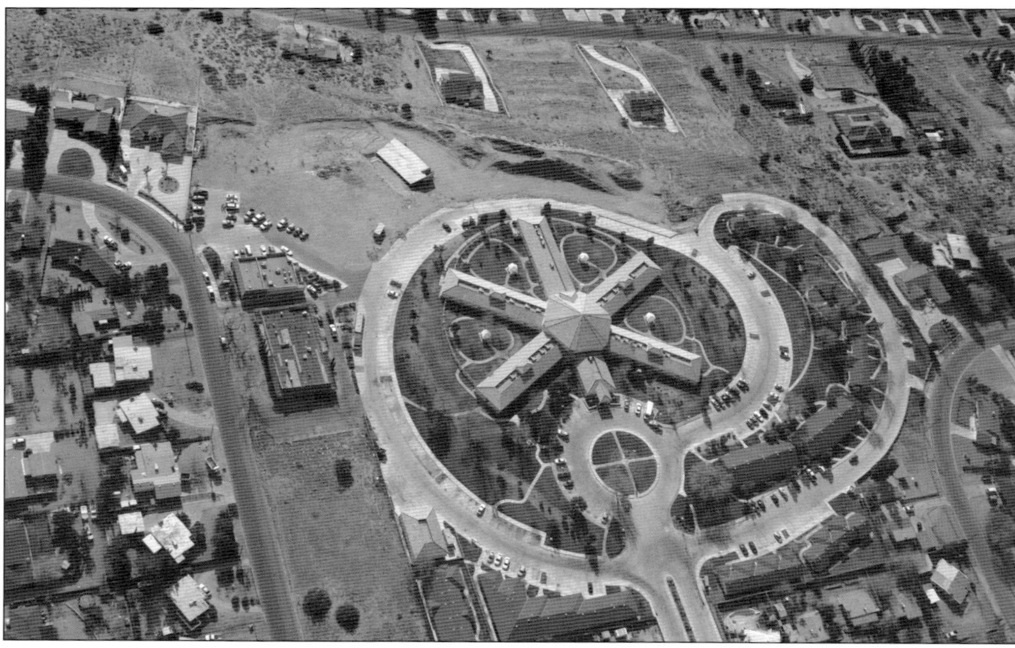

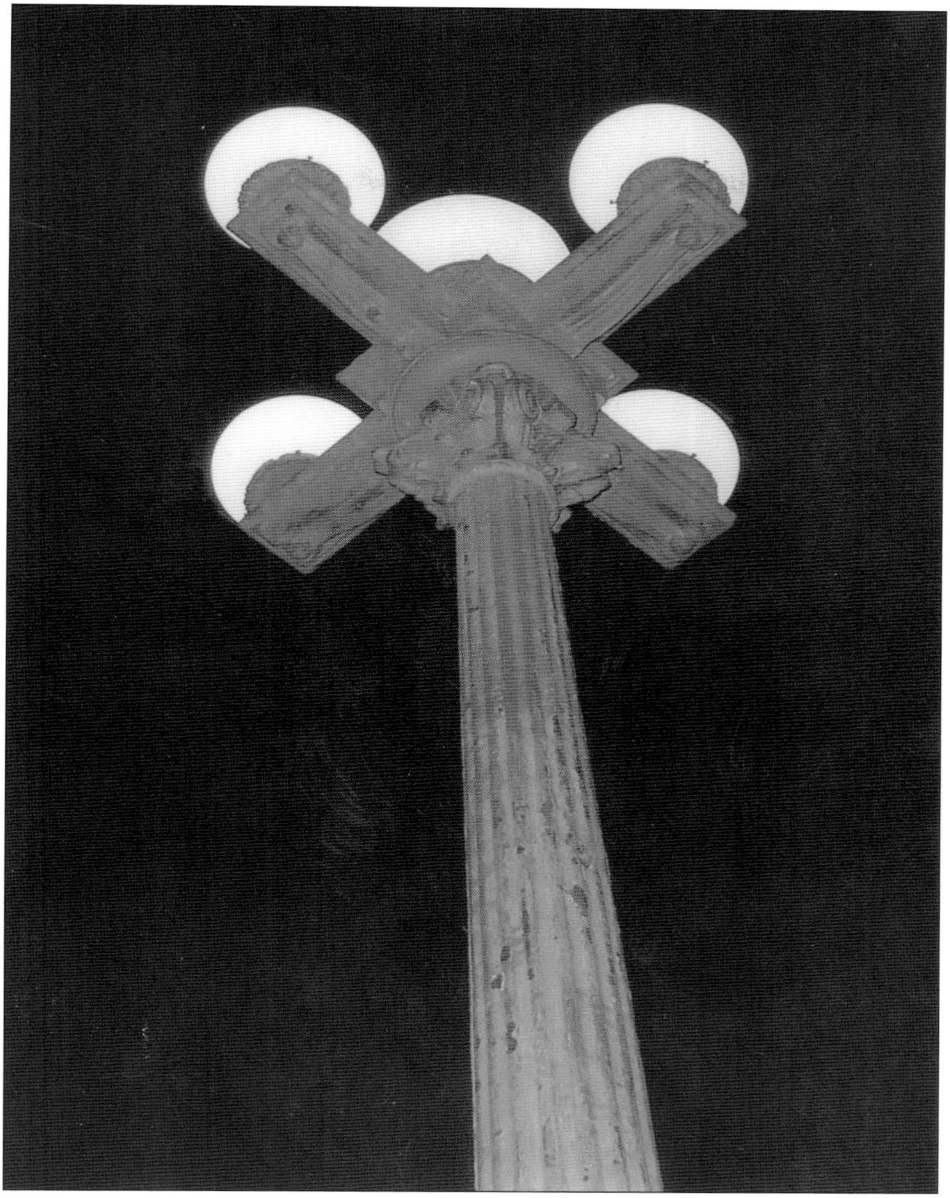

Here is one of the first 10 streetlights in Hesperia. They sit on Sultana Street in the Old Town Area. These lights were installed in the 1950s, when Old Town was built. The history of the light standards goes back even further than this. They were purchased used from the City of Los Angeles, where they had been used for many years. When the lights were installed, they were wired into the private homes that they sat in front of. Due to vandalism, the lights stopped being repaired in the early 1990s. When city leaders began to consider restoring the old lights, no one knew who actually owned them. Only after investigating the city records was it discovered that the streetlights were actually wired to each house—meaning that the private owners of these houses had been footing the bill for the electricity used by these streetlights for around 40 years. To this day, only two of the 10 light standards remain aglow, reminders of the days when Old Town Hesperia was the center of the "New Frontier." (Courtesy HOTM.)

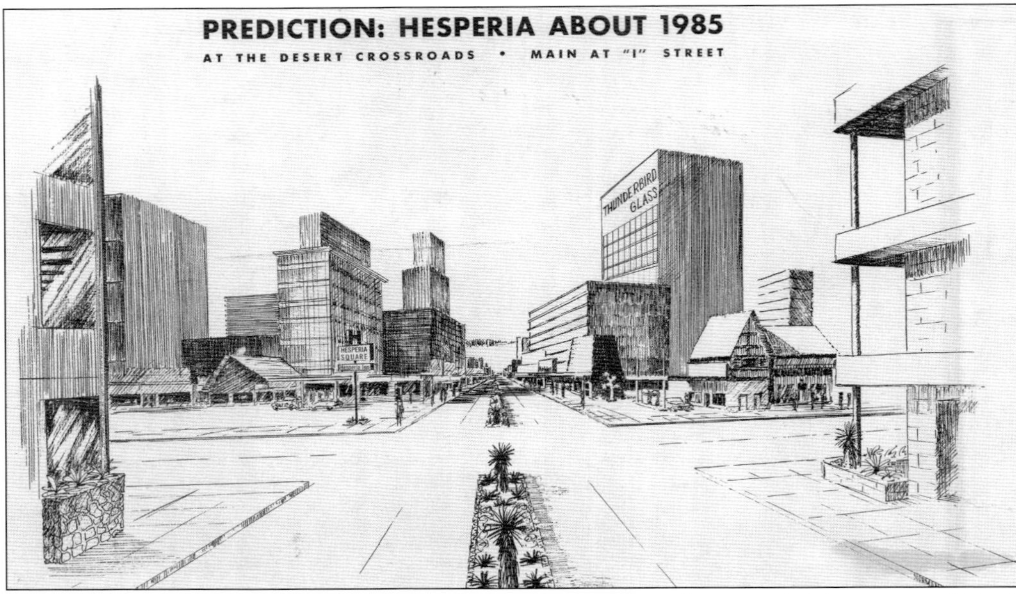

Norman Rangere's drawing is a prediction of how Hesperia at Main and I Avenue would look by 1985. The tall building on the right side has Thunderbird Glass on the marquee. This is the approximate location of Thunderbird Glass today. The oldest operating business in Hesperia, Thunderbird Glass is still owned and run by Jack and Clara Unger's daughter and son-in-law, Marsha and Dennis Nicklaus. The Unger family also owned Iron Horse Hobbies. (Courtesy HOTM.)

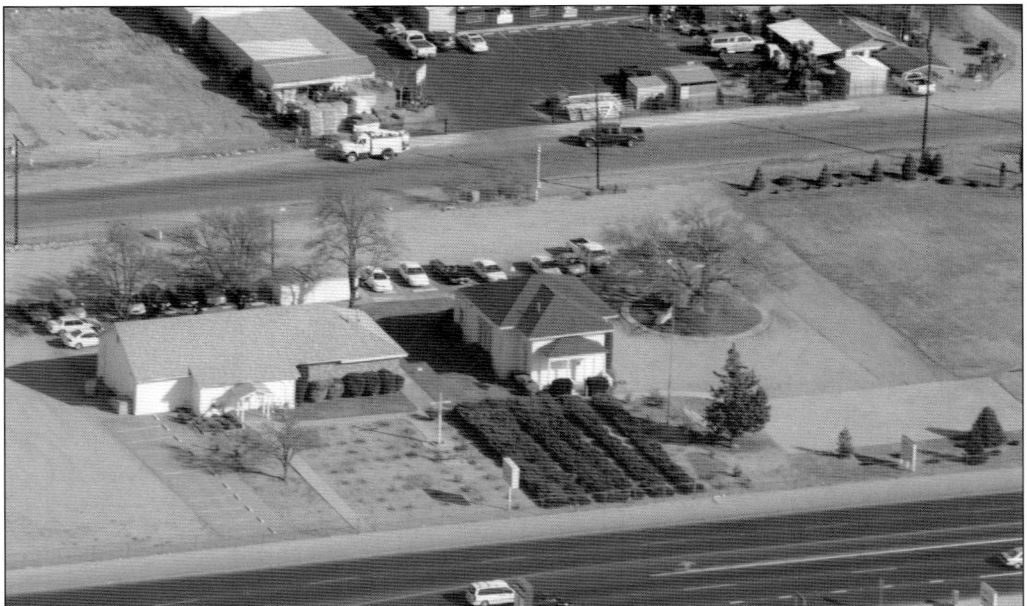

This aerial photograph was taken by the author in 2007. The original schoolhouse, built in the 1880s, still stands, as does the second schoolhouse, built in 1926—though the second schoolhouse had to be rebuilt and enlarged after a fire. Though the old buildings are no longer home to public schools, they are owned by a local church, and good lessons and values are still taught under their roofs. (Courtesy HOTM.)

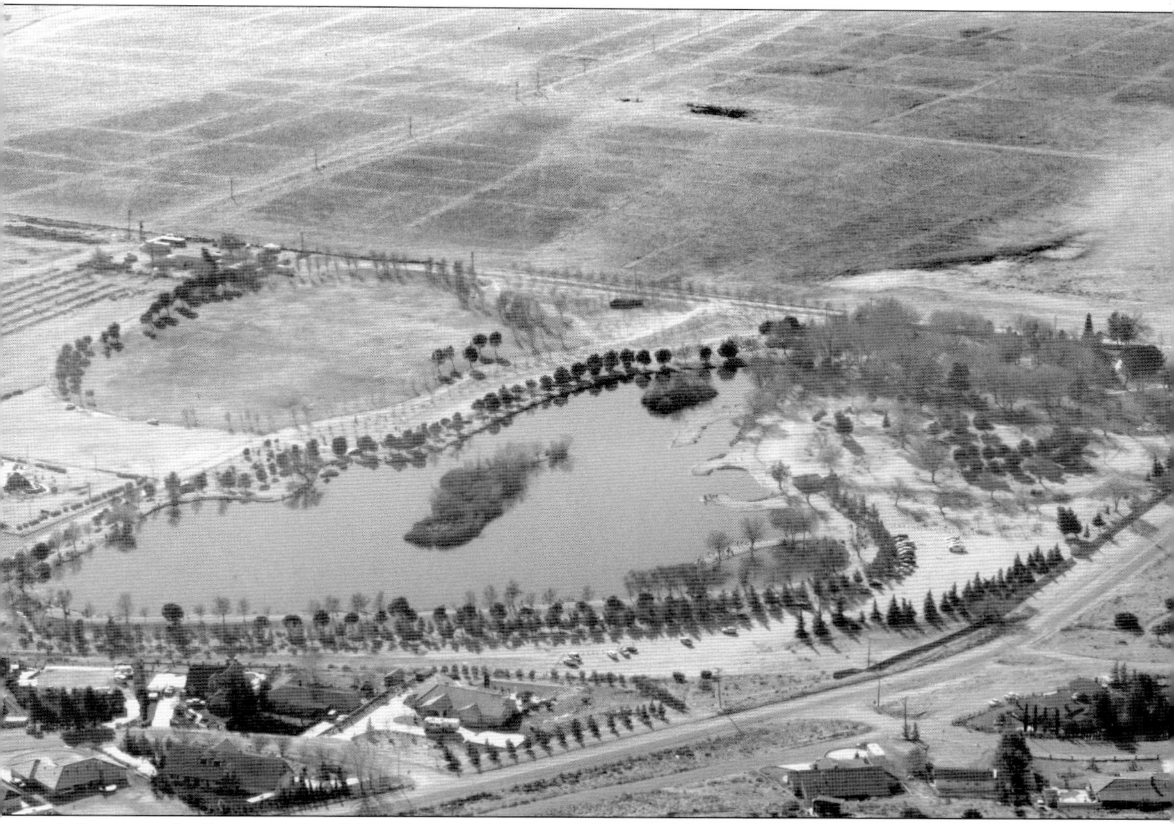

This aerial photograph of Hesperia Lake was taken by the author in 2007. From its humble beginnings as Mary Emery's Lake RoToBo and a trout farm, it has grown and matured under the Hesperia Recreation and Parks District. The lake is continuously restocked with a variety of fish. Soccer fields and equestrian areas have been added to its shores, and a nature center is under development. (Courtesy HOTM.)

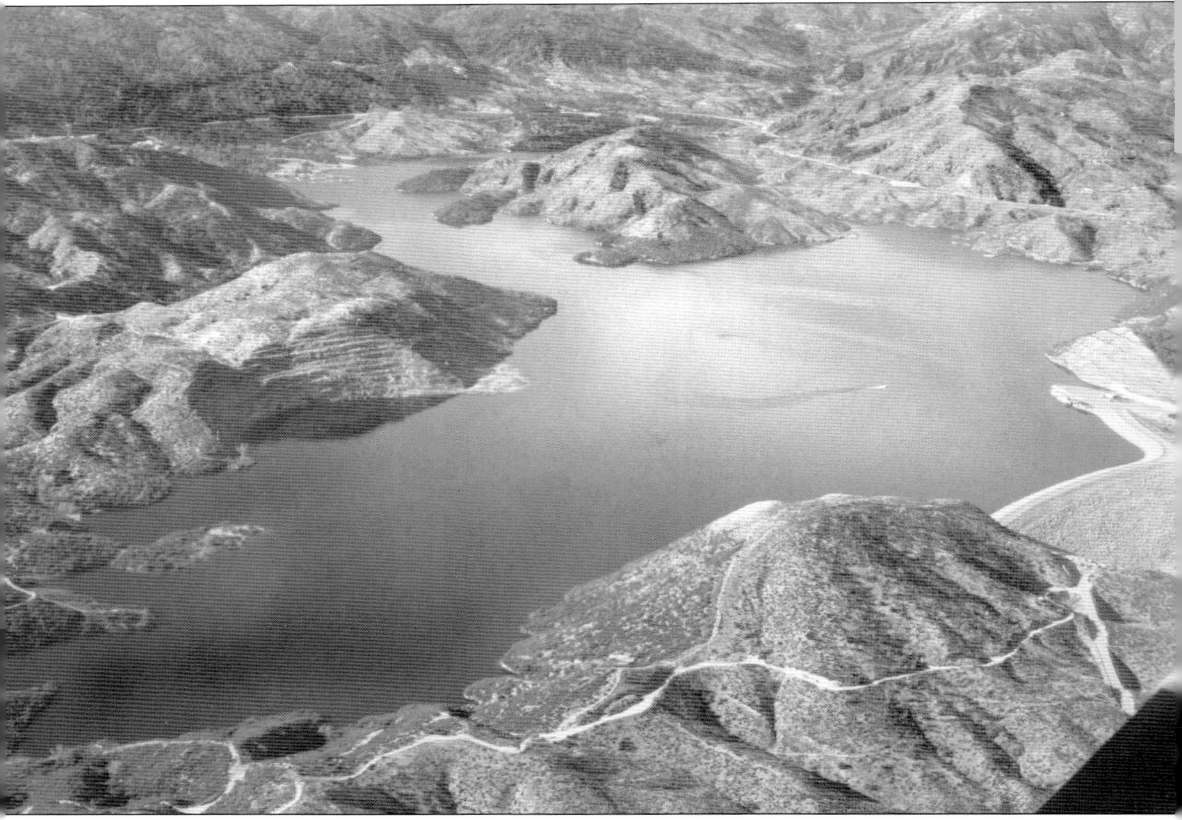

People from all over the Inland Empire come to Lake Silverwood for boating, fishing, and skiing. Beneath its waters, however, lies a bit of history—the town of Cedar Springs. The small community was evacuated and flooded after its namesake, the 249-foot-high Cedar Springs Dam, was built. When the lake was drained in the early 1980s, remnants of some of the old buildings could still be seen. (Courtesy HOTM.)

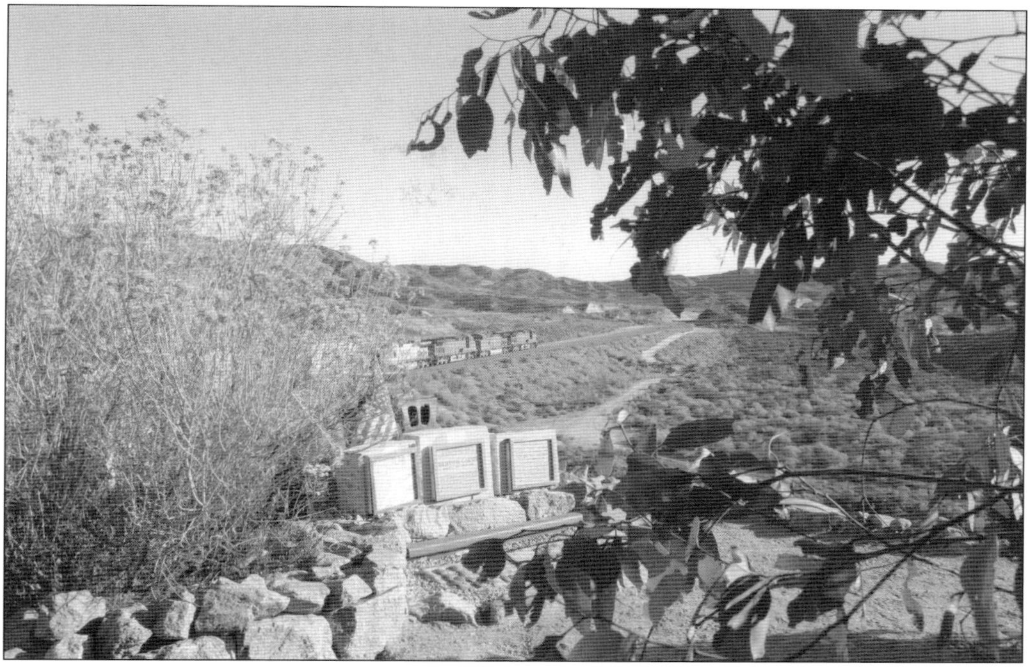

Hill 582 is a railroad viewing area built by train enthusiasts in 2000. This spot celebrates the efforts of all those involved in railroading over the past 150 years. The markers placed on the hill are the originals that marked tunnel No. 1, including a draw bar and the original signal mast reading "Hill 582." Several markers commemorate those who made the site possible. It is a beautiful location with an air of reverence to it. (Both, courtesy HOTM.)

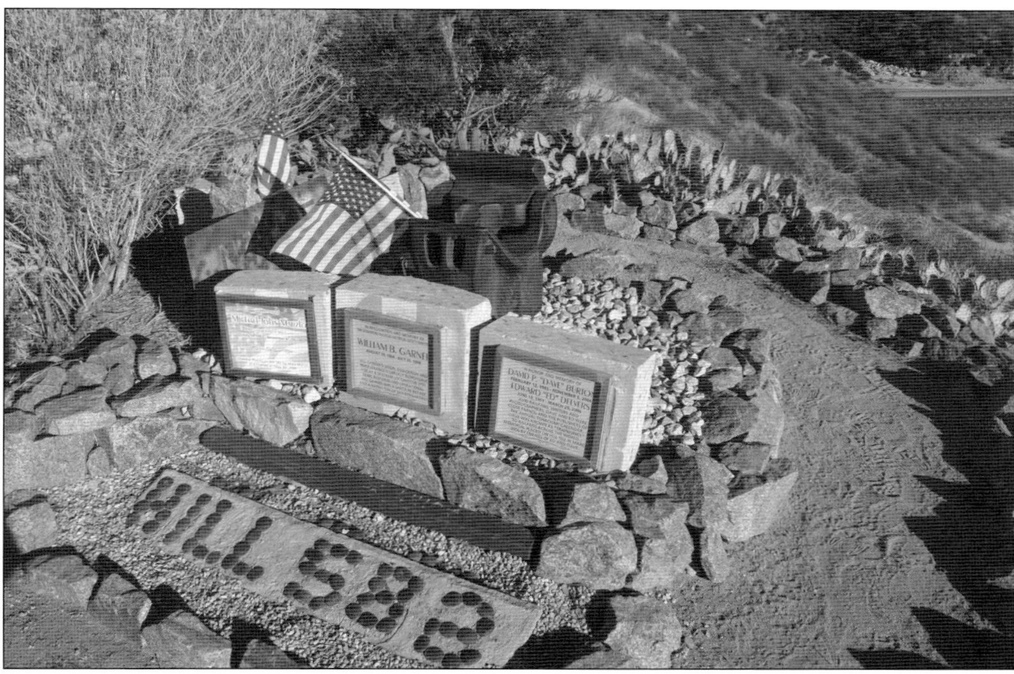

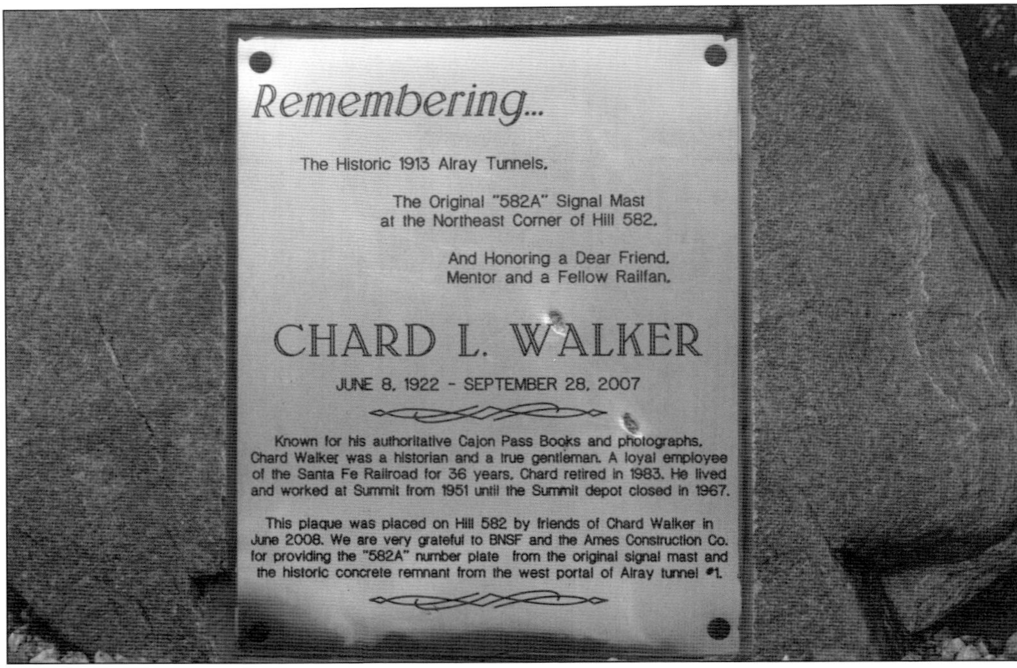

One plaque on Hill 582 honors Chard Walker, author of three rail-related books and compiler of a collection of railroading slides that may never be equaled. The slides can still be viewed at the Pacific Railroad Museum in San Dimas, and his books can still be purchased on the Web. Chard worked the Summit Valley station from 1951 to 1967 and lived in Hesperia until his passing in 2007. (Courtesy HOTM.)

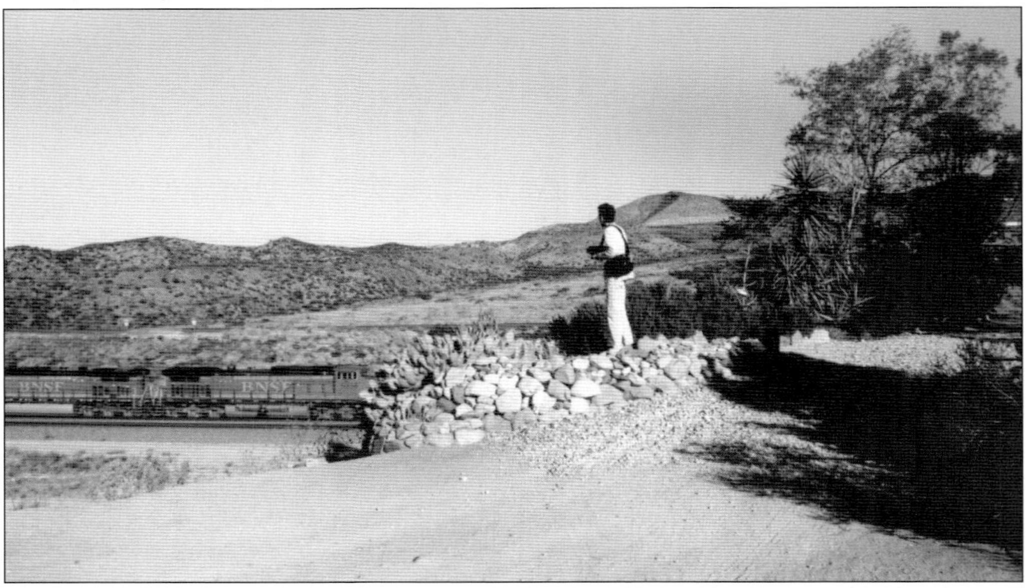

Though Hill 582 is just outside of the Hesperia area, it pulls together many railroaders from all over, and the railroad is a definite part of Hesperia history. The hill is known in many parts of the world; people travel to visit it and relive the history of railroading up the Cajon Pass. (Courtesy HOTM.)

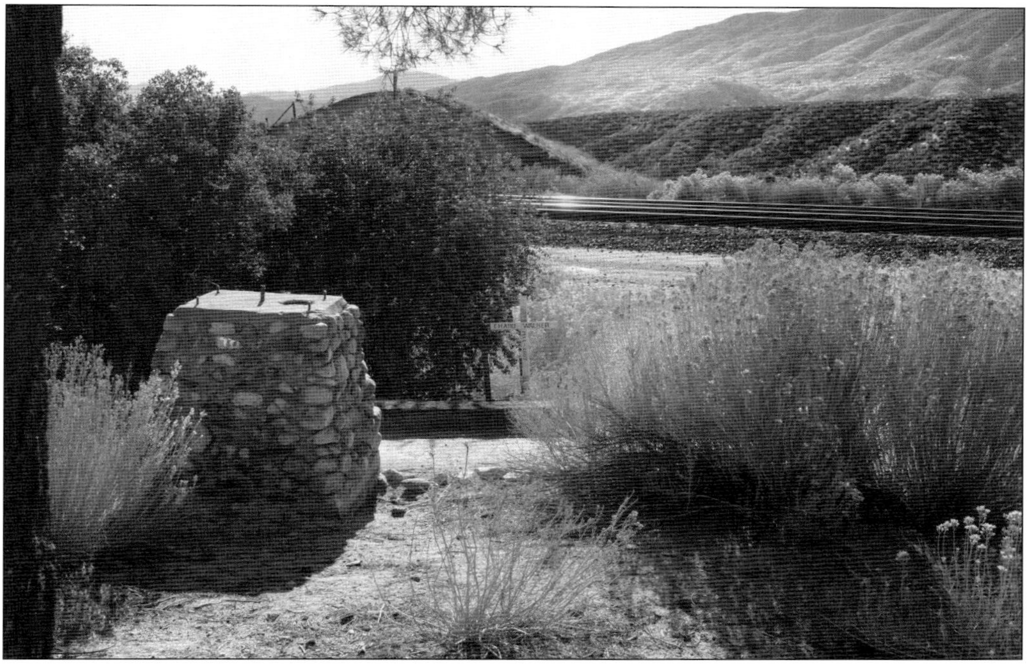

The *Descanso* was a funeral car brought to Summit Valley to serve as a meeting place for railroad enthusiasts in 1948. It was converted into temporary living quarters for Chard Walker at one point and remained on the Summit Valley site until the early 1960s, when it was taken to the Orange Empire Railway Museum and refurbished back into a funeral car. A lone cross remains here in memory of Chard Walker. (Courtesy HOTM.)

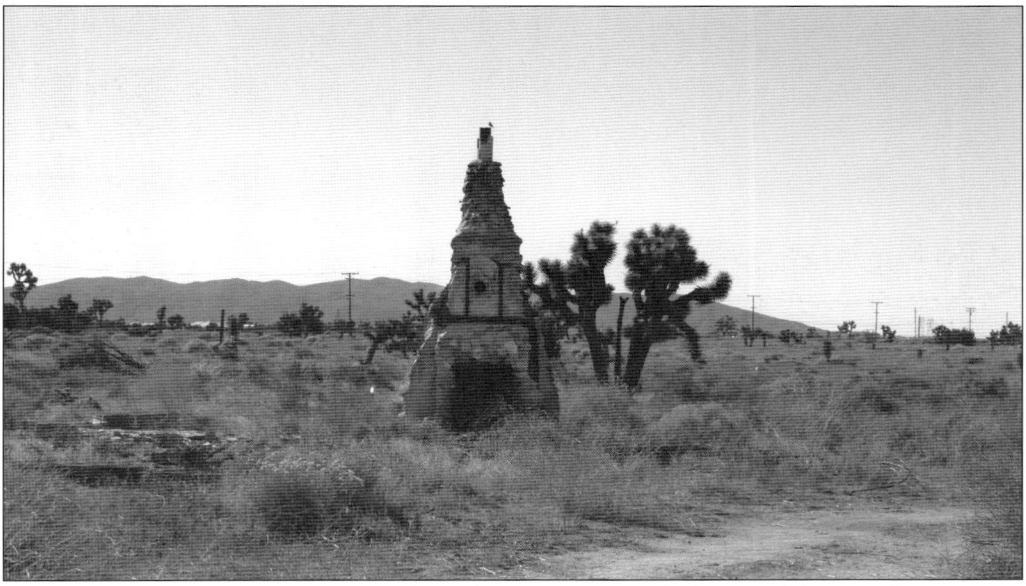

This chimney is the only remains of the Rolars gas station, which served the area from 1941 to 1949. A monument in the area remembers Leroy and Della Rolars for the service they provided to motorists. There was also a well on the property that was nicknamed the "whispering well." It has since been capped off, as it never drew a sufficient amount of water. (Courtesy HOTM.)

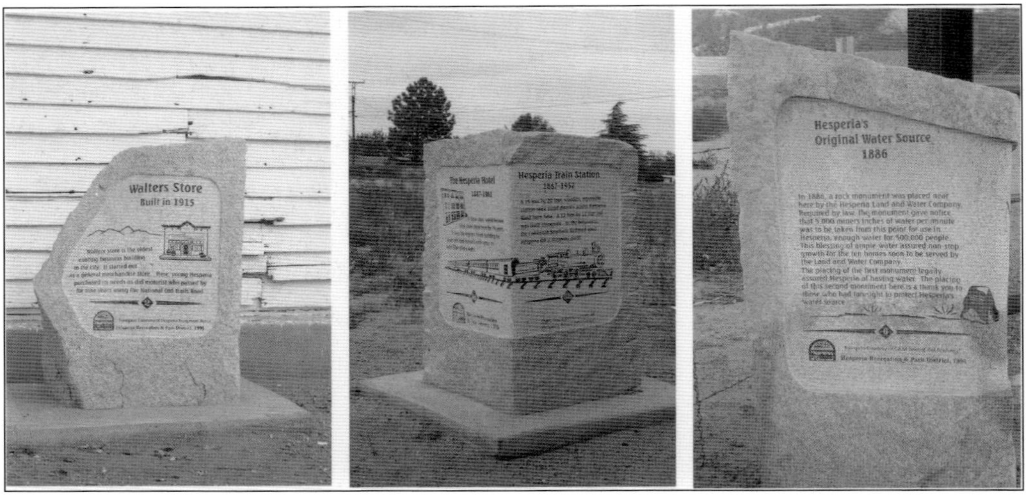

In the mid-1990s, the Hesperia Historical Preservation Committee, under the direction of the Hesperia Recreation and Parks District, formally identified 15 historical sites throughout the town. The monuments shown here comprise 3 of the 15 designated spots. A map showing the location of all 15 sites can be found at the parks district office. (Courtesy HOTM.)

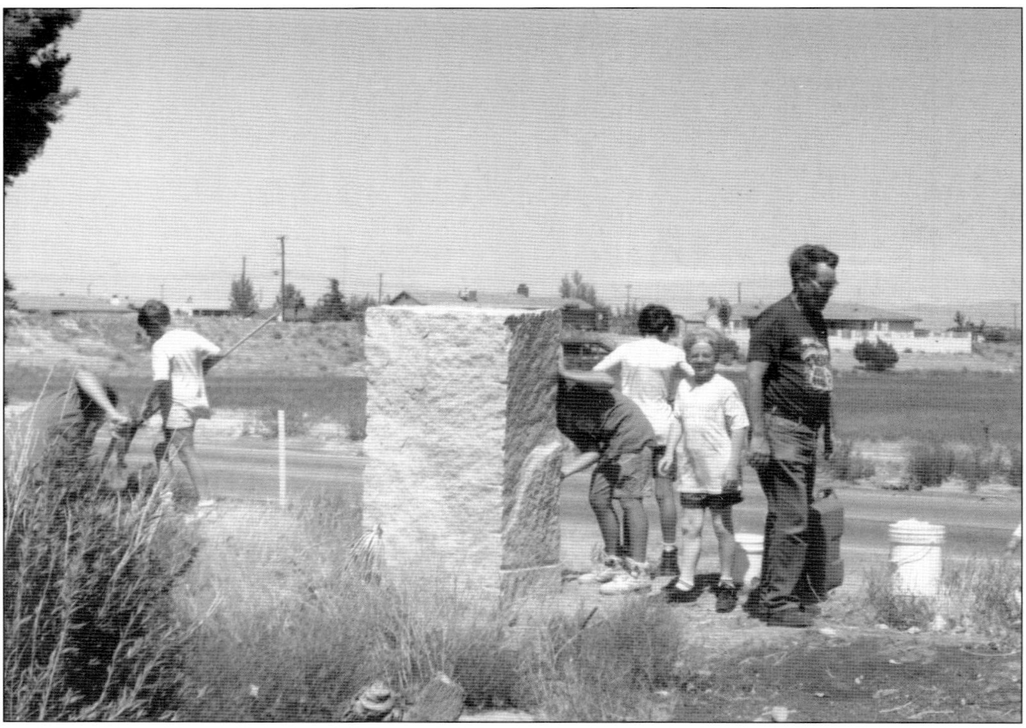

Pictured here is Boy Scout Troop 450 cleaning up around one of the city monuments in 1998. Many different community organizations periodically take care of the monuments. It is all part of preserving history, taking a little pride in the community, and teaching good values to youth. (Courtesy HRPD.)

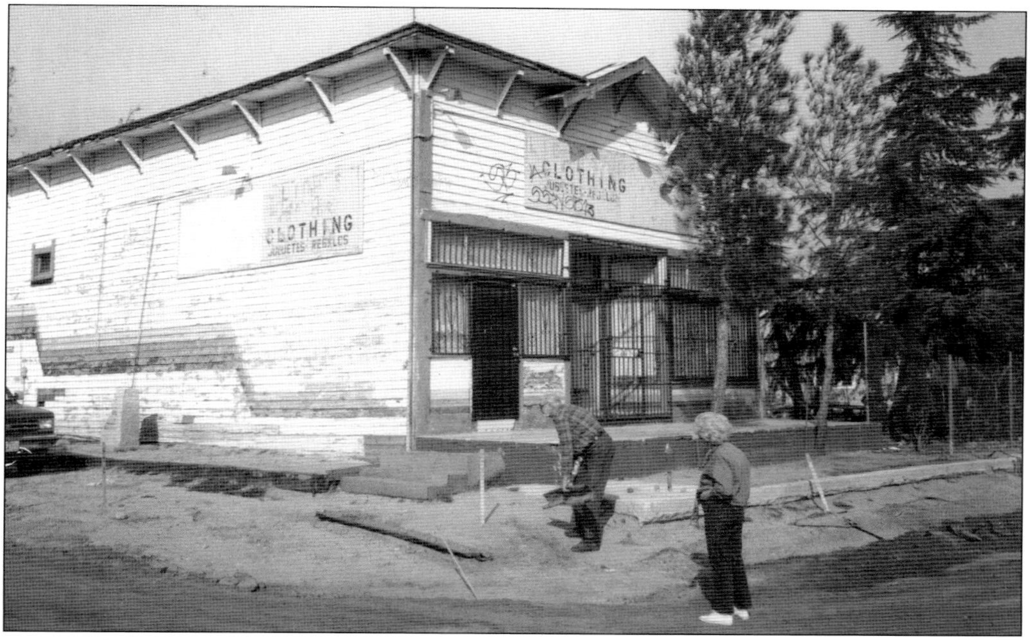

In 1998, the Hesperia Historical Preservation Committee noted that the structural integrity of the Walters Store was in danger. Under the direction of the Hesperia Recreation and Parks District, the committee accomplished the necessary repairs. (Courtesy HRPD.)

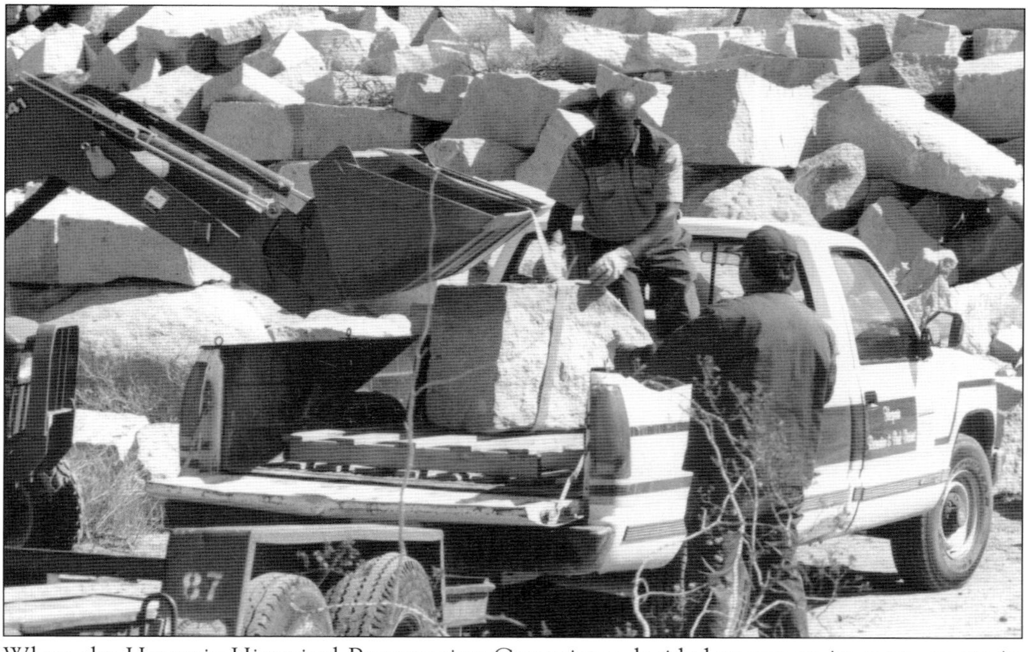

When the Hesperia Historical Preservation Committee decided to put up its monuments in the mid-1990s, the volunteer group got together and picked the granite markers by hand. After the markers were etched with the desired verbiage and art work, it was time to put them in place. With the aid of G&M Towing, the monuments were moved to the appropriate locations. (Courtesy HRPD.)

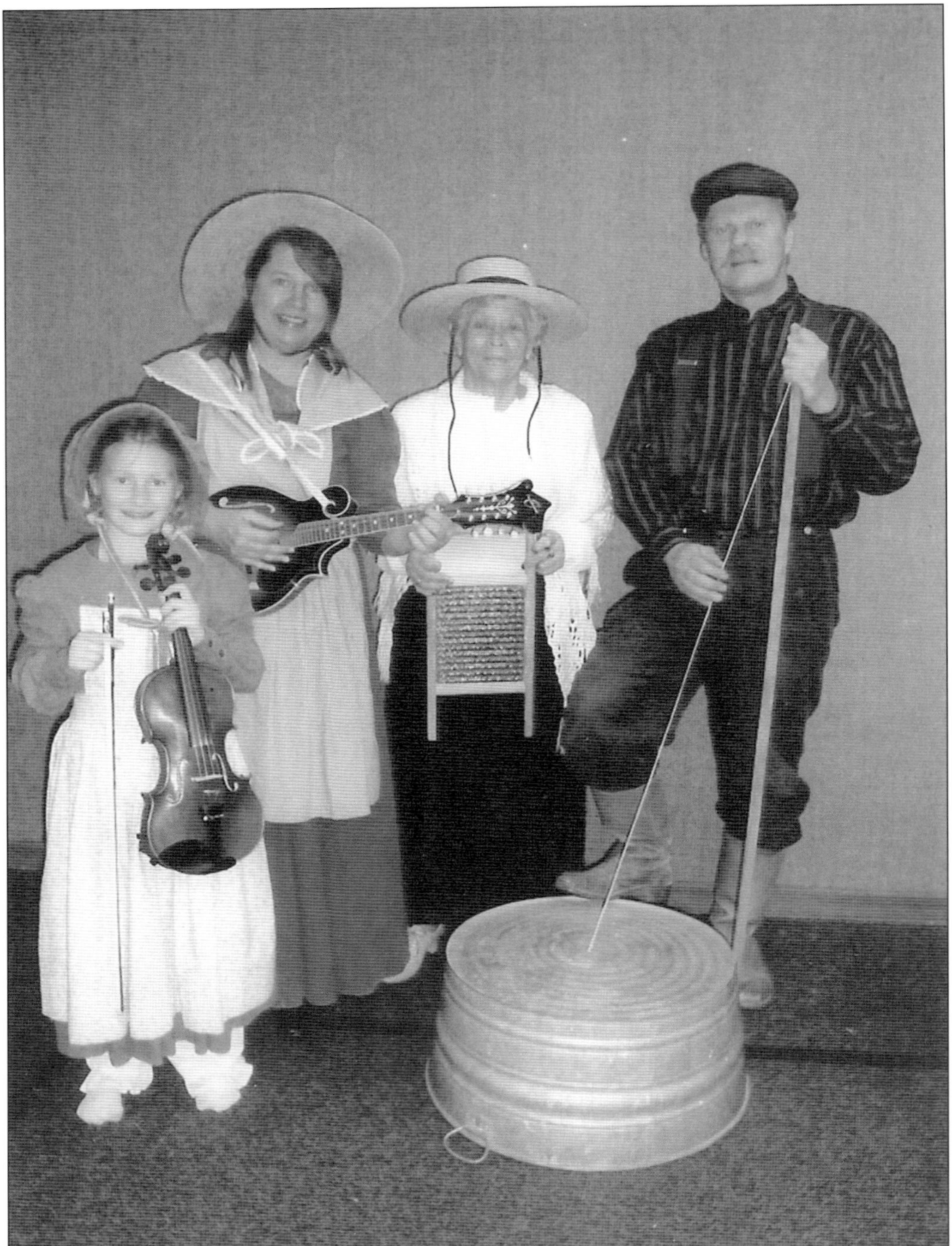

There are many ways of preserving history. Here members of the musically talented Bascom family perform with traditional country instruments. Pictured from left to right are Juliette on the violin, Lisa on the mandolin, 93-year-old Nadine on the washboard, and John on the washtub. (Courtesy BF.)

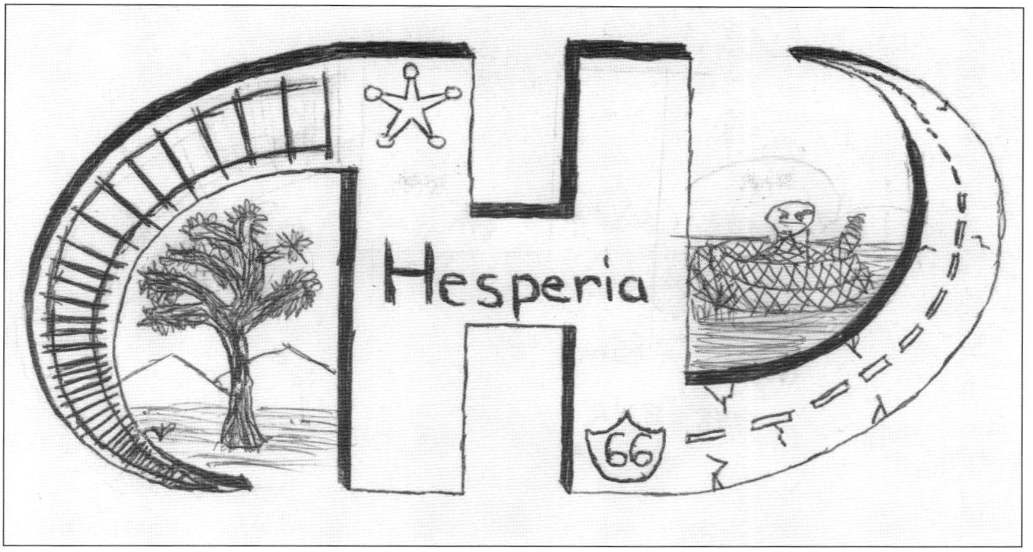

The original Hesperia Old Town Museum logo was designed by eighth-grader Brandon Gradillas at Ranchero Middle School in 2004. Brandon's design was chosen from among 125 entries by a panel of five judges from the chamber of commerce, city government, school district, and the author and his wife. Later the logo was colorized by a Sultana High audio-visual class under instructor Shawn Brown. (Both, courtesy HOTM.)

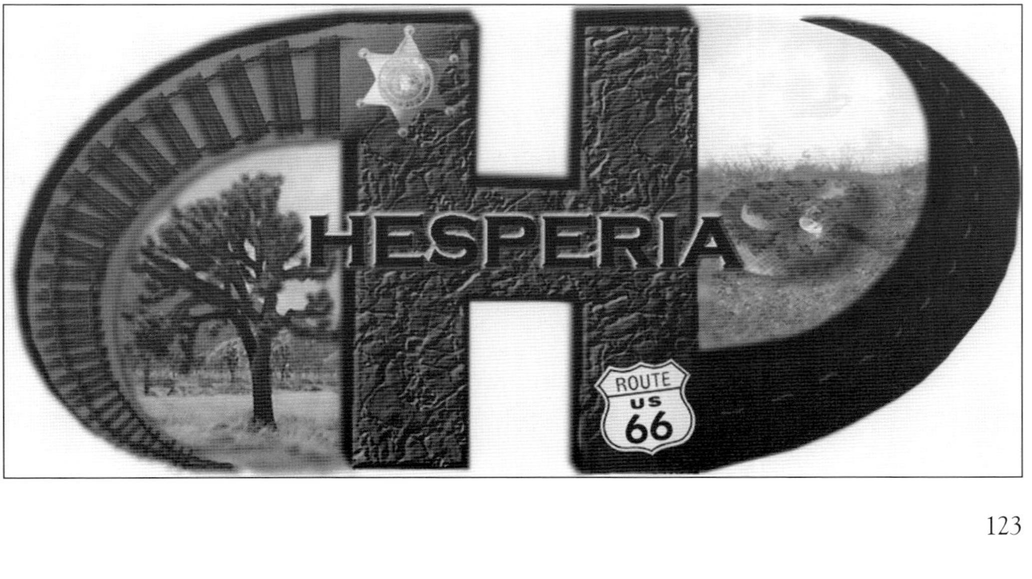

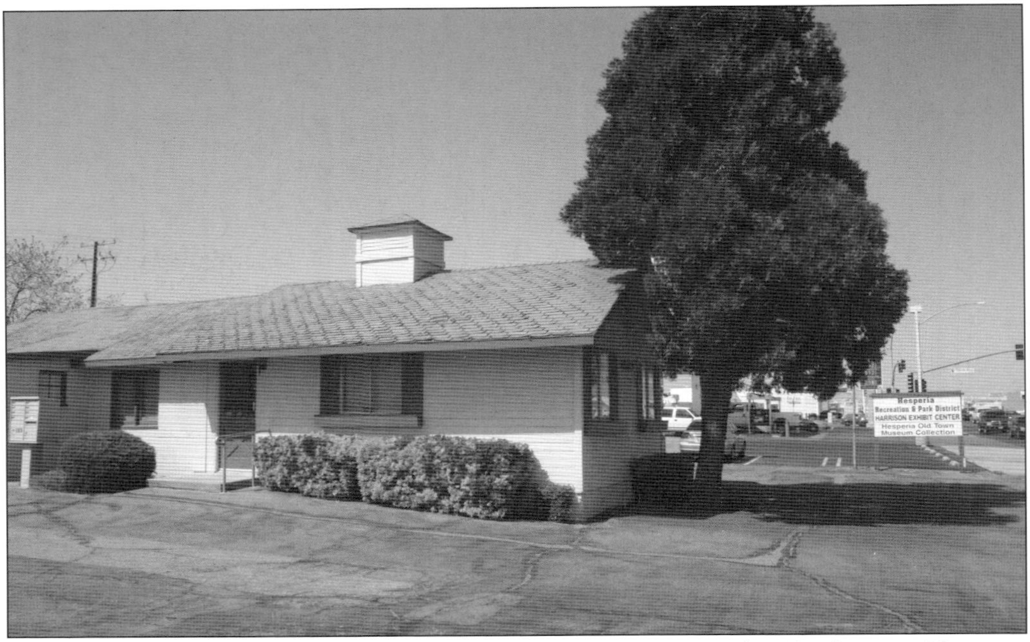

The Hesperia Old Town Museum is housed in the recreation and parks district's Harrison Exhibit Center. This building was the Stratton home from the early 1920s to the early 1970s. June Stratton Deutschman used it as her art studio. The house was remodeled some time after 1936. (Courtesy HOTM.)

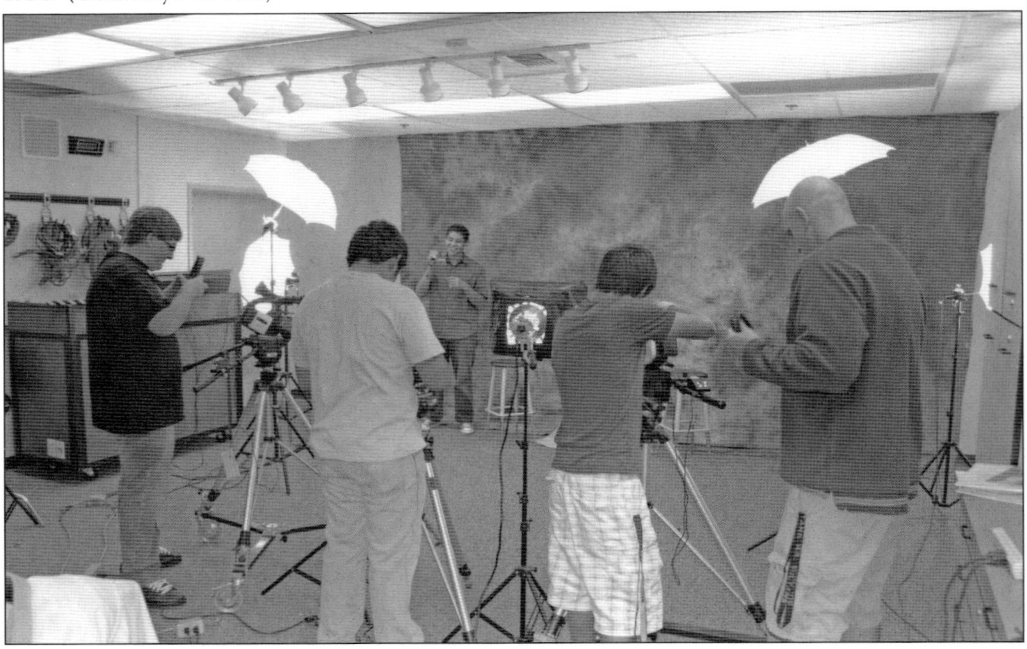

This photograph was taken inside the audio-visual classroom at Sultana High School. The students are setting up to film a portion of the *Potatoes and Pipelines* episode with narrator Old Town Griz and Jim Walker, who worked the potato fields with his father and the Tatums in the 1940s. (Courtesy HOTM.)

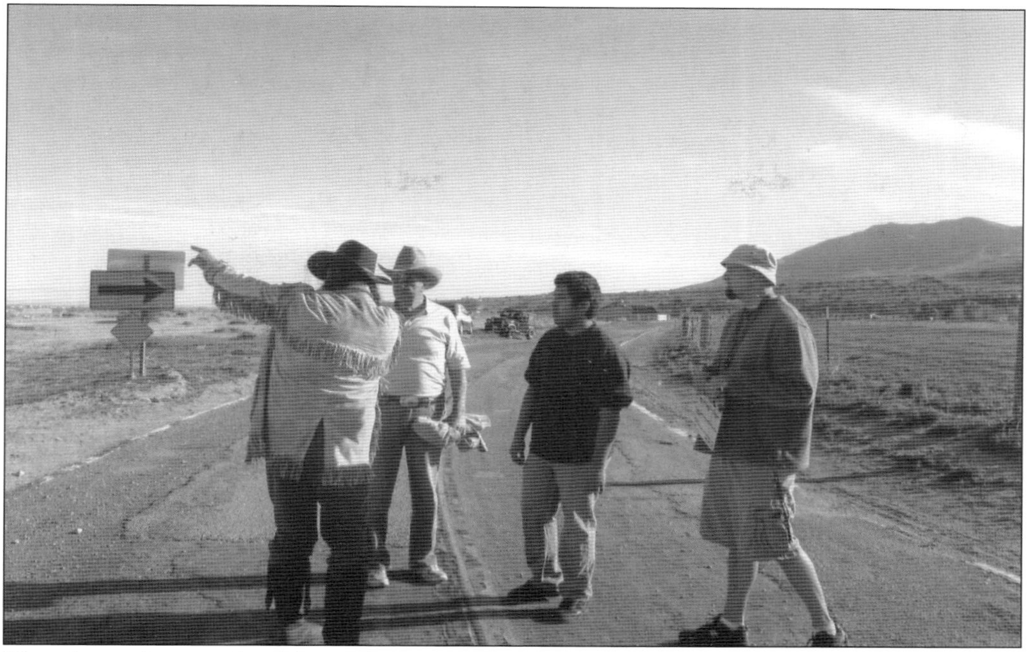

This above photograph of the author (left) was taken by Shelly Drylie out on location with instructor Jim Walker (second from left) and the students of his Sultana High School audio-visual class. This segment was filmed in Deep Creek just north of the spillway and in line with the 14-inch and 30-inch pipes that once ran from the ditch to the reservoir at Lime Street and Hesperia Road. A large portion of the old pipes is still visible from the ditch up toward Hesperia Lake and onto the mesa. Some of the 14-inch pipe can be seen at the intersection of Joshua and Chase Streets. The poster at right was created by the audio-visual class to advertise the history documentary projects *Schools: A Look Back* and *Potatoes and Pipelines*. The students have done a great job with these projects and have learned a lot of Hesperia history. (Above, courtesy HOTM; right, courtesy HUSD.)

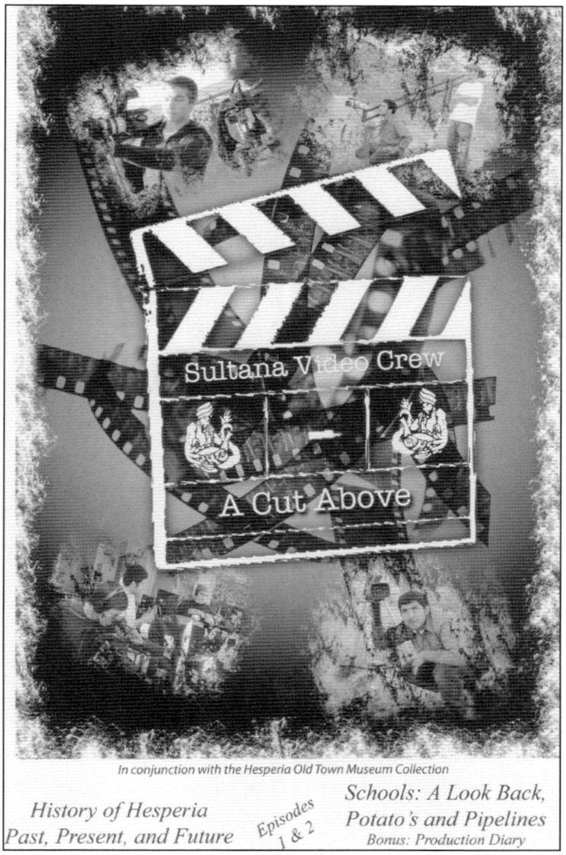

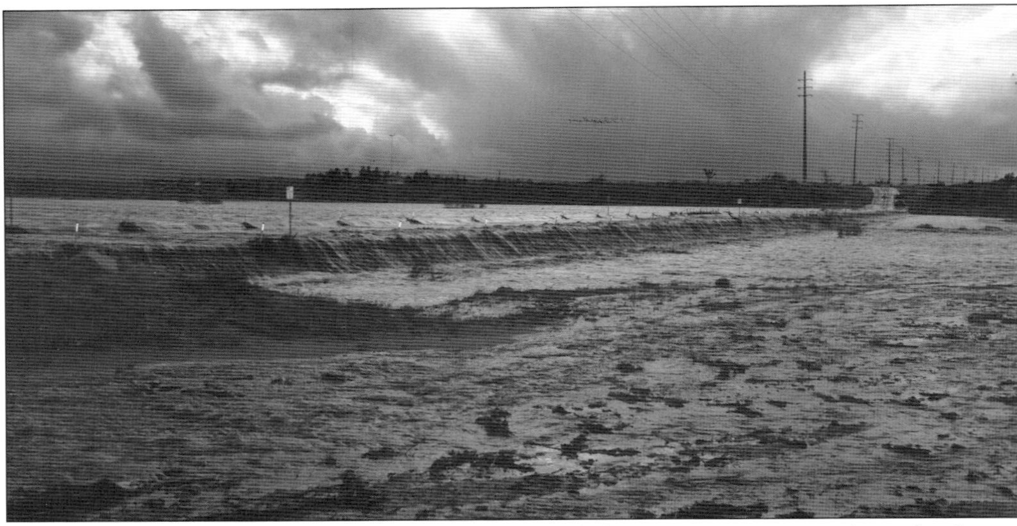

This photograph was taken in 2010 as the rains filled the Mojave River to its lower banks and flooded out Rocks Springs Road. At this flood level, trucks with scrapers could still traverse the road, as shown in this photograph. During the much larger floods of 1938 and 1861–1862, the water would have reached the upper banks, and even modern-day equipment would have been of no use. (Courtesy HOTM.)

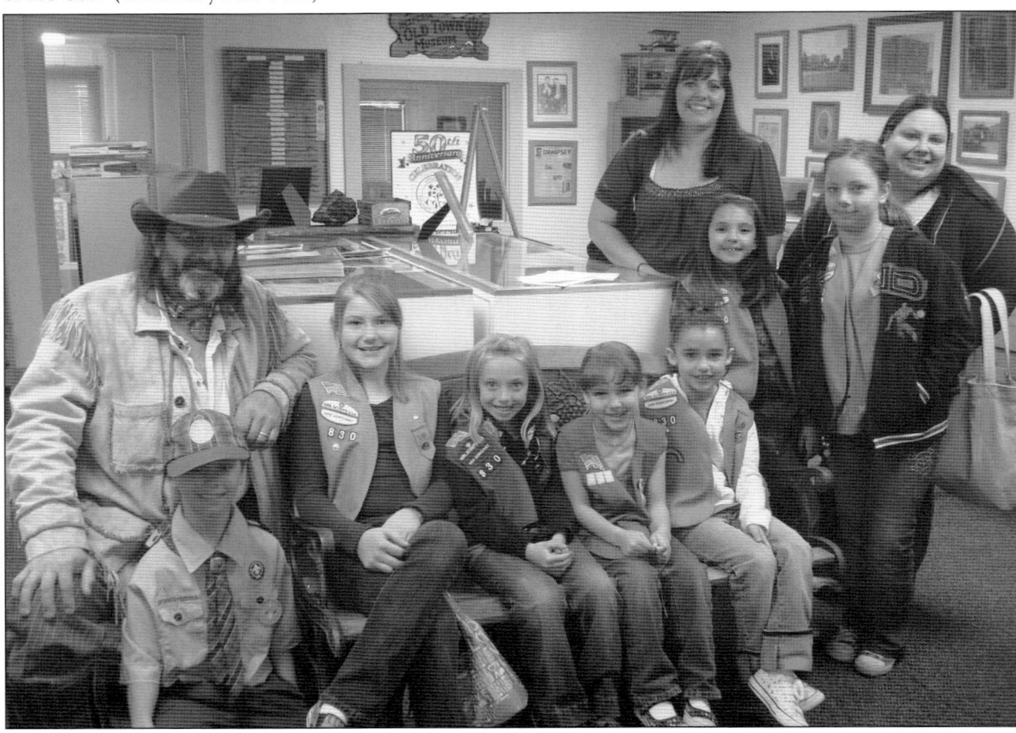

Troop 830 of the Hesperia Girl Scouts visited with the author at the Hesperia Old Town Museum. From left to right are "Old Town Griz," his grandson Krystiano Maldonado, Madisyn James, Kylee Rodriquez, Riley Fuller, Taylor Wamsley, Carli Fuller, Shelby Forgey, Marlene Fuller, and troop coleader Faith Forgey. (Photograph by Shelly Drylie; courtesy HOTM.)

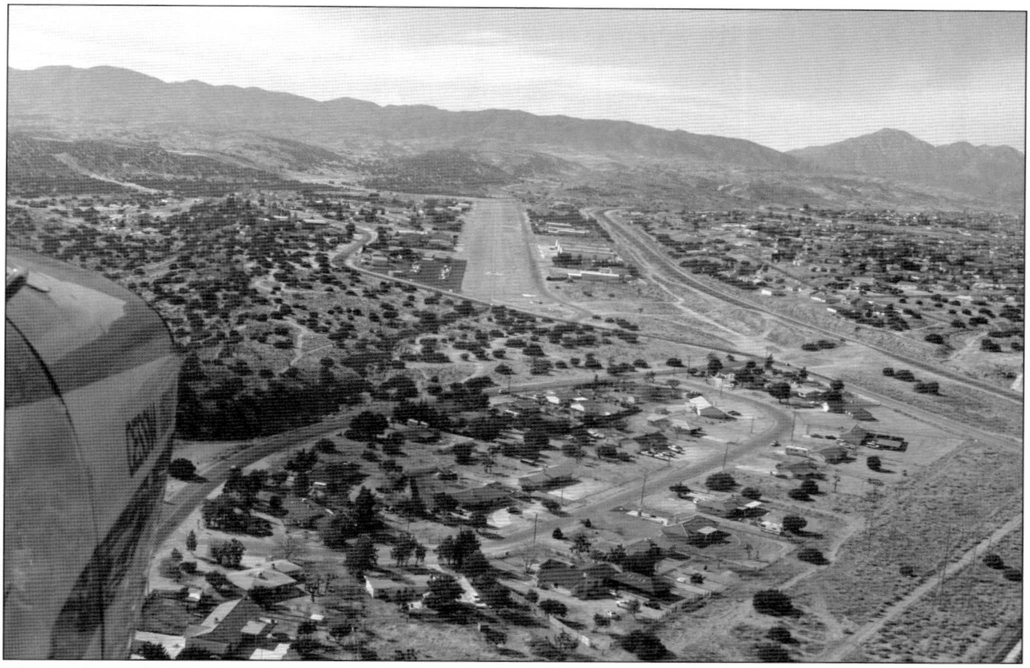

The author takes a photograph as his pilot comes in for a landing at the Hesperia Airpark. He is always looking for history to document and is almost never without his camera. (Courtesy HOTM.)

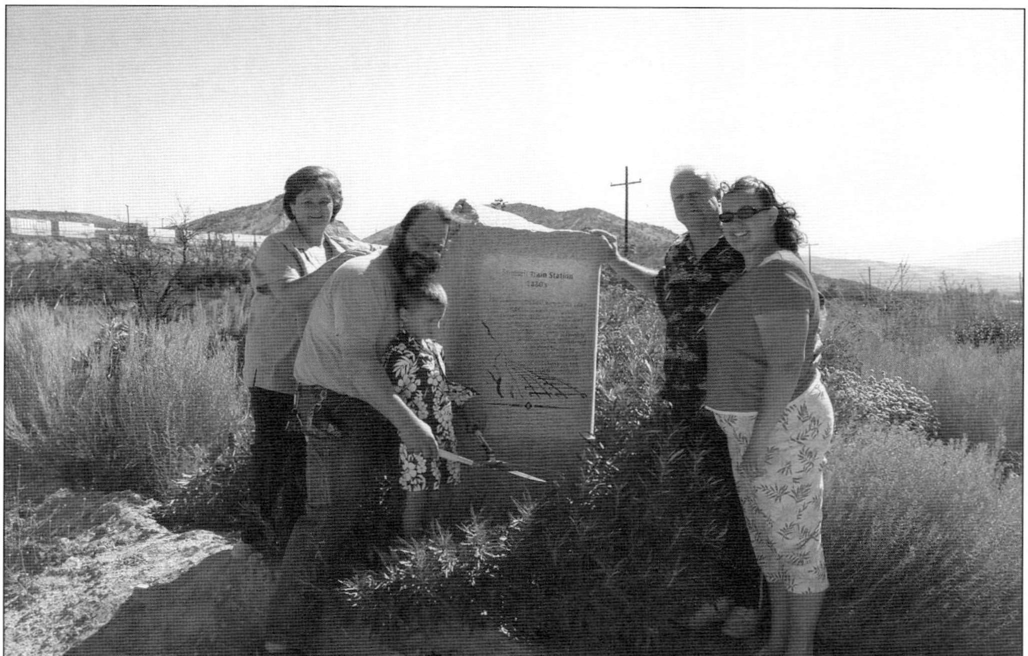

The author's family has been in the area since the late 1960s. His grandfather delivered mail to Hesperia by train back in the 1940s and 1950s. Pictured here are four generations of Drylies trimming around the Summit Valley Station Monument in remembrance of his grandfather. (Photograph by Shelly Drylie; courtesy HOTM.)

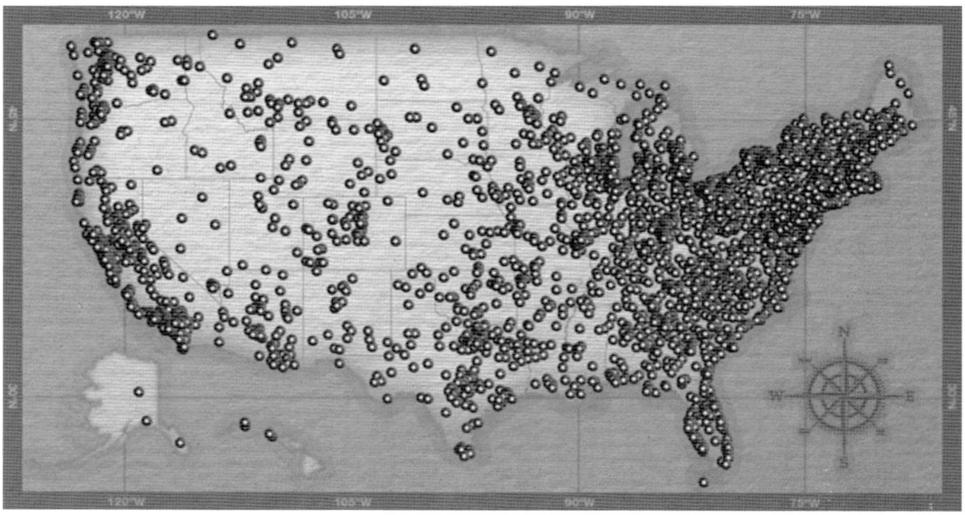